UNDERSTANDING
THE LAW

UNDERSTANDING THE LAW

Third Edition

GEOFFREY RIVLIN

OXFORD

UNIVERSITY PRESS

OXFORD
UNIVERSITY PRESS

Great Clarendon Street, Oxford OX2 6DP

Oxford University Press is a department of the University of Oxford.
It furthers the University's objective of excellence in research, scholarship,
and education by publishing worldwide in

Oxford New York

Auckland Bangkok Buenos Aires Cape Town Chennnai
Dar es Salaam Delhi Hong Kong Istanbul Karachi Kolkata
Kuala Lumpur Madrid Melbourne Mexico City Mumbai Nairobi
São Paulo Shanghai Taipei Tokyo Toronto

Oxford is a registered trade mark of Oxford University Press
in the UK and in certain other countries

Published in the United States
by Oxford University Press Inc., New York

Text © Geoffrey Rivlin 2004
Illustrations © Chris Burke 2004

British Library Cataloguing in Publication Data
Data applied for

Library of Congress Cataloging in Publication Data
Data available

ISBN 0-19-927023-6

1 3 5 7 9 10 8 6 4 2

Typeset by RefineCatch Limited, Bungay, Suffolk
Printed in Great Britain by Ashford Colour Press Ltd, Gosport, Hampshire

Outline Contents

Detailed Contents

Preface

Since the publication of the first edition of this book, a tornado of reforms has lifted the legal system off its base, and it is still flying through the air—the House of Lords (our most senior court), the future form of trials, the legal administration throughout the country, solicitors without wigs and barristers with them, even the exalted figure of the Lord Chancellor himself, their gowns flapping in the wind—all are spiralling away, and no one knows quite where they will land.

Major historic changes have already taken place, both to our constitution and to our laws. Scotland now has its own Parliament, Wales its own Assembly, the voting powers of hereditary peers have been reformed, and we now have a new Human Rights Act. But that is only the start of it. The House of Lords as the final court of appeal may soon be replaced by a new Supreme Court. The office of Lord Chancellor, a pivotal figure in our constitution, is under threat of abolition, as is the ancient rank of Queen's Counsel. Judges are soon to be appointed in a different way. Even the 'dress code' in court for judges, and the advocates who appear before them, is under review.

Then we have the Criminal Justice Act 2003, whose groundbreaking provisions are timetabled to come into force over the next three years. When they do, some long-standing (even cherished) principles of our criminal law may disappear. The Government proposes that juries will no longer be able to try certain cases, and Parliament has stepped (not so gingerly) into areas of sentencing offenders that have always been the jealously guarded preserve of an independent judiciary. With all this happening, and so much uncertainty about the future, much of it still but a dream, it may be that the most prudent course for this author would be to put down his pen, and make a run for it; but who could resist the challenge of an opportunity at this time to try to enable others to understand something of our system of laws, how we have arrived at this point, and what may happen in the near future?

One far less important change is that this book, originally *First Steps in the Law*, has been renamed *Understanding the Law*. This is because my esteemed publishers have persuaded me that the new title best illustrates what the book sets out to achieve. Whether it does so is for others to decide. My only anxiety is that anyone might think that I claim to 'understand' the law myself! I should confess that after far too long I still find some aspects of the law an enticing mystery, the end of the 'Yellow Brick Road' (for me, at least) always being just out of reach. I can only hope, therefore, that the journey we are about to take, and the people we are to meet, will at least help the interested beginner along the way to an understanding of the law, and better still, to a real enjoyment of it.

Geoffrey Rivlin
January 2004

Preface to the First Edition

Sometimes we do not know what to call our own country. Are we Great Britain? Are we the United Kingdom? Are we simply England, Scotland, Wales and Northern Ireland? In fact, we are all of these, and I hope that any young person who wishes to learn more about how our nation 'ticks', and how our laws affect so many different aspects of our lives, will find this book about our laws interesting and informative.

Whereas England and Wales have for many years had the same legal system —for example, the full title of the Lord Chief Justice is 'The Lord Chief Justice of England and Wales'—there are some important differences between this system of law and the Scottish and Northern Irish systems. A few of these are referred to in this book, and there is a chapter towards the end of the book where we look briefly at international law and the legal systems of other countries. However, this book is mainly about the law and lawyers in England and Wales, and from now on, with apologies to the Welsh, I shall for convenience refer to the 'laws of England'.

Our laws are vital to us. Without laws there would be no hope for our society, or for that matter any society; and without the constant development of the law there would be no chance for us to progress. I have attempted to give the reader a broad picture of what the law means to us, how we make our laws, and how the legal system works. In particular, we will be looking at criminal trials and punishment.

As we look at our laws and legal system we will from time to time delve into our legal history. Some people find history dreary. How can it possibly be relevant to the lives we lead today? It so happens that our legal history is a remarkable and colourful one. It is also a very bloody one. Oscar Wilde, poet, dramatist, wit (and convict) said '*As one reads history, one is absolutely sickened, not by the crimes that the wicked have committed, but by the punishments that the good have inflicted*'. There is some truth in this, as we will discover when we come to look at the story of our criminal law; but the best reason for the occasional historical sketch is that it is really impossible to understand how, or indeed why, we have the remarkable system which exists today, and which forms the basis of laws in countries throughout the world, without knowing something of its background.

Although aspects of our law have remained unchanged for many years, fundamental changes have taken place in the last few years, and the scope and importance of change are gathering pace; the nature of our constitution, the law relating to children, the duties of a judge, the powers of the courts, even the make-up of the legal profession—all these and more are undergoing such radical change that it may one day be said that the last decade of the twentieth century saw a greater change in the face of the law than the rest of the century put together. Lord Bingham of Cornhill, the Lord Chief Justice, said in July 1998, '*We are currently witnessing a degree of constitutional, institutional and professional change of which we have not in combination seen the like for 350 years*'. This may be stimulating, but it is also daunting. It certainly calls for a constant state of awareness, and the hope that not too much will have changed between the writing of this preface and publication!

Hopefully, you will find the law as set out in this book easy to follow, but that is not to pretend that our legal system is simple. Should you ever wish to go into the subject deeply—should you ever go into a court and watch a case yourselves, which anyone over the age of 14 can do—you will find that almost every important rule has its refinements and it exceptions. Many of these are fascinating, but I have dealt with only a few of them in this book, which is intended as an introduction to the law for those of you who wish to know how it works, but as yet know nothing about it. I would like to think that it will encourage you to find out more.

For Maureen, Emma, and Sophie

Acknowledgements

In the first two editions of this book I expressed my indebtedness to a number of people, who had given generously of their time, advice and encouragement. There were many, and I still owe them my sincere thanks. During the preparation of this edition I have been greatly assisted by Jonathan Creer, Matthew Gullick, Tony Hearne, Robert Kyriakides, Valerie Pearlman, Hayden Phillips, Laura Rosefield, Robert Taylor, Joan Ward and Paul Yates; and they too have my sincere appreciation for all their kindness and expertise.

The Act of Parliament on page 62 (Figure 5.1) is reproduced by kind permission of the Controller of HMSO, the map of the Circuits on page 109 (Figure 10.1) by kind permission of the Bar Council; the diagram of the court structure on page 116 (Figure 11.1) by kind permission of the Department for Constitutional Affairs (as it is now called); and the extract from the Young Witness Pack *Preparing Young Witnesses for Court*, on page 270 (Figure 21.1) by kind permission of the NSPCC.

I would like to express my particular thanks to Sarah Hyland and Sarah Silvester of Oxford University Press for their advice and encouragement in the preparation of this edition, and to Francine Morris and Jane Henderson for devising the 'Questions for the Reader'. Once again, I am delighted to express my gratitude to Chris Burke for his superb illustrations.

This book makes no pretensions to being an academic treatise. There are no footnotes; nor is there a detailed bibliography—although a short list of useful reading is included at the end.

1

Introduction — the Royal Courts of Justice

At the opening of the Royal Courts of Justice in 1882, the Lord Chancellor, Lord Selborne, called a meeting of the judges to discuss his address to Queen Victoria. When he read the phrase, 'Your Majesty's judges are deeply conscious of their own many shortcomings . . .', the Master of the Rolls, Lord Jessel, objected strongly, saying, 'I am not conscious of "many shortcomings" and if I were, I should not be fit to sit on the bench'.

*

The vast building of the Royal Courts of Justice, commonly known to lawyers as the RCJ, dominates the Strand in London like a great Gothic cathedral. Opened by Queen Victoria in December 1882, to celebrations of lavish splendour, the entrance takes us straight into the Central Hall, a cavernous space, impressive for its size and intricate mosaic tiled floor. Judges long forgotten look down from portraits high on the walls, or gaze from marble plinths in stony silence. They are wearing ceremonial court dress—wigs and gowns—intended symbols of ancient dignity and the majesty of the law.

The graceful old courts lead off the Hall, and when we enter their public galleries we might believe that some of these portraits have come to life. The judges who are trying the cases and the barristers who are presenting them are still wearing robes—seventeenth-century court dress of wigs and gowns. They are so used to wearing them that it no longer occurs to them that they might look in the least odd, and the remarkable thing is that in this setting they do not.

In these courts the judges, high above the lawyers, look down on a scene of order and calm. Surrounded by walls lined with leather-bound law reports, barristers address the judges in quiet and measured tones, punctuating their legal arguments with quaint old-world courtesies: *'With all due respect to my Learned Friend . . .'; 'If it pleases your Lordship . . .'; 'May I respectfully draw the court's attention to . . .'*. These and phrases like them come as naturally to the lawyers as any expressions we may use in our everyday lives.

The court staff—clerks, ushers, stenographers—play their parts; they perform their duties so discreetly that it is easy to forget they are there at all. Members of the public or media who are present are expected to remain still and listen to the proceedings in silence. Even those who are actually involved in a case, and their relatives and friends watching anxiously from the public gallery, are reduced to whispering.

In this atmosphere, tranquil and unruffled, it is difficult to believe that the business of the courts is often that of real human drama; but the fact is that these very people—judges and lawyers (barristers and solicitors)—working carefully and quietly in this historic building, may well be concerned with some of the most exciting, important, and relevant questions of our age. There may be an appearance of calm, but for all their courtroom courtesies the lawyers are likely to be fighting as fearlessly for those whom they represent as the stone cat and dog above the Judges' Entrance, representing battling litigants in court. The judges know that they are making decisions that may well vitally affect the lives of the people whose cases they are hearing. Some of these decisions may be so important that they will affect us all, for they will be adding to the great body of law that has to be followed by all the courts in the land.

Each day new, fascinating, and sometimes heartbreaking problems have to be faced. What might they concern? Whom might they affect? A seemingly endless procession of men and women come to the RCJ to have their cases heard. Each one has his or her own story to tell, and it is a story that could involve any one of the three main areas of the courts' work—crime, disputes between citizen and citizen, and disputes between citizen and the State.

Different courts with different judges try these cases. Here is a glimpse of just a few of them:

IN THE COURT OF APPEAL (CRIMINAL DIVISION)

- The judges are hearing an appeal by a man convicted of murder. He shot a youth, who, together with another, was burgling his home. He says that as his home was being burgled, and he feared that he was going to be attacked, his action was justified.

- A women, who has already served a long sentence of imprisonment for the murder of her young child, is claiming that her conviction was unsafe. She says that the child suffered a 'cot death' and the scientific evidence given against her at her trial was unreliable. She succeeds and she is released.

- A young woman is freed from a sentence of life imprisonment for killing her husband, who she claimed had mistreated her. The court has decided that her mental state at the time of the offence was not properly considered at her trial, and orders a re-trial.

- A man who has killed three pedestrians in a drunken motor accident is before the court because the Attorney-General has decided to argue that his sentence of two years' imprisonment was far too lenient. The court agrees, and the sentence is increased.

IN THE COURT OF APPEAL (CIVIL DIVISION)

- A magazine that published an article suggesting that the wife of a serial murderer knew that he was committing his crimes has been ordered to pay her a huge sum by way of compensation, and is appealing against the size of this order.

- A woman is fighting for permission to be allowed to try to have a baby with sperm taken from her husband before he died.

- A hospital authority is seeking permission to separate conjoined Siamese twins, claiming that if it does not, both twins will die; but their parents, who know that an operation will surely cost the life of one child, object to the operation on religious and moral grounds.

- The loving parents of a son, who has been lying in a coma for years, are seeking the permission of the court to allow him to die in peace.

IN THE HIGH COURT

- A judge is hearing the claim of a widow who is asking for compensation from her late husband's employers, following his death in a factory accident. Her case is that he was killed as a result of unsafe conditions at work.

- A father is fighting for a court order that his local hospital authority should provide expensive medical treatment for his sick child.

- A young student, who has been detained in England as an illegal immigrant, is claiming that he should not be deported back to his home country, where his life might be in danger.

- A singer has been in court for weeks fighting to be released from his contract with a record company.

All of these people, and many, many more—each with his or her own special and compelling story—have come to court to seek *justice*.

'**Royal Courts of Justice.**' These are the words on the sign above the arched entrance to the courts, which is so familiar to everyone who reads the papers or watches the news on television. What do they mean?

ROYAL

'Royal' is not just a fine-sounding title to make the courts seem more important and attractive. The courts are 'Royal' because, as we shall see, an important feature of our country's constitution, which directs the way in which we are governed, is that those who make our laws, those who govern us, and those who judge us should each owe allegiance to 'the Crown' (the Queen).

COURTS

There are over eighty courts in the RCJ, and their varied work gives us an idea of the enormous range of cases with which the justice system is concerned.

First, this is the home of the Court of Appeal, whose judges hear appeals in criminal and civil cases, where the judgment of the first court trying the case has not been accepted, and it is being argued either that it should be corrected or that the court should order a re-trial. Here sit some of the most senior judges in the land, including the Lord Chief Justice and the Master of the Rolls.

Then there are the courts of the three divisions of the High Court: the Queen's Bench Division, the Family Division, and the Chancery Division. The judges in these courts will be trying a great variety of cases—from 'running-down' actions (where people have been killed or injured in road traffic accidents) to collisions at sea; from the most complex commercial disputes to divorce and family matters; from cases where ordinary people are claiming that they have been unfairly treated by the State to battles over the property of those who have died.

The courts in the RCJ are only a small fraction of the many courts elsewhere in London and throughout the country, serving the needs of the communities in their areas. Many of them have quite different functions. These are just a few examples of the great volume of work they do:

- *Criminal courts*: judging whether people are guilty of crime, and if so, how they should be punished.

- *Civil courts*: deciding if and how people should be protected, whether against threats of violence or threats to break contracts, dishonest advertisements, or noisy neighbours, and whether they should be compensated (awarded money) for injuries or other harm they have suffered.

- *Family courts*: considering the welfare of children, who may have the simple need to be protected against cruel treatment, or from the effects of the break-up of their parents' marriage or partnership, and deciding upon the financial arrangements between them.

JUSTICE

'Justice' is a difficult concept, chiefly because everyone has a different idea of what it is. There is a strong notion that there are 'rules of justice'—rules that dictate that if we behave honourably we will be rewarded, and if we are bad, we will be punished—if not in this world, in the next. This is what many sincerely believe; unhappily, this idea is hardly borne out, at least by earthly experience.

Because ideas of justice can be so subjective, it is often much easier for us to agree upon a case of 'injustice' than it is for us to agree upon a case of 'justice'. The seventeenth-century French philosopher La Rochefoucauld expressed this another way when he said: '*In most men love of justice is only a fear of suffering injustice.*' We know that there is injustice in the world. It does not seem just that one person dies young and another lives to be one hundred, or that one person suffers appalling illness whilst those around him are in the best of health. It does not seem just that countless people have so little money that they find it virtually impossible to live, while others have so much they do not know what to do with it all. We know that the courts cannot be expected to deal with these kinds of 'injustice'. So what kind of justice can our courts provide? Let us take some examples from the short list of cases above to see how difficult this can be:

- The woman who has been wrongfully convicted and has spent years in prison before being released. She will say that at last she has received some justice, but she has lost years of her life away from her family. Can anyone believe that she has received justice?

- The woman who killed her husband, who she claims was violent towards her. She may think she was unjustly treated by being sent to prison in the first place, but her husband's grieving relatives may say that she should have been kept in prison for life, or even executed for his murder. Here, everyone may come away from court feeling a sense of injustice.

- The widow whose young husband has been killed in an accident at work. No award of money, however great, can possibly compensate her. How can the courts do justice to her?

- The Siamese twins are far too young to express any views as to what should happen to them. Their parents love them both. Where does justice lie here, and justice for whom? Their condition may be described as an 'act of God' (it was certainly outside the control of man), but the choice of what must now be done is a stark, human one—and it is left to the courts to face up to it.

- As for the young man in the coma, who can say whether he should live or die? Whatever happens to him, whether he is allowed to live or die, are he and his family given justice?

Of course, there are no simple answers to many of these problems. In some cases it may be wise to accept that there is no perfect answer at all, or that the answer must depend on ideas of what is morally right. These moral principles, known as **ethics**, may differ from person to person. We now have very different ideas of fairness and justice from the ideas of our ancestors, who lived in different ages and experienced different problems. This is to be expected, and we will see examples of it when we come to look at how criminals have been tried and punished throughout our history. We also have different ideas of fairness and justice from people who live in other parts of the world, and who have been brought up under different conditions and cultures. What is thought of as fair and just by Americans, Chinese, Russians, or other peoples throughout the world can be completely different from our own ideas of fairness and justice. This may even be said of people living in the next street. In the case of the boy in a coma, some may say it is morally right that he should be allowed to die; others may argue that society has a moral duty to keep him alive.

Nevertheless, despite all the difficulties, it is possible in most situations to give citizens who have been harmed through the fault of others, and those who are accused of causing that harm, the feeling that we are concerned with their misfortunes, and that we must and do try to see that justice is done. How do we attempt to achieve this?

Any society has a duty to its citizens to do the best it can to make **laws** which, if obeyed, will provide them with a reasonably safe and trouble-free environment. These laws will also form a framework in which to live their lives. It must therefore also provide **courts** that are able to deal with those who break the law, and give individual citizens a peaceful means of settling their differences. After all, when the law has been broken it is never possible to turn the clock back and wipe out what has been done. The only way of trying to put things right is for the courts first to decide by fair procedures what has happened; and then, if the law has been broken, to deal fairly both with those responsible and those who have suffered because of it.

Over a period of almost one thousand years we have built up a remarkable body of laws, and a legal system that, for all its faults, is generally admired and has been copied in many other countries. The laws that we have in place at any given time in our history represent what we believe to be right and necessary at that time. They are the foundations of our system of justice.

One simple idea of justice is the upholding of rights, and the punishment of wrongs, by the law. Most people believe that justice involves far more than that. We have a strong idea of the basic requirements of a fair hearing. These are sometimes called the **rules of natural justice**: an open hearing; an impartial court (whether judge or jury); giving each side an equal chance to state its case and to call evidence in support of it; listening to the arguments of each side before coming to a reasoned decision. This is what we mean by fairness, and the fair manner in which our courts deal with legal issues and problems, according to rules that are the same for everyone, is what we call 'doing justice according to law'.

※

We should accept that our legal system does not and cannot always provide justice, whatever that may mean. Any system operated by human beings, with all our failings, can only be fallible; and despite all the safeguards that have been built into it, cases do sometimes go badly wrong. Some cases take far too long to come to court. Judges and juries can and do make mistakes. People who should win their cases lose; and people who should lose them, win. Individuals or organizations who can afford the most able lawyers and the great expense of going to court may have an advantage over others. This has always been a problem. The great eighteenth-century satirist Jonathan Swift said: '*Laws are like cobwebs, which may catch small flies, but let wasps and hornets break through*'.

Our very methods of reaching decisions have also been criticised, for some people claim that we seem to be more concerned with procedures (the way in which we try to arrive at the truth) than with getting at the truth itself. Most serious of all, justice is always at risk when witnesses commit **perjury**—give false evidence. It therefore faces its greatest danger when people in a position of authority and trust (such as the police), whose evidence is likely to be believed, conspire together to give false evidence. It is hoped that these cases are rare, but they have been known, and still happen. It is said that the courts are sometimes too ready to accept without question the evidence of people in authority.

In this book we will come across illustrations of injustice, and examples of the ways in which Parliament and the courts are constantly striving to improve our laws and our legal system in their efforts to avoid it. Nevertheless, there is confidence that in the vast majority of cases the decisions of the courts are correct, and have been reached fairly. In other words, despite its many shortcomings and the shortcomings of those who operate it (which

Lord Jessel, who appears in the opening paragraph of this chapter, might have had the humility to admit), our legal system is generally regarded as a good and fair one.

It is also important to understand that our laws and legal system are forever in need of review and reform. Parliament is constantly looking at ways to improve our laws. In 1965 an Act of Parliament set up the *Law Commission*, a group of eminent lawyers and others concerned with the administration of justice, to '*promote the systematic development, simplification and modernisation of the law*'. This Commission regularly reports on the state of the law, and makes recommendations as to how it can be improved. There is always a healthy pressure from many different groups and individuals to advance and improve our laws, and adapt them to the changing needs of society.

This book, then, is about our laws—the kind of laws we have, and their importance to us all. It is about the people who make our laws, and how they are made. It is about those who must enforce and uphold our laws, and what happens when anyone breaks them. It is about the courts, and the lawyers who work in them, and how criminal cases are tried and how those found guilty of crimes are punished. It is about understanding how the legal system works, and understanding the roles of the people who try to ensure that it works properly and fairly.

2

The Law and its Importance

'Law, says the judge as he looks down his nose,
Speaking clearly and most severely,
Law is as I've told you before,
Law is as you know I suppose,
Law is but let me explain it once more,
Law is The Law.'

W. H. Auden. Extract from *Law is Like Love.*

'Where law ends, tyranny begins.'

William Pitt, Prime Minister, 1801.

᛫᛫᛫

WHAT IS LAW?

Human beings have always lived together under **rules** of one kind or another. It does not matter where in the world; it does not matter in what age, whether the society in which they lived was a simple or a complex one by our present-day standards—humans have always as a matter of necessity lived by rules.

These rules are likely to be influenced by nature and the natural environment of the society in which people live, and by the simple natural instinct everyone has for survival. They may be influenced by religious or secular beliefs, and they will cater for the ideas of right and wrong that have been developed over time to suit the society in which they live.

Think about yourself. If you form a club or society to include your friends, almost certainly the first move will be to choose a leader and make up some rules. You may find that they do not all work, and as time goes by you will change and adapt them to suit your needs, and any new ideas you may have; but you will not be able to manage without any rules at all. Even criminals who plan a crime will work to a set of rules of their making, however unpleasant they and their crime may be.

- Every sport has to have its own set of rules. Imagine what it would be like trying to play cricket or football, tennis, or netball without rules. Even the simplest sport such as running a race must have rules. If it had none at all, everyone would set off at different times and in different directions and stop at different places!

- Sometimes new rules are introduced into a sport to make it more enjoyable to play and watch: the 'off-side' rule in football and 'limited-overs' rule in one-day cricket are examples of this. After a while people forget about the changes and the reasons for them, and the new rules become as much a part of the game as all the old ones.

If we think about our own family and school, past or present, we will know that there are things that we have to do and things we are not allowed to do. Some of these rules will be very obvious and we would expect to find them in any family or school. Some may apply only in our lives. They may be sensible, or they may seem to us or to outsiders to be strange—even foolish. We may well question these rules, but we will be told that there is no point in doing so: this is how things have always been, and how they are—the *'Law is The Law'*!

Very often these rules will be in force because our parents and school are handing down to us a way of living which has been tried and tested, and which has suited them over many years. Whether they are sensible or silly, useful or useless, serious or fun, we still live by them, because it has become the **custom** to do so. Gradually, over a period of time, these customs may change to adapt to the new times, just like the rules of a sport.

In this country we have three main kinds of rules:

- Rules that are the basic commonsense rules of everyday life. We must have rules that forbid us to do things which almost everyone thinks of as plainly and morally wrong.

  We must not kill or rob. This all seems very obvious and we would expect to find the same rules in countries throughout the world. Nevertheless, we must have rules in our own country which make killing and robbing crimes, and provide a system of punishment for those who commit these and other crimes.

- Rules that govern things that have become important *in our particular community* and about which we have learned from experience.

  It is the rule that the driver and passengers in a car must wear seat-belts. This is the law in many countries, but of course it was not always so. We did not have any cars until the early 1900s. We did not have any motorways until the 1960s. We are required to wear seat-belts because there were so many road accidents, and we learned from experience that in most cases they provide protection from injury. Without a rule making people use them, they might not bother to do so.

- Rules which have gradually developed over a period of many years, because it has become the custom to do things in a particular way, and that custom has become a settled and accepted way of behaviour.

  An example of this is our 'mercantile law', which deals with the way people trade with one another. Mercantile customs are important not merely in a domestic setting. Trade between countries throughout the world is based upon customs, and international trading practices have been accepted as part of our own commercial law.

People do sometimes use the expression 'laws' when they are talking about the rules by which they live their own lives: 'This is the law in our family'; 'This is the law in our school'; 'These are the laws of football'. We all know what may happen if we break these 'laws'—there will likely be punishment or, in the case of sport, penalties of one kind or another.

In this country there are certain rules which are there to be obeyed by everyone—by you, by your parents and family, by your teachers—by everyone who is old enough to behave responsibly. As we shall see, many of these rules have grown up out of custom—the customs of town and country, which have developed over the centuries, and have been adopted by the judges sitting in their courts. Many more rules have been laid down for us all by Parliament. If any of us break these rules we may be brought before a **court of law**. We may be punished by the court, or ordered to make amends in some way. All the rules that could result in the **courts** deciding to take action against us if we break them are called **laws**.

HOW IMPORTANT IS THE LAW?

We live on an island with a population of nearly 60 million people, and now a vast number of laws affect almost every aspect of our lives.

- The laws that apply to *everyone*, wherever we may be, are called the **laws of the land**. It is the law throughout the whole land that no one should steal and no one should supply certain drugs.

- The laws that only apply *locally*, in the areas in which we live, are called **by-laws**. There are roads in your area and there may be a park near your home. There will be special local laws which govern the traffic that uses these roads, or the way in which those who visit the park should behave. These by-laws will apply only to your local roads and your local park, and not to all the roads and parks in the country.

Whether laws are laws of the land or by-laws, they are mostly inspired by the desire to improve our lives and protect us from harm. They give each of us **rights**, which should be respected by others. We also have **duties** to obey them, whether we like them or not; and when we do so we automatically protect the rights of the people about us. This simple balance, which gives everyone rights and imposes on everyone equal and opposite duties towards others, is one of the basic foundations of our laws:

- We have the *right* to own our own property and to be left in peace to enjoy it. Equally, we have the *duty* to let others own and enjoy their property; and so, we must not steal from others. We know that there are those who break this law, and cause much distress by doing so. It is not difficult to imagine the consequences if it were not against the law to steal. Society would swiftly descend into chaos and violence.

- We have the *right* to safety on the roads. There are speed limits on all the public roads in the country, because experience shows that road accidents are often caused by people driving too fast. Some drivers may be better than others; some cars are designed to go much faster than others; but we all use the roads together—and all drivers, however good or bad, have the *duty* to drive within the speed limits. If they do so, they will help all road users to travel in safety.

In Chapter 4 we will learn more about the duties we owe as individuals, not merely to one another, but also to the State. We will also learn that ignorance of the law can never be an excuse for breaking it. Of course, laws do not deal only with very obvious things, such as stealing and driving too fast; they affect us in very many ways. The laws that make up our constitution guard our basic freedoms and guard us against the tyranny of a dictator. The ordinary laws that affect the way in which we lead our lives are designed to protect us from many different kinds of harm.

Laws can and must change to achieve these goals. The laws we have today bear very little relation to those of centuries ago. The laws we have in force at any particular time reflect our thoughts and attitudes as a people at that time, and in many cases it is possible for historians to trace a thread through from our past laws to our present ones. When Justice Kennedy of the US Supreme Court posed the question, 'What is law?' he answered it, saying, '*Law links the past to the future. The law is a story of our moral progress as a people*'.

Not everyone appreciates the extent to which our lives are surrounded and governed by laws of one kind or another. They may or may not be effective, but they are there, and there is little we do that is totally unaffected by the law. We all have experience of school because it is *the law* that every child up to the age of 16 must receive an education, and almost all children are educated in school. Let us take a look at the law in the context of a day in school as it is today, to glimpse just a few of the wide range of laws that apply to this simple situation.

GOING TO SCHOOL

- First, we are doing something without even thinking about it. We are breathing. The very air we breathe is protected against some forms of pollution by the law.

- We wash and get dressed. The water we use must be of a certain quality as specified by the law. If we bought our clothes in this country, the 'contract' made with the shop when they were purchased gives us protection if they prove to be of poor quality, and if they were made in factories in this country, conditions of employment and safety for the workers there are provided by the law.

- Breakfast. The food we buy must be of a certain quality and standard, as laid down by the law. There are numerous laws relating to the production and preparation of almost every type of food. There is often controversy over how much the law should regulate our food, and whether we should be free to eat unhealthy food if we want to. The publicity given in the 1990s to the dangers from bovine spongiform encephalopathy (BSE) shows that, in fact, we have come to rely on the law to protect us, and there is much anger when it seems to have failed. The story goes on, with arguments today about genetically modified (GM) foods, and the responsibility of the Government to ensure our safety.

- Travelling to school. Whether we walk or go by transport, even a short journey to school will be affected by dozens of safety requirements: the quality of the road surface, the safety of the pavements, the speed of the traffic, the duty to obey road signs. They all are governed by laws of one kind or another.

- Arriving at school, we may be surprised to learn how many laws govern the day—from the safety of the school premises and equipment to the hygiene of the kitchens. Then the law provides guidelines for the type and quality of education which everyone attending State schools must receive. Teachers must have certain qualifications before they can teach. Students up to the age of 16 have to follow the National Curriculum laid down by Act of Parliament. Primary school pupils have the exact form of their English and maths lessons ('literacy' and 'numeracy' hours) set out by law.

• The law also controls the ways in which teachers may or may not punish us if we misbehave. It even has something to say about the way in which teachers and pupils should behave towards one another. It is now a vital part of the law that they must not allow prejudice to result in different treatment, for it is against the law to discriminate against anyone because of his or her sex, colour, or race.

It is possible to go on with more and more examples of the ways in which our lives are governed by laws. It is interesting to think about them, and it is worthwhile doing so, for the law is not only concerned with crime and criminals. In a well-organised and complicated society, where there are so many things to do, and so many things could go wrong, the law has to be concerned with almost every aspect of our lives. The only way in which we can hope to live with one another in peace and security is by having *laws* made by people of good will, which provide for our safety and well-being. These must be laws that seem to be right and just, and which ordinary people will respect and obey because they seem to be right and just. If they do, they will expect others to obey them too—by being *law-abiding* citizens.

3

The Invisible Palace—Part 1 'Judge-Made' Law—Common Law and Equity

'The Common Law of England has been laboriously built about a mythical figure—the figure of "The Reasonable Man".'

A. P. Herbert, *Uncommon Law.*

Who is the ordinary reasonable man? Lord Justice Bowen in 1903 famously described him as 'the man on the Clapham Omnibus'. Lord Justice Greer in 1933 pictured him as 'the man who takes magazines at home and in the evenings pushes the lawn mower in his shirt sleeves'. In 1940, Lord Chief Justice Goddard was less romantic: 'Searching for the reasonable man is like a blind man looking for a black hat in a dark room.'

*

England is rich in castles and palaces and, if we were taken on a guided tour of some of the greatest, we would quickly discover that the fine buildings we see today were not all constructed at one time, but grew over the centuries as alterations were made to them. A visit to one of the most famous royal palaces, Windsor Castle, may help us to understand something about the foundations and development of our law.

Windsor Castle was built as a royal fortress by William the Conqueror towards the end of the eleventh century. The great round tower was built in the twelfth century in the reign of Henry II. Massive stone fortifications were added in the twelfth and thirteenth centuries. A chapel was built in the fourteenth century and then replaced, by the one we see today, in the early days of the Tudors. Important additions to the palace were made in the reign of the Stuart King Charles II, and the royal apartments were later rebuilt or restored many times under the direction of George III, George IV, and Queen Victoria.

Even now, following the great fire of 20 November 1992, much work has been done to restore and improve Windsor Castle. Historians know that literally dozens of major additions and alterations have been made over the years, but they have been carried out with such care and skill that anyone visiting Windsor today will see a magnificent and beautiful royal palace.

The beginnings and the development of the law in this country have been very much like those of Windsor Castle. The importance of William the Conqueror, not only to our island history but also to the story of our legal system, is seen by the fact that some of the foundations of the law which we know today were being laid in the very days that William's workmen were laying the foundation stones of his castle at Windsor.

William was the Duke of Normandy, before he became King of England, and the great 'legal' foundation which he laid was an import from northern France, the *Curia Regis* (King's Court). This was not just a court of law, but a royal household. Its Council comprised the king and some of the most powerful men in the land. William used it as an instrument both to govern the country, and as a court for deciding disputes.

Just as Windsor Castle has been added to and improved over the centuries, so have a succession of kings and queens, governments and parliaments and judges, built up, added to, altered, and improved our laws. New courts have been built to provide justice in areas where justice was not available before. New ways were invented to enable people who had been harmed to commence legal **actions** (proceedings)—to bring their grievances before the courts and have them remedied.

This too has been done with such care and skill that our laws have been adapted and used as the foundations of the laws of many other nations. As some of these countries were once part of the British Empire, this is hardly surprising; but the fact is that today the legal systems of countries as far apart as Canada, Australia, Hong Kong, Israel, and Kenya draw on our system of laws. In the USA, English law is the basis of the law in every state except Louisiana (where the civil law, like that of France and many other European nations, is based upon Roman Law).

The supreme law-making body in this country is **Parliament**, and this has been so for centuries. Parliament passes laws in the form of **Acts of Parliament**, which are known as **statutes**. The law created by Parliament is known as **statute law**. Whenever there is any question about the meaning of a law passed by Parliament it is for the judges in the courts to decide what the true meaning is—that is, to interpret it.

During the nineteenth and twentieth centuries Parliament has passed a vast number of statute laws, and its law making, both in volume and importance, has greatly exceeded that of the courts. Nevertheless, judges play an essential part in the lives of individual citizens—presiding over cases of those accused of crime, deciding disputes between citizen and citizen and disputes between citizens and the State. We have a system of law in which those very decisions—at least the most important ones decided by the senior courts— have for hundreds of years been carefully recorded in **law reports**. These reports first appeared in what were called Year Books, but there are now dozens of different publications containing detailed reports of leading cases in every area of the law. Each report begins with a 'headnote', which provides an expert summary of the facts and the court's decision. This summary is followed by the exact words of the judgments given by the judges. Edited by qualified lawyers, their accuracy is confirmed or 'approved' by the judges themselves. The principles of law as stated in these cases must normally be accepted and followed by the next court which has a similar case.

Many thousands of cases have come before the courts, and the decisions of the judges, like the individual stones of a palace—case by case, year by year—have added to the gradual build up of the law. In this way, over the years and running alongside the laws passed by Parliament, a great body of law, known as **judge-made law**, has been developed. It is not possible to see it, as we can see a royal palace such as Windsor, or indeed the Palace of Westminster, where Parliament passes its laws. It is an *Invisible Palace*, but still it exists—and it plays a vitally important part in the life of our nation.

Another and equally crucial part of our national life is the way in which the country itself is governed. This may not be widely known, but here also the courts play an essential role. Our country is governed according to the rules of our **constitution**. This too cannot be seen, for unlike many other countries, we do not have a written constitution that we can take out and study (although we do now have an important statement of our 'human rights'). If our Invisible Palace has a throne room, the constitution is it, and as we shall see, the judges may be called upon, and counted upon, to protect it should the need arise.

We will be looking in Chapter 5 at Parliament, our chief law-making body, and the way in which it passes new laws. In this and the next chapter we will concentrate upon our system of judge-made law, and the constitution. Judge-made law has over the centuries been divided into two main types: **common law** and **equity**. In this chapter we will examine something of the beginnings and nature of each of them.

THE COMMON LAW

In very early times—before King Alfred the Great (reigned 871–99)—there was no system of justice that applied to the whole of the country. It was not ruled by a single monarch. The population was small. There was no transportation as we know it today and communications were available to the few. Most people never travelled more than a few miles from their homes, and only a tiny number could read and write. There were no law books. It was not possible for the whole country to be ruled according to a single set of laws. Nevertheless, despite the limitations of the time, the Anglo-Saxons created the Kingdom of England and its counties (or shires) headed by sheriffs.

When William the Conqueror invaded England in 1066, he took over the most efficiently governed kingdom in Europe, but he soon grasped the need to reinforce its system of central or national government. This meant trying to provide some central system of justice over which the king had control, for William understood that it was only by making laws which had to be obeyed and could be enforced throughout the land that he could exercise real power and control over all his subjects.

For centuries English monarchs had governed the outer reaches of their kingdoms through sheriffs and their officials, but to secure their authority they would have to travel, or 'progress' through the country, taking their court and courtiers with them. When William's court progressed, he and the most powerful courtiers attached to his *Curia Regis* would listen to those who came to him with their 'grievances'—their complaints or accusations—and they would give judgment. Almost all the main courts we have today can be traced back to William's *Curia Regis*.

The king would literally sit on a *bench* to hear cases in his own court. This is why one of the most important courts became known as the **Court of King's Bench**; but not every monarch made a good judge, or for that matter was particularly interested in his system of justice. In the years that followed, kings delegated their work in the courts to others. They and their advisers in the King's Council set up **royal courts**, appointing men who became known as judges to sit in them, and leaving it to them to decide many cases which they might previously have tried themselves.

King Henry II (reigned 1154–89) was particularly interested in law and order, and played an outstanding part in the development of the legal system. He understood to a greater extent than his predecessors that a single system of justice for the whole land under the control of the king would not only help to unify the country, but give him great power. He studied how best to achieve this.

Henry set the foundations of 'professional' judges, members of the clergy or laymen 'learned in the law' upon whom he could depend to uphold his laws. There were then 18 judges in the country. He ordered five of them to remain in London and take over from him the task of deciding cases. This resulted in the creation of the King's Bench of judges, who sat at Westminster.

In 1166 Henry issued a Declaration at the Assize of Clarendon (an **assize** was an early form of King's Council; it later became a 'sitting' or session of the court) that the remaining judges should be sent out on **circuits** to travel different parts of the country. When they did so they had to apply the laws that had been made by the judges at Westminster. In this way many local customary laws were replaced by new national laws. As these national laws would apply to everyone, they would be 'common to all'. These laws therefore became known as the **common law**.

> Henry II himself fell foul of the law. He was accused of ordering the death of his Archbishop of Canterbury, Thomas Becket. The murder of Becket in Canterbury Cathedral by four of Henry's knights made him very unpopular, and in an effort to make amends, and avoid a rebellion, Henry accepted the punishment of a public whipping—perhaps one of the first very dramatic illustrations of the principle that even kings are not above the law.
>
> Henry died on 6 July 1189, and was succeeded soon afterwards by Richard I 'the Lionheart'. 1189 is a date is of some legal interest, for it is the origin of the phrase '*from time immemorial*'. This is because in the reign of Edward I (1272–1307) Parliament decided that 'legal memory' should run from the date of Henry's death, and the courts would take no account of any legal transactions which had taken place before it. With the passage of time this was also taken to mean that the courts would not recognise any laws made before 1189.

The system which developed, of judges sitting in London and also travelling the country, became known as the 'Assize system'. It survived in that form for 800 years—until 1971. Although the present 'Circuit system' may have a different name, to this day High Court judges still sit in London for part of the year and then travel the country to hear cases in much the same way as they have done for centuries.

Although judges, when travelling on Assize, would wherever possible put into force the same laws as were being applied at Westminster, they would not altogether ignore the customs of the region. They would learn from them, and if they approved of them they would be prepared to accept them as the law, sometimes even carrying them on to other parts of the country, and back to Westminster itself. The judges sitting in London held their courts in Westminster Hall. In his book *Westminster Hall* Dorian Gerhold says: '*The English legal system, and thus also the related legal systems of the United States and many other countries, was largely developed in Westminster Hall, and for almost seven centuries the Hall was the centre of that system.*'

The Norman and Plantagenet kings spanned the period 1066–1399. During this time three separate Royal Courts grew out of the *Curia Regis*. They dealt with cases involving the royal revenue and the collection of taxes (**Court of the Exchequer**), criminal and civil cases in which the king was concerned (**Court of King's Bench**), and cases which concerned disputes between private individuals (**Court of Common Pleas**). In addition to these three main courts, yet more courts were created to deal with many other aspects of local life, and courts of one kind or another gradually became a focal point in the everyday lives of most citizens. In his *Social History of England* the historian Alan Harding refers to the use to which courts came to be put in binding together the affairs of the nation: *'The medieval constitution might be described as a network of courts. Everyone had to attend some court regularly . . . England was in effect a conglomeration of "countries", held together by its legal system.'*

The courts of the Exchequer, King's Bench, and Common Pleas kept their names and continued to hear cases for many centuries—until 1873. (We still have a division of the High Court which, in the reign of a queen, is called the **Queen's Bench Division**.) Each court was based at Westminster. King's Bench and Common Pleas occupied a part of the Great Hall, with Exchequer in an adjoining building. So we must picture courts sitting at the same time in different parts of the Hall. King Richard II rebuilt Westminster Hall in its present form at the end of the fourteenth century. The scene of many famous trials, including that of King Charles I, it was the chief law court of England for well over 600 years, from the reign of Henry II until the opening of the Royal Courts of Justice in 1882.

The common law, originally based upon the common customs of town and country and gradually developed over the centuries, has become one of the most prized features of our national way of life. Many of our most famous judges have been known as 'great common lawyers', committed to the advancement of our laws and the rule of law. The common law has been aptly described as *'The common-sense of the community, crystallised and formulated by our forefathers'*. This is because, as we shall see, many of our laws have been based upon what the courts would expect the 'reasonable' man to do and think in certain situations.

THE REASONABLE MAN

The common law is still very much part of our law. It is applied in courts throughout the country. In many instances, when developing the law and deciding cases, in particular in the civil law, judges have tested the behaviour of the people whose cases they were trying against the standards of what might be expected of an 'ordinary, reasonable' person faced with similar circumstances. In Chapter 12 we will see examples of this in both the civil and the criminal law.

In *Uncommon Law*, a parody of the law and legal system written in 1935, A. P. Herbert puts the following words into the mouth of a fictional judge:

> The Common Law of England has been laboriously built about a mythical figure—the figure of 'The Reasonable Man'. He is an ideal, a standard, the embodiment of all those qualities we demand of the good citizen. No matter what particular department

of human life which falls to be considered in these courts, sooner or later we have to face the question: Was this or was it not the conduct of a reasonable man?

In considering how this test should be applied in any particular case, the courts are prepared to hear evidence so that they might better understand all the problems involved. They do not expect standards of conduct that are unreasonably high; nor have they allowed people to be judged by standards that are unreasonably low. Their ideas of reasonableness may be based upon 'common sense'; but it is not common sense simply because it is the individual judge's impression of what is right; it is common sense that makes sense, and is reasonable because it has survived the test of thorough argument, and has the force of reason. This is why the common law has a reputation for sound common sense and justice.

EQUITY

We have learned that with the passage of time new courts were added to our system of justice, to provide justice where the ancient royal courts had failed. The common law may be admired and copied today, but in centuries gone by it was primitive, and became rigid while circumstances changed. In consequence it came nowhere near to satisfying the growing needs of the people. In his book *England under the Tudors*, the distinguished historian G. R. Elton writes:

> *The common law is certainly one of the glories of England, and it was perhaps the chief legacy of the Middle Ages. But by the late fifteenth century the courts were in a bad way ... The procedure of the common law courts was slow, highly technical and very expensive: a trivial mistake in pleading [setting out the case] could lose a good cause, and a good lawyer could drive a coach and four through the law by exploiting technicalities.*

Another serious problem was that the use of juries became widespread, even in civil cases, and juries could be intimidated, bribed, and 'packed' (filled with the friends of one of the parties).

How could people obtain justice, if not in the common law courts? The answer seems almost to echo the beginnings of the common law courts. Even after the formation of the common law courts it was always open to those who felt that they could not receive justice, or afford the expense of going to court, to appeal to or **petition** the king to '*redress their grievances*'. This meant pleading with him directly to hear their complaints and provide a remedy for them. At first kings would consider these petitions themselves, or leave it to their Councils, or 'Parliaments', to decide them, but during the fifteenth century this work was delegated to one of the Council members. This was the Chancellor—later to receive the title Lord High Chancellor.

Because the Lord Chancellor decided petitions addressed to the king, he became known as the 'Keeper of the King's Conscience'; and because there were so many petitions, he came to preside over his own court. It was called the **Court of Chancery**. The Chancellor did not try criminal cases. He dealt only with civil disputes concerning, for example, matters of property and breaches of contract. He set out to do justice in these cases where the **parties** (people involved in a case) were able to show that the common law courts were not able or prepared to do justice. The law that was applied in the Court of Chancery was known as **equity**, a word meaning even-handedness and fairness.

Eventually, the work of the Court of Chancery grew to the point where it became a rival to the common law courts. No one knows precisely when it first came into being, but it was well established by the time of Henry VIII— and it too came to occupy a space in Westminster Hall. There is a touching account of Sir Thomas More, upon his appointment by Henry as Lord Chancellor, on his way to his Court of Chancery, stopping to pay his respects to his aged father, Sir John More, who was also sitting in the Hall as a King's Bench judge. According to Sir Thomas's son-in-law, this he did by *'reverently kneelinge downe in the sight of them all duely aske his father's blessinge'*.

The essential principle by which the Court of Chancery acted was that everyone should receive fairness and justice. There were three important conditions that a person seeking justice from the Court of Chancery had to meet:

- He had to show that he could not receive justice in the common law courts.

- He had to show that he was himself without blame. This was called 'coming to court with clean hands'.

- He had to show that he had not delayed in bringing his case before the court.

If he was able to do these things, and to satisfy the court that he had suffered as a result of some wrongdoing by another person, the court would give him a **remedy**, meaning that it would devise some way to ensure that if possible something was done to put right the wrong that had been done to him. In this way, to use an expression well known to lawyers, it was able to 'redress his grievance'. This example may help to illustrate how the Common Law courts and the Court of Chancery could differ:

- If two people made an agreement (a contract)—one (the seller) to sell a house and the other (the purchaser) to buy it, and the seller broke his side of the bargain and refused to sell, the common law courts would grant the purchaser a sum of money to compensate him for the harm done or inconvenience he had suffered.

In these circumstances, however, money might not be enough. After all, on the promise of a house sale the purchaser might have sold his own house and made many plans. The Court of Chancery assumed the power to order the guilty party (the seller) to keep his side of the bargain fully. He would be made to keep his side of the contract, sell the house, and allow the purchaser to move into it.

The first and most influential of the new courts added to the 'Invisible Palace' was the Court of Chancery, but it was by no means the only one. Several other new courts appeared, and in some cases later disappeared. These included another court of equity, the Court of Requests, a younger sister for the Court of Chancery.

The Court of Requests—'The court for Poor Men's Causes'

For many years the Court of Chancery had a good reputation for delivering justice, but as its popularity grew it could not cope with the volume of petitions presented to it. A second 'court of conscience' was created. Known as the Court of Requests, its judges were men trained in the civil law—bishops, doctors of law, and almoners.

This court was established to provide justice to those who were too poor to have their cases heard in the other courts. By the 1530s the Court of Requests was extremely busy. Known as 'The court for poor men's causes', it operated on similar lines to the Court of Chancery. In 1580 the Elizabethan, William Lambarde, wrote, '*In that the Court of Requests handleth causes that desireth moderation of the rigour which the common law denounceth, it doth plainly participate in the nature of the Chancery*'.

The Court of Requests came under mighty attack from the common law courts. Jealous of its success, for it attracted much business away from the common lawyers working in the Court of Common Pleas. They cast doubt on the validity of its judgments. In 1599 the Court of Common Pleas declared that '*Requests has no power of judicature*' (no power to make judgments which the parties must obey). In 1606 Sir Edward Coke, when Chief Justice in the Court of King's Bench, refused to convict of perjury a man who had lied on oath in the Court of Requests, on the ground that it was 'not a court'.

In these ways, people who had been ordered by the Court of Requests to redress some grievance were encouraged to claim that as they had not been tried in a proper court they were free to disobey its orders. The judges in the Court of Requests were not men of great influence. They did not have the authority to fight off these attacks. Its work gradually diminished, and by 1643 it had ceased to exist.

As the years went by the Court of Chancery (now the **Chancery Division of the High Court**) tended to specialise in certain areas of the law. In Chapter 11 we will see the main types of work done by the different courts. The work of the Chancery Division is now confined mainly to cases of company law, partnership, conveyancing (transfer of land and buildings), wills and probate (administration of the property of persons who have died), patent and copyright law, and revenue (taxation). As we will see in Chapter 12, another important aspect of Chancery work is the administration of trusts.

There were, however, serious problems with the old Court of Chancery too—the reverse side of the legal coin. In contrast with the common law courts, where judges were obliged to follow the decisions of their predecessors, the Lord Chancellors in their Court of Chancery were free to do as they thought right in each individual case. This depended entirely on their own personal ideas of justice—their own 'consciences'. This meant that although lawyers who had to advise people of their rights at least knew what the common law courts were likely to do in a particular situation, it was much more difficult to predict what the Lord Chancellor would do in his court. In the Court of Chancery the law had no certainty, and lawyers therefore felt unable to advise their clients properly. This is why it was said with scorn that decisions of the Court of Chancery *'varied according to the length of the Chancellor's foot'*. The historian John Selden (1584–1654) in his remarkable book *Table Talk* wrote: *'Equity is a roguish thing. For law [common law] we have a measure, know what to trust to; equity is according to the conscience of him that is Chancellor and as that is larger or narrower so is equity.'*

There developed another and even greater problem. Despite its good intentions and early popularity, as the work of the Court of Chancery grew, it earned a bad reputation for expense and delay. This became critical during the long period in office of one Lord Chancellor, Lord Eldon, who was Chancellor from 1801 to 1827. For many years, both as a politician and judge, Eldon opposed law reform and religious liberty. He was a slow and ponderous judge, and he hated the jibe about the Chancellor's foot.

Under Eldon's influence the Court of Chancery, like the common law courts, did have to regard, and follow, its previous decisions. Its work became increasingly formalised, or, as we would now say, bound up in 'red tape'. Cases became bogged down in interminable delays. In 1823 the House of Commons debated delays in this court. When Lord Eldon was asked why he had not yet given judgment in a case which he had heard in 1817, he admitted that he had *'entirely forgotten it'*. (One hundred and eighty years later, in 1998, a judge of the Chancery Division resigned following severe criticism by the Court of Appeal that he had kept the parties waiting 20 months for a judgment.)

- The failures of the old Court of Chancery were savagely satirised by Charles Dickens in his novel *Bleak House*. There he relates the case of *Jarndyce* v *Jarndyce*. This was a probate action (in which the parties were arguing about their rights to property left in a will). It lasted so long and was so expensive that eventually all the property, which had been left in the will, was spent on paying the lawyers' fees. Describing the progress of the case, Dickens said: '*Equity sends questions to Law [the common law courts], Law sends questions back to Equity; Law finds it can't do this, Equity finds it can't do that; neither can so much as say it can't do anything, without a solicitor instructing and this counsel appearing*'. He ends a tirade of abuse against the Court of Chancery with the words: '*Suffer any wrong that can be done to you, rather than come here*'.

- There is a hold in wrestling — it is called 'a Chancery', and it means getting your opponent's head locked under your arm. This expression stems from the days of the bare-fisted fights, when it was said that once a man got his case into the 'Chancery' court, the lawyers had him in a stranglehold and could pummel him for as long as they liked, and he would not be able to get free.

In 1873, the Judicature Act 'merged' common law and equity, and although one of the divisions of the High Court is still called the Chancery Division, since that time all the courts have been permitted to administer both. Parliament decreed that where there was a conflict between the common law and the laws of equity, equity should be supreme.

✳

We now have a system of laws, whether common law or equity, in which cases decided by judges have been handed down from generation to generation. They are laws which relate to many different aspects of our lives. Judges have usually (but not always) respected and followed the decisions of their 'brethren' — a term used for their fellow judges (we would now say 'sisters' and 'brothers'). In particular, where legal **rulings** (decisions) have been made by the highest courts in the land, as we will see in Chapter 11, they *must* be accepted and followed by the lower courts. Only Parliament can change these laws.

Our judge-made laws are one of our national treasures. The efficiency and popularity of the common law courts and the courts of equity may have varied from century to century, and we should not become too starry-eyed about our judges, some of whom, by modern standards, exhibited a terrifying insensitivity to human suffering, and made few concessions to changing times. Nevertheless, over the years the judges in our courts have handed down many remarkable judgments, examples of independent and careful thinking, which have led to much important social change. The result is that our legal history is paved with landmark cases in which judges of the common law courts in particular, now revered as 'great common lawyers', have recognised and advanced the causes of freedom.

In the course of this book we will come across some notable cases of judge-made law. One is *Bushell's Case* (Chapter 15). Heard in 1670, it decided once and for all that a jury could return any verdict it believed to be right. Almost exactly one hundred years later another great case put an end to slavery in this country. This was the case of James Somerset:

Somerset's Case

James Somerset was an African who was transported as a slave to Virginia in America. There he was sold to a man called Charles Stewart. In 1769 Stewart brought his slave with him on a journey to England. Once in England Somerset looked after his master for two years, but when Stewart decided to return to Virginia, he escaped his master's control. Stewart employed men to re-capture him, and he was taken to a ship called the *Ann and Mary*, which was bound for Jamaica. There Somerset was kept in irons.

Word of Somerset's plight leaked out before the ship set sail, and a writ (claim) of *habeas corpus* was issued to bring him before a court. *Habeas corpus* literally means 'you must have the body' and the ancient writ of habeas corpus (which still survives today) commands any person holding someone in custody to bring that person before the court and justify his detention.

The case was heard by Lord Mansfield. It was argued that there were over ten thousand slaves in England at this time, and if he let Somerset free the result would be to abolish slavery altogether. This would cause great economic loss to many people. Lord Mansfield ended slavery in England with these words: *'The state of slavery is so odious that nothing can be suffered to support it, but positive law [meaning an Act of Parliament]. Whatever inconvenience, therefore, may follow from the decision, I cannot say that the case [in favour of slavery] is allowed or affirmed by the law of England. The air of England is too pure for any slave to breathe. Let the black go free.'*

It is not within the scope of this book to give a detailed history of the courts, or to recount the many stories which might be told of important judge-made laws; but it is necessary to understand that the courts are still constantly advancing the law to meet the ever-changing demands of society. Some dramatic examples of this are to be found in cases involving difficult questions of medical ethics—ranging from artificial birth and 'cloning' to the artificial prolonging of life. Doctors may have their own and varied views about these life and death issues, but it has been left to the courts to devise the sensitive rules which govern these situations. Another recent illustration of the courts being prepared to move with the times concerns the offence of rape:

• For centuries it had been the (common) law of the land that a man could not be found guilty of raping his wife. In a case heard in 1992, the courts decided that in this day and age, where a husband and wife had separated, and she wished to have nothing more to do with him, the husband would be guilty of rape if he had sexual intercourse with her without her consent.

Modern judges are not, however, always prepared to change the old common law themselves, even if they think this is desirable. Usually they will not do so where it is thought best that Parliament should consider carefully the social consequences of change; but even if they are not prepared to alter the law, judges may make recommendations for change; and Parliament will normally take their views seriously. Here are two recent examples of cases where the courts have refused to alter the law, but Parliament has done so in the wake of their recommendations:

- It was the ancient (common) law that a person could only be charged with murder if his victim died within a year and a day of his attack. With the advance of medical science a person might be subject to a murderous attack, and kept alive in hospital, possibly on a life-support machine, for years. Under the common law, if he then died, the attacker could be charged with serious assault, but not murder. The courts decided that this old rule was still the law, and would remain so until Parliament changed it. In fact, the *Law Commission* (responsible for suggesting reforms of the law) did recommend that it should be abolished, and by an Act of Parliament passed in 1996 its abolition was effected.

- Another old (common) law rule was that children between the ages of 10 and 14 were presumed to be incapable of committing a crime unless it could be proved by clear evidence that they knew that what they were doing was seriously wrong. As recently as 1995, judges sitting in the House of Lords, the highest appeal court in the land, were asked to decide whether this law still applied. The 'Law Lords' said this was a law with important social consequences, and that it must be for Parliament to decide whether it should be changed. Parliament has now abolished this ancient law, so as to make it easier for the authorities to prosecute children.

These are not the only examples of laws that have been shown to be out of date, for just as a great palace requires constant maintenance and renovation, so does the common law—and it does not always get it. Many people are concerned that because the common law has served us so well in the past, we have been too ready to revere and preserve some of our ancient laws, and believe that much needs to be done by Parliament to simplify and modernise certain parts of our law. Of these, the criminal law is thought to be in the greatest need of reform. Here both the common law and statute law have become outdated. Over 140 years after its enactment, the Offences Against the Person Act 1861 still governs the majority of cases of violence (covering more than 80,000 cases each year). In 1999 Mr Justice (now Lord Justice) Carnwath, then Chairman of the Law Commission, referred to it as a *'tired and confused old workhorse long overdue for reform'*. There is a move towards the creation of a Criminal Code which would, as in other European countries, set out in one document in an understandable and straightforward way the main principles of our criminal law.

*

With few exceptions, judges have never liked to see themselves as creators of laws, regarding that as the province of Parliament. They are happy to be seen as applying and interpreting the law as it is, but no more. Some of the most creative judges who have played a significant part in the evolution of the law have preferred to regard themselves as guardians of the common law, rather than as makers of new law. Perhaps understandably, they prefer the public perception of Parliament, as opposed to judges, making new law, and they find comfort in that illusion.

There is, however, no doubt that over the centuries judges have been responsible for making a great deal of law, and our senior judges are still doing so. If not how could the common law and the law of equity have developed? As we will see in the next chapter, and Chapter 19 (Human Rights), it is to be expected that the influence of the judges in the making of new laws will increase, and that in future they will come to play an even more active and important part in the development of our laws.

4

The Invisible Palace—Part 2
The Constitution

'Be you never so high, the law is above you.'

Thomas Fuller, chaplain in the army of King Charles I and chaplain to King Charles II.

'May she defend our laws,
And ever give us cause
To sing with heart and voice,
God save the Queen.'

Extract, second verse, the National Anthem.

＊

The Throne Room of our Invisible Palace is the **British Constitution**. The way in which a country is governed, and power is organised and distributed, is called its **constitution**.

In many countries the constitution is written down. They therefore have what is known as a **written constitution**. One of the oldest examples of a written constitution is the Constitution of the United States of America (USA) which was written in 1787. Among the most recent are the Constitution of South Africa, which was drawn up in 1992, and that of the newly independent State of Ukraine, whose Parliament passed its written constitution in 1998.

In the countries of the United Kingdom we do not have a written constitution to tell us how power is to be divided up and exercised. The way in which we are governed is of course known, and has been written about in many books, but we do not have one document which sets it all out for us. Until October 2000 we had no single document to guarantee our rights as citizens, but that at least has changed. We do now have a statute which guarantees our 'human rights'—the Human Rights Act 1998, which came into force on 2 October 2000, and we will be looking at the rights which it confers later in this book.

Our **unwritten constitution** has been developing for over 700 years, and it continues to do so. It is in part founded upon statute and case law, but mainly upon custom and **convention**—the widely accepted view of proper behaviour, which has become hardened into accepted rules of law. According to Halsbury's *Laws of England*, our constitution is based upon the idea that '*no body or political party has a monopoly of wisdom, that State bodies should be democratically and legally accountable, and that they should promote good government in the general interest, rather than in their personal interests or the interests of limited sections of society.*'

In practice this means that no one person should be given so much power that he or she can become a dictator and tyrant, whether that person be the sovereign, a politician, an army general, or anyone else. Power is separated and distributed in such a way that this cannot happen. This principle is called the **separation of powers**.

The **British Constitution** is therefore unwritten and it is flexible. It is open to change by Act of Parliament to meet the gradually changing needs of the nation. This is one important difference between our system and that of the USA, which, being written, is more rigid, and can only be changed by special procedures.

Alternatively, a written constitution is intended in the most open way to be a blueprint for the way in which a country is to be governed, and to guarantee individual rights; and the US constitution has, in a way for all to see, given rights and provided a means by which judges have the power and duty to oversee the protection of those rights. They have the power and duty to protect the series of checks and balances built into the constitution which limit the power of the US government. This means that US judges can even 'strike down' laws if they are contrary to the constitution.

*

In the United Kingdom (UK), power is divided so as to ensure that it never becomes dangerously concentrated in the hands of one person, or even a small group of people. At one time, power and responsibility were said to reside in the 'Three Estates of the Realm': the Crown, the Clergy, and the Laity (non-clergy). The 'Fourth Estate' was Edmund Burke's ironical phrase for the Press, in whom resides '*power without responsibility*'. The present constitutional theory, which has grown into hardened practice, is that power is divided between three main organisations. Each is to a greater or lesser extent independent of the others, but at the same time owes allegiance to, and is under the nominal control of, the Crown.

In due course we will see some practical examples of the way power is separated in our constitution. Figure 4.1 shows, in a simplified way, how it is supposed to work:

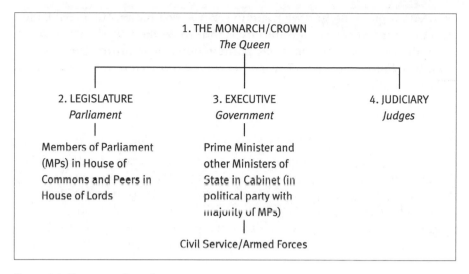

Figure 4.1 The separation of powers

We will look first at the roles of the legislature, executive, and judiciary in our constitution, and then at that of the monarch.

2. THE LEGISLATURE

The **Legislature** means our law makers. In this country our chief law maker is 'The Queen in Parliament', and in the next chapter we will see how this works. All those responsible for making laws in Parliament, whether they are Members of Parliament in the House of Commons or Peers in the House of Lords swear an oath of allegiance to the Queen on taking office, and all Acts of Parliament must receive the Royal Assent—the Queen's agreement and her signature, before they can become law. The two Houses of Parliament also hold the Government (executive) to account for its actions, by making it answer questions and explain itself.

3. THE EXECUTIVE

The **Executive** is the power which can take the initiative for change: it can take action.

LOCAL GOVERNMENT

In the 'town and country' the local authority in each area decides such matters as who should clean the streets, what the traffic speed and parking restrictions might be, and what sort of school organisations we should have. The executive in the Local Authority is formed by the political party which wins the local elections, and has greatest number of **councillors** on each county or borough council. The local executive is therefore voted in (and can be voted out) by the people.

NATIONAL GOVERNMENT

The national executive is always known as the **Government**. It is formed from the winning political party at the nationwide General Election. This is the party which has the most members in the House of Commons. These are **Members of Parliament** (MPs). The national executive is therefore also voted in (or out) by the people.

The leader of that winning party becomes Prime Minister. He or she chooses other members of that party to be in charge of different aspects of government—for example, foreign affairs (the Foreign Secretary), money and taxation (the Chancellor of the Exchequer), law and order (the Home Secretary). The most important of these **Secretaries of State** are the Senior **Ministers** who form the **Cabinet**. This is the top committee of government; but there are many (more than 100) other members of the Government doing different jobs. These are the Junior Ministers. All Ministers are assisted in their government departments by thousands of permanent officials in the Civil Service.

The Government makes the day-to-day decisions about the public life of the country: foreign policy—even war and peace; the level of taxation; expenditure on roads, hospitals, education, and welfare. The policies of the executive in these areas provide the framework within which we live our everyday lives. It is the executive which decides how that policy is to be carried out, and the executive is actually responsible for carrying it out. It is helpful to take an example:

LAW AND ORDER

- We know that if anyone is accused of committing a crime, he is first charged and then brought before a court. The court will decide if he has committed the offence, and if so what the punishment should be; but there is much more to a system of 'law and order' than that. 'Law and order' involves making laws to protect people from any form of crime or disorder, providing a police force to investigate and enforce these laws, and the means of rehabilitating or punishing anyone who breaks them—for example, the probation service and prisons.

  The Home Secretary is the Minister responsible for law and order. He is a member of the Cabinet and part of the executive (Government). The

Home Secretary obviously cannot do all this work on his own. He is in charge of a great **Department of State** (the Home Office), and together with his junior Ministers who have special responsibilities in the Department, he must make the major decisions as to how it is run. The Home Office is the Government department in which civil servant employees (all persons employed by the State or 'the Crown' are called civil servants) deal with matters of law and order and the reform of the criminal law.

The Home Secretary, his Home Office ministers, and the thousands of civil servants who work in the Home Office are the branch of Government which must be responsible for law and order matters. This of course includes how we deal with the problems of crime and criminals. They will put forward legislation (new laws) to tackle crime. This will include the various ways in which criminals can be punished. Parliament will then decide whether to pass these laws.

The executive, in the form of the Home Secretary and the Home Office, is in overall control of all the other tens of thousands of civil servants who are concerned in keeping law and order—the police service, the probation service, the prison service. It decides how they should do their work and how that work should be organised. That is the purpose of government.

4. THE JUDICIARY

The **Judiciary** (judges) has two vital roles in our constitution. First, where there is any dispute about constitutional law, the judges must decide what the law is. Their most important role, however, is to act as an independent check on the powers of the executive. Only the courts have the authority to stop any individual or body of persons from exceeding their powers, or making improper use of their powers. This is known as preventing an **abuse of power**.

There is no doubt that the Prime Minister and his Ministers, who are part of the executive, do have enormous power, and that power is all the greater when the Government has a large majority in the House of Commons. What happens, then, if it is believed that any member of the executive is about to abuse his powers and act unlawfully, or that he has already done so? Here again is a simple example:

- The Home Secretary has executive powers, exercised by his civil servants, to detain any person who enters the country as an illegal immigrant, and deport him back to his own country. What if an immigrant has been detained and is about to be deported, but he claims to be lawfully entitled to remain in the UK? How can he ensure that the Home Office deals with his case properly?

The answer is that the Home Secretary is responsible for the actions of all the civil servants employed by the Home Office; and however powerful he may be, if it is thought that he or anyone in his department has acted unlawfully—in excess (abuse) of his power or without reason—the Home Secretary himself may be taken to court.

The court will then have to decide if he has acted lawfully or not. If the court decides against the Home Secretary, it will make a **court order**—an instruction to him not to do anything unlawful, or to put right any unlawful thing that he has done. In this case, if the court decides in favour of the Home Office, the immigrant will be deported. If it decides in favour of the immigrant, he will be released from detention, and allowed to remain in the UK.

Few people are aware of this aspect of the courts' work. It may not be well known; but it is of great importance. It concerns deciding disputes between citizens and the State, and these cases are heard in London in a special part of the Queen's Bench Division of the High Court, called the **Administrative Court**.

It is not unusual for Ministers to be taken to court; neither is it unheard of for Ministers to lose. For instance, from time to time the courts do indeed decide that the Home Secretary has exceeded his powers; and so even the Minister in charge of 'Law and order' is not above the law.

Judges have not always acted boldly to control the executive, but in a famous judgment in 1942, Lord Atkin expressed the need to do so:

Liversidge v Anderson

In that year a case came before the House of Lords. During both world wars the Home Secretary (as part of the Executive) took power under laws called Defence Regulations to detain without trial any 'person of hostile origin or associations', or anyone whose conduct was 'prejudicial to the safety of the country'.

John Perizweig, also known as Robert Liversidge, was arrested and imprisoned on the orders of the Home Secretary (Sir John Anderson). Anderson had him detained under the Defence Regulations, but gave no reasons for this. Liversidge brought an action in the courts claiming that he had been falsely imprisoned and requesting his immediate release.

The House of Lords ruled by a majority of 4–1 that his detention was lawful. Lord Atkin strongly disagreed with his fellow judges. Although this was at the height of the war and a time of great national peril, he was convinced that the detention of Liversidge without any reason being given was unlawful, and condemned it as an abuse of executive power.

He also made this blistering attack on his fellow judges, which at the time caused great offence:

> *I view with apprehension the attitude of judges who . . . when faced with claims involving the liberty of the subject show themselves more executive minded than the executive . . . In this country, amid the clash of arms, the laws are not silent. They may be changed, but they speak the same language in war as in peace. It has always been one of the pillars of freedom, one of the principles of liberty for which on recent authority we are fighting, that the judges are no respecters of persons and stand between the subject and any attempted encroachment of his liberty by the executive, alert to see that any coercive action is justified in law. In this case I have listened to arguments which might have been addressed acceptably to the Court of King's Bench in the time of Charles I.*

These words have rung down the years as a call to all judges to protect the rights of the individual against any abuse of power by the State. In more recent years the courts have developed a special procedure to enable individuals to challenge decisions by the executive. They can ask the courts to 'review' these decisions, and this procedure of **judicial review** is the special responsibility of the Administrative Court. More and more of these cases are being heard. They are not merely of interest and importance to the individuals concerned in them, but amount to a check on the power of the Executive, which should also be seen as a vital expression of our constitution in action.

1. THE SOVEREIGN/MONARCH/CROWN

We may think of the Queen as being very important but we do not think of her as being very powerful. We tend to see her as the figurehead of power, and a natural focus of loyalty. To an extent that is true, but the position of the monarch or **Crown** in our constitution is extremely important. *Halsbury* describes it as follows:

> *The Head of State, and the supreme executive officer in the State; . . . the titular head of the Church of England, the Law, the Navy, the Army and the Air Force, and the source of all justice and titles of honour, distinctions and dignities; foreign affairs are conducted, declarations of war and peace made, and the law executed and administered, solely in her name, although the monarch acts in such matters only on the advice of her ministers.*

Referring to the numbers in Figure 4.1, we should therefore understand that:

2. *Legislature.* The Queen is a part of the legislature—here she is known as 'the Queen in Parliament'. It is the Queen who opens and dissolves (closes) Parliament. Laws passed by Parliament can become laws of the land only

when she signs her assent to them. It is, however, her constitutional duty always to do so.

3. *Executive*. The Queen is head of the executive. Government operates in her name. It is the Queen who invites a new Prime Minister to form a Government. The Government Ministers are chosen by the Prime Minister, but they are formally granted their 'seals of office' by the Queen, and are called 'Ministers of the Crown'. Even the leader of the largest 'minority' party, which opposes the Government in Parliament, is called 'Leader of Her Majesty's Opposition', and is paid a special salary for holding this office.

4. *Judiciary*. It is in the 'name of the Queen' that our system of justice is administered. The sovereign is the 'fountain of justice and mercy'. The actual power of doing justice in the courts has been placed in the hands of the judges but they are all called 'Her Majesty's Judges'; they receive their 'Warrants of Appointment' from the Queen and all courts display the Royal Coat of Arms to show that they do their work in the name of the Queen. All criminal prosecutions are brought in the name of the Queen. The cases are called *R* v *Smith*, or Jones or whatever the defendant is called. Here '*R* v' means 'Rex versus' or 'Regina versus'—'The King against' or 'The Queen against'—depending on whether we have a king or queen on the throne. Even the prisons are 'HM [Her Majesty's] prisons'.

(Only one other person in our constitution has held a position that has straddled the legislature, executive, and judiciary. He is the Lord Chancellor, but his active role as a party politician and Minister in charge of a large department, Speaker of the House of Lords, and Head of the Judiciary is no longer considered acceptable in a modern democracy, because it breaches the separation of powers. In this it differs from the Queen's *ceremonial* role in presiding over all three arms of the State. We will be looking more closely at the Lord Chancellor's functions, and their recent development in the next chapter and Chapter 13.)

Therefore, although the Queen's position in the constitution may be a largely ceremonial one, its great importance is that she is uniquely placed to bind together the most powerful bodies in the country under a vow of loyalty to her. They must work together in the Crown's best interests. These are always considered to be the best interests of the nation as a whole, rather than of the Queen as an individual. At the same time the position of the Crown helps to divide up their powers, and keep them separate. In this way, in theory, no one can acquire too much power. This is the constitutional role of the monarch, a job that kings and queens have now done for centuries.

In the seventeenth and eighteenth centuries our island story featured a succession of battles between the Crown and the executive. Each resented the other for having and wanting too much power; and each fought for more power—quite literally in the Civil War (1642–8) between Charles I's Royalists and Oliver Cromwell's Parliamentarians. These wars ended with perhaps the most famous trial in our history, and one which was to become a great constitutional landmark.

The Trial of Charles I

The trial of Charles I took place in Westminster Hall on 9 January 1649. He was charged as 'a tyrant, traitor, and murderer, and public and implacable enemy to the Commonwealth of England'. Lord President John Bradshaw, the senior judge, announced that *'The House of Commons, assembled in Parliament, being sensible of the great calamities brought upon this nation, and of innocent blood that hath been shed in this nation . . . have constituted this High Court of Justice'*.

Charles immediately challenged the right of the court to try him: *'I would know by what power I am called hither . . . I would know by what authority, I mean lawful authority . . . Remember I am your king, your lawful king, and what sins you bring upon your heads, and the judgment of God upon this land [if you try your king] . . . I have a trust placed in me by God, by old and lawful descent . . . a king cannot be tried by any superior jurisdiction on earth.'*

Bradshaw, who was described as *'short tempered and long winded'*, replied to the King: *'How far you have preserved the privileges of the people, your actions have spoken it . . . you have written your meaning in bloody characters throughout the whole Kingdom . . . There is a contract and a bargain made between the king and his people, and your oath is taken: and certainly, Sir, the bond is reciprocal . . . the one tie, the one bond, is the protection that is due from the sovereign . . . Sir, if this bond is broken, farewell sovereignty!'*

Charles remained steadfast to his challenge to the court's authority throughout the trial, but he was convicted and beheaded. Eleven years later, when his son Charles II ascended the throne, a number of those involved in the trial, including eleven of the 'Regicides' who had signed his death warrant, were condemned and executed. Cromwell and Bradshaw were already dead, but that did not deter the new regime. Their bodies were exhumed from their honoured tombs in Westminster Abbey and executed for treason. They were first hanged in chains; then their heads were stuck on poles on one of the Hall's towers. This macabre revenge may have been in keeping with the times, but nothing could undo the fact that Charles's trial had brought to an end in the most dramatic way possible the idea that the monarch was above the law.

George II (reigned 1729–60) was a king who had a good understanding of the power of the executive when he complained that *'Ministers are Kings in this country'*. At the beginning of George's reign, the French writer and philosopher François Arouet, who assumed the name Voltaire, was in England. He had fled from Paris in 1726 after his release from imprisonment in the Bastille.

Nearly three hundred years ago Voltaire was quick to perceive the nature of English constitutional government, and to stress its advantages over the absolute monarchy of France, where the king was all-powerful. In his *Letters on the English* he remarked upon the wisdom of the British system *'which leaves the King all-powerful to do good, but ties his hands if he tries to do evil'* and he praised the House of Commons, which *'though second in rank, is the first in influence'*.

- In Figure 4.1 the Queen is seen above the judges. Does this mean that she is above the law, and can do whatever she likes without fear of the courts? Some constitutional lawyers would argue that this is still the position — that the Crown still enjoys the 'prerogative of perfection', which means that the 'Queen can do no wrong', and that any blameworthy act by her must be imputed to her advisers. They would argue that legislation does not normally bind the Crown, who as the Head of State enjoys immunity from prosecution. Others would say that the answer was given in 1608 by Sir Edward Coke who, as Chief Justice of the Common Pleas, and when face to face with King James I, met James's claim that *'The King is the Law speaking'* with the brave retort *'The King is under God and the Law!'* and it was repeated by Thomas Fuller, chaplain in the reigns of Charles I and Charles II: *'Be you never so high, the law is above you'*. They would recall Charles I's execution.

  Therefore, although the matter would no doubt be hotly debated by constitutional lawyers, and would surely be the subject of much learned argument, it is interesting to reflect that if, having been investigated by *Her Majesty's Constabulary* and the *Crown Prosecution Service*, Her Majesty the Queen was charged with committing a crime, she would have to be prosecuted *In the name of the Queen*, in one of the *Queen's courts* by one of *Her Majesty's counsel learned in the law* (Queen's Counsel). She would be tried by one of *Her Majesty's judges* and, if convicted, might be sentenced to a term in one of *Her Majesty's prisons*!

  Perhaps we need not worry that she would spend much time there, for to continue our wild constitutional imaginings, as the sovereign is 'the fountain of justice and of mercy', as soon as sentence was pronounced Her Majesty would be able to grant herself a *Royal Pardon*, and the whole sorry business would be at an end.

The British Constitution, as it is known, may be complicated; it may be unwritten; it may even be something of an illusion made up of myths and theories, customs and traditions — a magnificent 'magic trick', with the Crown having every appearance of enormous power and influence, but in reality having very little, except for the appearance. The Queen may not be above the law, but that presents no problem for constitutional lawyers, for who could contemplate Her Majesty breaking the law? Anyone would know this could not happen: it is unthinkable, and if it is unthinkable, the thought need not shatter the illusion. Or need it? In 2002 the illusion came perilously close to being shattered, not when the Queen was in danger of being prosecuted, but when she was at risk of being called as a witness in a criminal trial.

The Queen has a special relationship with the courts. They are essentially 'hers', in the sense that justice is done in her name—hence the description the *Royal* Courts of Justice. The ancient legal principle that the monarch cannot be compelled to give evidence in his or her own courts stems from the constitutional theory that as the monarch is the highest authority in the land, there is therefore no higher authority than the monarch to issue an order requiring her to attend court. Until 2002 this has never been a problem, simply because there never was a time when the interests of justice required the monarch to appear in court, but this question loomed large during the dramatic trial of Paul Burrell, butler to Diana, the late Princess of Wales.

The trial of Paul Burrell

Between 1992 and her death in 1997 Paul Burrell had been butler to Diana, Princess of Wales. In October 2002 he stood trial at the Old Bailey charged with the theft of over 300 items associated with her, many of which had been taken into his possession after her death. His defence to the charge was that he had merely taken them for safe-keeping. After several days the trial came to an abrupt end, when the Queen herself revealed that after Diana's death she had had a conversation with Burrell in which he had told her that he was removing items belonging to Diana 'for safe-keeping'.

One of the many questions raised following this revelation was that of the Queen's legal immunity from giving evidence in the courts. How could Burrell have a fair trial if the Queen might have confirmed his innocence, but (as everyone appeared to accept without question) she had a legal immunity from appearing in her own courts? This could have presented a huge problem as it meant, for example, that she could not be compelled to give evidence as a defence witness. The matter, however, was not resolved by any legal ruling because as soon as it was known that this conversation had taken place, the case against Paul Burrell was dropped by the prosecution, and he was acquitted.

The constitution may be an illusion, but it is an illusion that works, and is made to work. It is so convincing and well established by practice and tradition that it has become an accepted fact, which must be guarded and protected. It is the province of the courts to guard and protect the constitution; and, if it becomes necessary, they will do just that. In this way the judiciary plays an essential role not only in the lives of individual citizens, but also in the running of the country as a whole.

✳

HUMAN RIGHTS

We will be considering human rights in Chapter 19, but by way of introduction to this subject, it is important to understand that this is an aspect of constitutional law, for it is under the constitution that individual citizens have duties to their 'Queen and Country' (the State) and the State has certain duties to protect the human rights of its citizens.

DUTIES OF THE CITIZEN

The duties of the citizen include serving in HM Forces when it becomes necessary, as in time of war. Citizens must also serve on juries, and give evidence in criminal or civil proceedings when required to do so. There are duties relating to the registration of births and deaths, or notifying the authorities of certain infectious diseases; and of course individuals must pay their taxes.

It is also the duty of every citizen to obey the law. This should be quite easy when we know what the laws are, but how is it possible when there are many thousands of laws, and we may know only a small fraction of them? In fact, contrary to popular belief, we are not all presumed to know the law. As long ago as 1846 a judge said, *'There is no presumption in this country that everyone knows the law; it would be contrary to common sense and reason if that were so'*. Again, in 1937, Lord Atkin said, *'The fact is that there is not and never has been a presumption that every one knows the law'*. Lord Atkin said the rule is *'that ignorance of the law is no excuse'*, and that is the position. This means that if anyone offends against the law, it is no answer to say that as they did not know the law they should not be responsible for breaking it. Genuine ignorance of the law may be a matter that the court can take into account when deciding how to deal with a case, but if ignorance of the law could always be an answer to any charge, the entire justice system would be unworkable.

DUTIES OF THE STATE

The duties of the State include giving citizens their civil liberties, which include all the civil and political rights recognised by English law. There are many of these, and they include the right to life, the right to personal liberty, and the right to freedom of expression and of conscience (for example, freedom of religion). Freedoms of expression and of assembly mean, for example, that people are free to demonstrate, provided that they do not break any laws when doing so. Then people have the right to be involved in government, to vote, and to stand for election to Parliament or local councils.

They have the freedom to own property. They also have the right to the protection of the law, which includes the right of anyone accused of crime to a fair and speedy trial.

Until recently, the human rights enjoyed by every citizen in this country were not easy to find. They were contained in numerous Acts of Parliament, and in cases which form part of the common law. Three of the most important landmarks in our human rights history span the centuries. After a wait of over three hundred years we now have another—the Human Rights Act 1998.

- *Magna Carta (The Great Charter) 1215* was signed by King John in June of that year on a small island near Windsor called Runnymede. Most of the 63 clauses in this famous document handed over power from the king to his barons; but by clauses 39 and 40, as we will see in Chapter 15, King John promised that no freeman should be imprisoned without a fair trial according to law, and that no one should be denied justice. The Magna Carta has been called the foundation of our constitution.

- *The Petition of Right 1628* was passed by both Houses of Parliament and reluctantly signed by King Charles I. It brought a new promise that no one should be imprisoned without trial. The king also confirmed that the Crown would not tax the people without the authority of Parliament. Part of the reason for the Civil Wars and Charles's trial was that he was said to have broken this contract with the Parliament and the people.

- *The Bill of Rights 1689*, signed by King William III (William of Orange) was a reaction against the disastrous reign of his father-in-law, King James II. James had by a series of arbitrary acts shown his determination to overthrow the constitution and the Church of England. One of these acts was the prosecution of the 'Seven Bishops' (see Chapter 15). The Bill of Rights, passed within weeks of William's accession to the throne, provided for free elections and freedom of speech in Parliament, and ended the royal power to suspend laws which Parliament had passed. It also prohibited '*excessive bail and fines*' (see Chapter 12 for bail) as well as '*cruel and unusual punishments*'.

- *The Human Rights Act 1998*, which came into force in October 2000, gives to the citizens of this country the rights given to individuals by the European Convention on Human Rights. When he introduced the new law Lord Irvine of Lairg, the Lord Chancellor, said: '*The Government this week has taken a major step in its programme of constitutional reform. It has introduced into Parliament a Human Rights Bill to incorporate the European Convention on Human Rights into British law.*' Professor Sir William Wade QC, an eminent constitutional lawyer, has described the Human Rights Act as '*one of our greatest constitutional milestones*'.

The European Convention guarantees a number of basic human rights, which are now part of our law. They cover many fundamental matters: the right to life; rights against torture or degrading treatment or punishment, slavery, and forced labour; rights to liberty and security of the person; the right to a fair trial and protection against retrospective criminal laws; respect for private and family life, home, and correspondence; freedom of thought, conscience, and religion; freedom of expression; freedom of peaceful assembly and freedom of association, including the right to join a trade union; the right to marry and to found a family; and rights against discrimination in the enjoyment of all these rights and freedoms. Citizens now have a code of rights which they can enforce in the courts—the nearest thing we have to a written constitution.

In his book *The Family Story* published in 1981, Lord Denning, one of the greatest of our twentieth-century judges, wrote:

> *In our constitutional theory Parliament is supreme. Parliament can take us into the Common Market. Parliament can take us out of it—by a simple majority. Parliament can pass a Bill of Rights. But it can also repeal it or any clause in it—by a simple majority. We have no entrenched clauses. We have no fundamental constitution by which other laws can be tested. No matter that a law may be unreasonable or unjust, nevertheless if it is clear on the point, the judges have no option. They must apply the statute as it stands. The people of this country, however, trust Parliament—and the members of it—always to be guided by those instincts for justice and liberty of which I have written.*

When we come to look more closely at human rights, we will see that there has been a move away from this statement of principle. Judges still do not have the power to 'strike down' Acts of Parliament as unconstitutional, but senior judges now have the power and duty under the Human Rights Act to '*declare*', if it be the case, that any laws passed by Parliament are '*incompatible*' with the rights given by the European Convention. When this happens, Parliament will be expected to reconsider these laws, and may repeal them to bring them in line with the rights granted by the Convention. All judges have the duty to ensure that the rights to a fair trial given by the European Convention are respected. The courts therefore now play a major role in the field of human rights.

The Human Rights Act has already made a real difference to the approach of our courts to the issue of human rights. Its principles have also caused the Government to think hard about the constitution, even to the point of considering whether the ancient office of Lord Chancellor, with its wide range of powers spread across the legislature, executive, and judiciary, is unconstitutional. When it comes to the development of our constitution, we are indeed living in interesting times.

5

The Palace of Westminster
Our Chief Law Makers—Parliament

'One Honourable Member imitated the crowing of a cock so admirably that you could not have distinguished it from the performance of a real chanticleer. Not far from the same spot issued sounds marvellously resembling the bleating of a sheep—blended occasionally with an admirable imitation of an ass by an honourable Member a few yards distant. There were yelpings worthy of any canine animal, and excellent imitations of the sounds of sundry musical instruments.'

Taken from a contemporary report describing heckling during a speech in the House of Commons, July 1835.

◦

Who makes our laws? We have already seen the way in which the judges have made and still make law, but for hundreds of years the supreme law-making body in this country has been Parliament. Since the European Communities Act 1972, the United Kingdom has been a member of the European Union, and until that Act is repealed (abolished) its laws (which we will look at in Chapter 24) must take priority over our own national laws. Apart from this, Parliament is supreme, because it is the only body which has the right to enact a new law, or alter or reverse a law which Parliament itself has passed. Any law passed by Parliament which clashes with, or alters or reverses any part of the common law automatically takes precedence, and becomes the law of the land.

Parliament has two main duties. In the first place, it **legislates**—it makes the laws of the land. (It also gives to Government Ministers the power to confirm by-laws before they can come into force.) In the second place, it **debates** matters of urgent public importance. In this way the public are given the chance to know what is happening, and what our leaders think about it.

PARLIAMENT, AND HOW IT MAKES LAWS

There are two 'Houses of Parliament'. These are the **House of Commons** and the **House of Lords**. They occupy another huge Gothic building standing by the Thames in London. This is famous for its clock tower, which houses the great hour bell known as 'Big Ben'. This building is usually called the Houses of Parliament, but its correct name is the Palace of Westminster.

Before the reign of Henry VIII, the Palace of Westminster was for centuries the home of the monarch. Most of the building we see today was designed by Sir Charles Barry in the nineteenth century, but its Great Hall, Westminster Hall, has survived for nearly one thousand years, and was the original Great Hall of the Norman Kings. Our early kings and queens not only held their feasts in Westminster Hall but, as we have seen, also held their courts there. The Palace of Westminster is still one of the Royal Palaces, although the Queen permits Parliament to occupy and run it. Unlike the palace in Chapter 4, it is a very visible one.

THE HOUSE OF COMMONS

The House of Commons is the chief source of our laws. It became known by this name because those elected to serve in it, as **Members of Parliament** (MPs) were not members of the nobility but ordinary common people, known as *'commoners'*. Even to this day a noble, or *'peer'* who is still a member of the House of Lords is not allowed to become an MP. If he wishes to become an MP he must first disclaim (give up) his peerage.

Tony Benn MP

The first person in the history of Parliament to disclaim a peerage was the Labour MP Tony Benn. He was the MP for Bristol South East. In 1960 his father, Viscount Stansgate died, and because he was a 'hereditary peer' Tony Benn automatically 'succeeded to' (inherited) his title.

Tony Benn wanted to remain an MP, but as a new member of the nobility he was not allowed to do so. He took the case to court (another illustration of the courts deciding constitutional issues). He was not represented by a lawyer, but appeared on his own behalf, arguing that he should be permitted to remain a 'commoner' and MP, and incidentally earning great praise from the judges for his conduct of the case. The court decided that under the constitution he could not disclaim his peerage. Only Parliament could alter this ancient law.

Soon afterwards an Act of Parliament was passed which enabled any hereditary peer to disclaim his or her peerage and 'stand for election' to Parliament. Tony Benn immediately did this. He was again elected an MP, and remained an MP for many years. He retired from the Commons at the General Election in 2001.

The United Kingdom, consisting of England, Scotland, Wales, and Northern Ireland, is divided up into 659 geographical parts. Each part is known as a **constituency**. At least once every five years a **General Election** is held, in which everyone who lives in a constituency and who is over the age of 18 and entitled to vote, has the opportunity to elect his or her MP. Those who wish to stand for Parliament are called **candidates**, and whichever candidate gets the most votes in a constituency is elected to become its MP. Almost every MP who is elected belongs to one of the political parties, and is voted into Parliament generally as a Conservative or Labour or Liberal Democrat MP. Each political party will canvass for election on the basis of its **manifesto**—a document setting out its aims, and the policies it proposes to implement to achieve them. The party with an overall majority of MPs will be asked by the Queen to form the next Government.

Some candidates, however, stand as **independents**, because they are independent of any political party. In 1997, the journalist Martin Bell, wearing his trademark white suit, stood as the independent 'anti-sleaze' candidate for Tatton. In 2001, Dr John Taylor became the independent MP for Wyre Forest, having campaigned, not on behalf of a political party, but on behalf of Kidderminster Hospital.

Candidates are voted for as people. Therefore if, for example, a Labour MP resigns or dies while he is in office, another Labour candidate will not automatically take over. There must quickly be a new election in his constituency. This is called a by-election, and voters in a by-election may choose to elect as their new MP a man or woman who supports a different party from the last one.

The 659 MPs who make up the House of Commons decide which laws to pass. They do this by voting in Parliament when each new law is debated. It is the duty of an MP to look after the interests of all the people in his constituency, whether they voted for him or not. If the people do not like what their MPs are doing or the way they are doing it, they may change them by 'voting in' different ones at the next General Election.

This method of voting—by the people for MPs, and by MPs on behalf of the people—is our way of ensuring that the country is governed according to the wishes of the people. The system of government by the people is called a **democracy.** The word 'democracy' stems from the Greek words for 'people' and 'rule'. It is government in which the supreme power rests with the people—in our case, through our representatives (MPs and local councillors). The system was aptly described by the US President Abraham Lincoln (Gettysburg Address, 1863) in his famous phrase '*Government of the people, by* *the people and for the people'*. The modern concept of democracy assumes, as Voltaire wrote, that, '*In the long run the people can be trusted to judge what is best for them'*. It provides for the political equality of all individuals, and their rights to private freedom and to petition for redress of grievances.

Any system of government must be as efficient as possible and this requires leadership. There will always be leaders whose job it is to decide what new laws should be passed, and to make sure that old laws are still relevant to the times in which we live. In the House of Commons leadership must be provided by the Government. This is formed by the political party which has the majority of MPs. The leaders of the Government are the Prime Minister, and the other Ministers, the most senior ones being members of the Cabinet. MPs hold Ministers to account by asking questions in Parliament. The Prime Minister comes to Parliament to answer questions once a week at 'Prime Minister's Question Time'.

The Cabinet is the senior committee of Government Ministers. The Prime Minister's headquarters is 10 Downing Street, where the Cabinet meets. The Government (executive) directs policy and proposes new laws to carry it into effect, and is therefore immensely powerful; but it is Parliament as a whole which decides whether to pass new laws or not. There have been times when Parliament has refused to pass Government legislation. On occasions the Government of the day has felt unable to govern, and been brought down as a result. When this happens the Prime Minister asks the monarch to dissolve Parliament, and call a new General Election. Then the people, making up the electorate which has the right to vote, decide who the next Government should be by electing MPs again.

The House of Commons is presided over by the **Speaker**, whose job it is to keep order in the House and ensure that its rules are obeyed. Betty Boothroyd, the first woman Speaker in the history of that office, was elected in 1992. The present Speaker is Michael Martin. He has a residence in the Palace of Westminster itself. He is also the MP for Glasgow Springburn, and as such must look after the interests of his constituents. When we come to look at legal dress, we might bear in mind how traditions can change. When Speaker Boothroyd took office she refused to wear the Speaker's full-bottomed wig when presiding over debates in the House; now Speaker Martin has continued that practice, and he is the first male Speaker in very many years not to wear a wig.

DEVOLUTION—NORTHERN IRELAND, SCOTLAND, AND WALES

Of the 659 MPs who sit in the House of Commons at Westminster, 529 MPs represent constituencies in England, 40 represent constituencies in Wales, 72 in Scotland, and 18 in Northern Ireland.

In 1998 the new Northern Ireland Assembly was created, and this was followed in 1999 by the Scottish Parliament and the National Assembly for Wales. The first two bodies have the power to pass laws for Northern Ireland and Scotland, but not laws which relate to matters that are 'reserved' to the Parliament at Westminster, such as foreign policy. They cannot therefore declare war against a foreign country, but for example, the Scottish Parliament can pass laws for Scotland relating to a number of domestic matters including education, health, the environment, local government, and food standards; and it may raise or lower the basic rate of income tax by up to three pence in the pound. The Welsh Assembly does not have the same power to pass laws, but it can decide priorities and allocate funding for all 'devolved' matters.

THE HOUSE OF LORDS

The House of Lords is made up of the **Peers of the Realm**. There are two main groups of Peers. These are called the **Lords Spiritual** and the **Lords Temporal**.

- The Lords Spiritual are the Archbishops of Canterbury and York, and a number of other leading Bishops. They are all representatives of the Established Church, the Church of England. There are 26 in total

- The Lords Temporal are made up of two types of peer, Hereditary Peers and Life Peers.

Hereditary peers are those whose titles are passed down from generation to generation. They include the Dukes, Earls, and Viscounts (and their female equivalents). They are known as 'peers by succession', because they have 'succeeded' to the titles of their ancestors. About 775 men and women are peers by succession. Until recently they were all allowed to sit and vote in the House of Lords, but in 1999 the House of Lords was reformed.

Following the House of Lords Act 1999, hereditary peers lost the right to sit and vote in the House of Lords, although under a compromise 92 hereditary peers were allowed to remain in the 'House' for a transitional period. Also, a small number of hereditary peers have accepted an invitation to continue to sit and vote in the Lords.

Life peers are, as their name implies, made peers for their lifetime only. They cannot pass their titles on to their children. There are now approximately 560 Life Peers. They are usually men and women who have had distinguished careers in such fields as politics, education, business, medicine, and the law. Leading figures in the arts, and a variety of other walks of life, have also been made peers.

- Lord (Richard) Attenborough (actor and film director), Lord (Andrew) Lloyd-Webber (musician), and Lord (Richard) Rogers of Riverside (architect) are celebrated examples of this. Lord (Brian) Rix was a fine comic actor who later became head of the charitable organisation for the mentally handicapped, MENCAP. Lord (Sebastian) Coe is a famous athlete. He became a Conservative MP after he retired from athletics, and received his peerage for political services.

All this means that the membership of the House of Lords will always include a wide range of highly talented men and women. They may not be truly representative of those who have made a contribution towards the life of the nation, but they at least have each done so, and continue to do so in a different way by being members of the House.

In November 2001 proposals were placed before Parliament to further reform the House of Lords. If these had been passed by Parliament they would have had far-reaching consequences, but they were not. A strong body of MPs believes that the House of Lords should be much more representative of the nation, and that a large majority, if not all of its members, should be elected by the people rather than appointed. In 2002, when new proposals were laid before Parliament, the House of Lords voted in favour of an all-appointed House; the House of Commons could not agree on any proposal, and the reform process stalled. Then, in September 2003, the Government announced its intention to abolish the right of the remaining hereditary Peers to sit and vote in the Lords. New peers will not be elected, but a new Appointments Commission answerable to Parliament will be set up to recommend the appointment of new peers. Its task will be to ensure that the House of Lords will be broadly representative of the gender, age, ethnicity, and disability mix of the nation; and new peers will be able to resign their appointments easily, and become eligible to vote and stand for election as MPs.

The members of the House of Lords have a duty to examine the laws proposed by the House of Commons, and to suggest amendments if they think they are necessary. They also have the power to block and delay a new law of which they disapprove; but this power is very limited:

- The Lords are not able to change or delay any laws (known as 'Money Bills') which relate to finance and taxation.

- The Lords only have the power to hold up legislation of which they disapprove for a certain period of time; for under the Parliament Act 1911 if a Bill is passed by the House of Commons but rejected by the House of Lords twice in two successive years, it may immediately be presented to the Queen for her Assent without obtaining the Lords' further approval. In December 2000, after a two-year battle between the Commons and Lords, Mr Speaker Martin informed MPs that the Parliament Act was being invoked to pass the Sexual Offences (Amendment) Bill, which then immediately received Royal Assent and became an Act. It reduced the age of consent for homosexuals from 18 to 16.

The power of the House of Lords to check, and in some cases influence or even alter, legislation may be limited but it is still a very real one, and the Lords have scored some notable successes. Its fierce opposition to the Mode of Trial Bill, which was designed to remove the rights of citizens to trial by jury in many cases, resulted in the Government abandoning that measure. Its opposition to certain provisions in the Anti-Terrorism, Crime and Security Bill, drawn up in haste following the terrorist attacks on New York and Washington on 11 September 2001, resulted in a number of them being withdrawn, including the power to hold suspected terrorists without giving them access to the courts, and the introduction of a new offence of inciting religious hatred.

The House of Lords has its own Speaker, the **Lord Chancellor**. He too occupies a residence in the Palace of Westminster. The Lord Chancellor still holds a unique position in the constitution, because in addition to presiding over debates in the House of Lords (legislature) he is a senior member of the Cabinet (executive), and as Head of the Judiciary, has the power to recommend to the Queen the appointment of new judges. Until very recently he was also entitled to sit as a judge in the Court of the House of Lords (judiciary). This too was part of the 'constitution magic'—about which Lord Bingham quipped, '*three in one and one in three—the finest flowering of British constitutional ingenuity*'. For a long time leading judges and lawyers have argued that the right to sit as a judge should not survive, for however honourably and carefully the Lord Chancellor may exercise his powers, his position in the constitution was incompatible with the principle of separation of powers. On 12 June 2003, the following historic statement was issued from the Prime Minister's Office at 10 Downing Street:

> *As part of the continuing drive to modernise the constitution and public services, the Prime Minister has today announced far-reaching reforms including the creation of a new Department for Constitutional Affairs. This will incorporate most of the responsibilities of the former Lord Chancellor's Department, but with new arrangements for judicial appointments and an end to the previous role of the Lord Chancellor as a judge and Speaker of the House of Lords. Once the reforms are in place, the post of the Lord Chancellor will be abolished, putting the relationship between executive, legislature and judiciary on a modern footing.*

Immediately following the publication of this statement, Lord Falconer of Thoroton was appointed to the position of Secretary of State for Constitutional Affairs and Lord Chancellor. He has already signalled his intention to end the office of Lord Chancellor.

The Lord Chancellor has custody of the *Great Seal,* which is literally a large seal with a unique design, used for sealing and authenticating a variety of State documents. These include writs to elect and summon Parliament, all Acts of Parliament, and treaties with foreign states. As a Minister of State, the Lord Chancellor holds one of the highest offices in the land. On State occasions, only the Royal Family and the Archbishop of Canterbury are entitled to take precedence over him.

When he was in office the last Lord Chancellor, Lord Irvine of Lairg, still wore his elaborate costume—of wig, gown, silk tights, cotton breeches, and buckled shoes—while presiding over debates in the Lords. He did, however, receive the permission of the House to dispense with his costume when he moved from the Speaker's chair on the Woolsack to speaking from the Government front bench as a Minister.

MAKING A NEW LAW (LEGISLATING)

The laws passed by Parliament are called **Acts of Parliament** or **Statutes**. Before a law becomes a statute it has to pass through a number of stages of debate and discussion in both the House of Commons and the House of Lords. There are seven main stages and each of them is given a special name. Some of these stages are more important than others. The headings of the most important ones are given emphasis in the following pages.

1. Introduction and first reading

First the law is presented to the House of Commons. At this stage it is called a **Bill**. All that happens at the first reading is that MPs are informed about the proposed legislation, and a date is given for the next stage. The Bill is then printed.

2. **SECOND READING**

The Bill is discussed or **debated** in the House of Commons and a vote is taken as to whether it is in principle a law of which MPs approve, or whether it should go no further. In this debate **front-bench** Government Ministers and their Opposition counterparts, who occupy the front benches of the debating chamber, will make the opening and closing speeches. The rest of the debate will be given over to the **backbench** MPs, who occupy the remaining benches. Any MP with a special interest in the new law or whose own constituency is particularly affected by it will usually have priority in the queue of MPs wishing to speak.

3. COMMITTEE STAGE

The Bill is now examined line by line, or 'clause by clause', in great detail by a small committee of MPs. These MPs may be chosen to serve on the committee because they have a special interest and experience in the subject. At this stage the committee may agree to receive representations and suggestions for and against the proposed new law from anyone who is likely to be particularly affected by it. It may also hear evidence and take the advice of experts. Alterations to the Bill known as **amendments**, made at the Committee stage, will be passed if a majority of the committee members vote for them. Most of the amendments passed at this stage will be proposed or supported by the Government, often in response to concerns raised in the Second Reading debate. The party in power is likely to have the most members on the committee, and voting is generally along party lines; but this is not necessarily so, for committee members should be concerned to listen carefully to all the arguments, in the hope of producing as good a Bill as possible.

4. REPORT STAGE

A report is made to the House of Commons on what has happened at the Committee stage, and all MPs are given the chance to discuss the changes that have been made by the committee. Even at this time it is possible to make amendments to a Bill, and experience shows that this often happens.

5. Third reading

At this stage little is done. It is a final debate, frequently held immediately after the Report stage. A vote is taken on whether the Bill, as amended in the Committee and Report stages, should proceed or not. If the vote is for proceeding, the Bill is officially passed from the House of Commons on to the House of Lords.

6. THE HOUSE OF LORDS

The House of Lords then considers the Bill in much the same way as the House of Commons. Once again the Bill goes through a number of stages, but this time it is carefully examined by members of the House of Lords. They too may make amendments to the Bill. If this happens, the Bill is sent back to the House of Commons for further consideration.

Not all Bills begin their lives in the House of Commons; many (usually less controversial Bills) are introduced in the House of Lords. Then they make a similar journey, a mirror image of that taken by Bills starting in the Commons, this time passing through the Lords first and then through the Commons.

7. THE ROYAL ASSENT

After a Bill has passed through all its stages in Parliament, it is sent to the monarch. It does not become law until the Queen has 'assented' or agreed to it. This **Royal Assent**, as it is called, is given by the Queen signing the Bill. If the Queen disapproves of a new Bill, must she always agree to it? The answer is that in practice the Queen always signs her assent to laws passed by Parliament. That is her constitutional duty. She is entitled to comment upon them, or, as was explained by Walter Bagehot, the great nineteenth-century constitutional expert, she may *'advise and warn'*; but if she chooses to do so, this will always be done privately. Her views will be considered, but if they are rejected, she must then sign the Bill. It is said that during the late 1880s, when Parliament proposed a law making homosexuality and lesbianism a crime, Queen Victoria advised (successfully) against the inclusion of lesbianism, on the grounds that she could not believe that it existed.

When the Queen has signed a Bill it is sent back to the House of Lords, where in an ancient ceremony the Clerk of the Parliaments pronounces the Norman-French words which signify that she has given her assent: *'La Reine le veult'* — 'The Queen wishes it'. (The form by which the Queen would refuse to give her consent is *'La Reine s'avisera'* — 'The Queen will consider'; but the last time a monarch refused to give assent to an Act of Parliament was in 1707, when Queen Anne refused to agree to a Bill for settling the army in Scotland.) At this point the Bill automatically becomes an Act of Parliament (or Statute). It is now the law, and everyone must obey it.

Bills which have to go through all these stages may take many months to become Acts of Parliament. Some Bills are well over a hundred pages in length. There is much thinking and talking to be done. After all, the word *Parliament* derives from the French verb *parler*—to talk. When a Bill receives the Royal Assent it becomes an Act, but the new laws contained in it do not necessarily come into force on the very day the Queen signs it. Sometimes, where an Act contains a large number of new laws, they may be timetabled to be **implemented** (come into force) over a period of time. The Criminal Justice Act 2003, which we will come across later in this book, is an important illustration of this:

• The Criminal Justice Bill 2003 set out to make many major reforms in the criminal justice system. After much debate, the Bill was passed through Parliament in early 2003, but it was not scheduled to receive Royal Assent and become the Criminal Justice Act 2003 until November 2003. Some of its reforms (relating to sentencing) came into force in January 2004, but others (relating, for example, to reforms of magistrates' powers, the types of evidence the court may receive, and non-jury trials) are not scheduled to be implemented until 2005–6.

It does not, however, always take a long time to debate and pass new laws. In times of national crisis, as in wartime, or for other urgent reasons, quite simple but important Bills have been rushed through all of these stages in both Commons and Lords. They received Royal Assent and were implemented in a matter of days.

- On 10 July 1998 the Landmines Bill, banning the use of landmines, went through all its stages in the House of Commons. This was done so that it would become law before the first anniversary of the death of Diana, Princess of Wales, and as a tribute to the Princess who had campaigned against the use of landmines worldwide. Less than a week later, the Bill had passed through all its stages in the House of Lords.

- In September 1998, following the Omagh bombing in Northern Ireland, Parliament was recalled from its summer recess, and within two days had passed the Criminal Justice (Terrorism and Conspiracy) Act 1998, giving added powers to arrest and prosecute suspected terrorists.

*

Parliament has enormous powers. It can, in practice, pass any law it wishes—even an unfair one (although we should recall that the Human Rights Act 1988 will affect this power). Anyone who breaks a law passed by Parliament will be taken to court. The fact that the person who breaks the law believes it to be wrong or unfair does not matter. Even if the judge agrees with him, if the law is expressed in clear terms, he has no power to alter it or make exceptions; all he can do is recommend that Parliament should consider changing it.

The only sure way of changing unpopular laws is for the people to vote out of office the political party responsible for making them, and to vote into office the party which promises to change them. Until Parliament itself changes the law and **repeals** (cancels) a statute, all Acts, no matter how old, remain the law of the land. They are said to be '*on the statute book*'. Lawyers still occasionally refer in court to the *Magna Carta 1215* (see Chapter 4).

The Act which is set out in Figure 5.1 is the *whole* of one of the shortest and most important statutes passed within the last century, for which many women fought so hard and courageously. It was finally passed by Parliament shortly after the First World War and gave women the right to enter Parliament as MPs. Within a year, Nancy Astor had become the first woman MP, being elected to succeed her husband as MP for Plymouth.

1918. *Parliament (Qualification of* CH. 47
Woman) Act, 1918.

CHAPTER 47.

An Act to amend the Law with respect to the Capacity
of Women to sit in Parliament. [21st November 1918.]

BE it enacted by the King's most Excellent Majesty, by and
with the advice and consent of the Lords Spiritual and
Temporal, and Commons, in this present Parliament assembled,
and by the authority of the same, as follows:

1. A woman shall not be disqualified by sex or marriage *Capacity of*
for being elected to or sitting or voting as a Member of the *women to be*
Commons House of Parliament. *members of Parliament.*

2. This Act may be cited as the Parliament (Qualification of *Short title.*
Women) Act, 1918.

Figure 5.1 The Act of Parliament permitting women to become MPs

All Acts of Parliament bear the Royal Coat of Arms. This also appears above
the bench in almost every court in the land. The Coat of Arms is supported by
the English lion and the Scottish unicorn, and it bears two mottos, both in
French. Each has its origins in the mists of time:

- *Dieu et mon droit* ('God and my right'). This is another relic of the days of
  Richard I. This was the watchword used by his soldiers at the Battle of
  Gisors (1198), and was intended to signify that Richard owed his allegiance
  to God alone, and not the French. Gisors was a great triumph for Richard,
  and he adopted this password as the royal motto of England.

- *Honi soit qui mal y pense* ('Shame on him who thinks evil of it'—often translated as 'Evil be to him who evil thinks'). The tradition is that Edward III gave a great court ball. One of the ladies present was the beautiful Countess of Salisbury. As she was dancing, her garter of blue ribbon accidentally fell off. The King noted the sniggers of some of his courtiers. He was not amused. He cried out these words, and then bound the ribbon around his own knee, proclaiming that he would one day *'bring it about that the proudest noble in the realm shall think it an honour to wear this band'*. Few present can have taken him seriously, but Edward was right, for since 1348 the Order of the Garter has been the senior order of chivalry.

All Acts of Parliament commence with the words in the second paragraph of this illustration, beginning 'Be it enacted'. These ancient words may seem rather grand and pompous, but to this day they neatly summarise what we have been considering—except that the persons mentioned are no longer in their true order of influence. There is also a reference to the 'short title'. Every Act is given a short title by which it is generally known, but sometimes, as in this case, it is hardly shorter than the long title.

BOW STREET RUNNER
1749 – 1829.

PEELERS
1829.

METROPOLITAN POLICE.

6

Our Chief Law Enforcers—the Police

'The Police Service has a role to play in shaping the next generation of citizens. By helping to keep children safe, aware of their rights and responsibilities and by helping them to understand and respect the law, we contribute to their development as active citizens.'
Introduction to Police Secondary Schools Involvement Programme.

'It is most distressing to us to be the agents whereby our erring fellow-creatures are deprived of that liberty which is so dear to all—but we should have thought of that before we joined the force.'
W. S. Gilbert, *The Pirates of Penzance*, Sergeant of police.

*

In this country a large number of agencies or departments are responsible for enforcing laws of one kind or another. Most of the people who do this work are called **Inspectors**.

For example, the Inspectors of *HM Inland Revenue* assess most taxes, and investigate the cases of those who do not pay. The Inspectors of *HM Customs and Excise* collect all Value Added Taxes (VAT), and customs duties payable on goods brought in from abroad. They are also responsible for ensuring that goods are not smuggled into this country, and are now particularly concerned with the importation of illegal drugs, such as heroin, cocaine, and cannabis, which are almost always produced from plants grown abroad.

There are many more Inspectors of one kind or another employed by different government departments. These include:

- Department for Environment, Food and Rural Affairs Inspectors, who must guard against pollution and other damage to the environment. Inspectors also supervise the quality of food, and are concerned with animal welfare.

- Department for Education and Skills Inspectors, who watch over the standards and management of schools.

- Department of Health Inspectors. This department employs a large team of Medical Officers (usually qualified doctors), whose job it is to watch over all aspects of health care.

All these people are specialists in their own fields, and their job is to make sure that the laws relating to their particular responsibilities are enforced; but by far the largest and best-known law enforcement agency in the country is the **Police Force**.

THE POLICE

The Police have the most important part to play in the keeping of public order and the protection of persons and property. It is their job to enforce the law, that is, to make sure we obey it. To do their work effectively they need the necessary powers. If the police see that the law is about to be broken they have the power to intervene to prevent that happening. If their orders are not obeyed, they may arrest the people involved. If the police have reason to believe that someone has broken the law, they have the power to arrest the suspect and bring him before the courts.

Centuries before the formation of any official police force, attempts were made to provide some means of 'community policing'. The keeping of law and order was the special responsibility of **Justices of the Peace** (JPs). They had a system of conscripting ordinary citizens known as petty constables, later simply called 'constables', to walk the streets or visit certain public houses to report any disorder. They were also employed to keep order at public executions and other punishments. The office of constable, still held by all police officers today, is now one of the oldest in the kingdom. The characters Dogberry and Verges in Shakespeare's *Much Ado About Nothing* were constables.

Keeping law and order has always been a difficult task, and in the days before the modern police force it was a pretty hopeless one. In their desperation Justices of the Peace would also employ *thief-takers* to catch criminals. Thief-takers were often no better than the criminals themselves. Sometimes they were criminals, who knew the criminal underworld well, and in return for payment would help the authorities to bring other criminals to trial.

The Thief-taker General

The most notorious thief-taker of all was Jonathan Wild, who operated in the early part of the eighteenth century. Nick-named 'the Thief-taker General' he began his career in a small way, informing on criminals who were suspected of crime. Eventually he built up a criminal empire of his own. His speciality was the organisation of robberies and burglaries. He was then paid rewards by the victims for securing the return of their property. Wild would in turn pay the thieves a commission out of this money!

In 1719, as a direct result of activities of this kind, Parliament passed the Second Transportation Act, which laid down that anyone taking a reward for receiving stolen goods, who did not also help to arrest the thief and give evidence against him, was guilty of a 'felony' (serious crime which could result in sentence of death).

Eventually, Wild was himself caught and prosecuted. He had for a reward returned some stolen lace to its owner. He was acquitted of the charge of stealing the lace, but found guilty of failing to give information which would lead to the capture of the criminals he had paid to steal it. He was executed at Tyburn in 1725, and his skeleton is now displayed in the museum of the Royal College of Surgeons.

Despite the cruel penalties inflicted upon criminals, the state of lawlessness in the seventeenth and eighteenth centuries was appalling. By the second half of the eighteenth century, the general population lived with a terrifying sense of insecurity. Gangs of criminals roamed the towns. Any form of transport was risky. Highwaymen held up stagecoaches in broad daylight. The fear inspired by these criminals may not have been much worse than that experienced by certain vulnerable sections of the community today, but it was far more widespread, and afflicted the whole country.

The Fielding brothers

In 1748, the novelist Henry Fielding took up appointment as a magistrate at Bow Street, London. His arrival there coincided with a new and terrifying crime wave. Only four years later, Horace Walpole, author and son of Britain's first Prime Minister, complained of the state of crime in London, saying, 'One is forced to travel, even at noon, as if one were going into battle'. Among the unpaid 'parish constables' of Westminster, Fielding found half a dozen men 'of public spirit' and formed them into a corps of honest thief-takers. They were first known as 'Mr Fielding's People', and later as the 'Bow Street Runners'. To everyone's astonishment, they cleared the streets of robbers.

Henry Fielding's success as a reformer in the fight against crime was followed by many years of hard work by his blind half-brother, Sir John Fielding—known as 'The Blind Beak'. At the age of 33, Sir John succeeded Henry as magistrate at Bow Street. He had been completely blind since an accident in his youth, and following his brother, was for 26 years in charge of the tiny unofficial force of 'policemen' in London. He was said to be able to recognise three thousand thieves by their voices. He produced a weekly list of wanted criminals, which was later published under the name Hue and Cry—the forerunner of the Police Gazette.

The Fieldings provoked much public discussion about having a force of armed men to catch criminals and bring them to trial, but all their efforts to create a regular force failed. This was in part due to another scandal of thief-takers who themselves turned to crime, which brought their schemes into disrepute, and in part due to all the campaigners who opposed the Fieldings' ideas of maintaining law and order on the grounds that it would infringe civil liberties. When he died in 1754, Henry Fielding left behind a detailed plan which was to be used by Robert Peel 75 years later as the blueprint for the first professional metropolitan force.

The first police force to become an organised body of men wearing uniforms and given special powers was the Metropolitan Police Force ('The Met'), named because it policed the metropolis of London. This force was created by the Metropolitan Police Act 1829. At that time Robert Peel was the Home Secretary, and policemen were therefore known as 'Peelers' or 'Bobbies'. The new police force first went out on duty at 6 p.m. on 29 September 1829. Its Instruction Book stated, *'the first duty of a constable is always to prevent the commission of a crime'*. The force made a poor start. By the end of the year, of the 2,800 men recruited, 2,238 had been dismissed, 1,790 of them for being drunk on duty.

It is hardly surprising, then, that in the early days of the police force, public opinion was very much against it. Newspapers complained bitterly that the police behaved with brutality in their enthusiasm to make arrests. At the same time the police were blamed for failing to clear up crime. Nevertheless, the value of an organised police force soon became apparent. In the 1840s police forces were formed in most of the counties, and the first plain-clothes detectives were used to infiltrate gangs of criminals and 'gather intelligence' on their activities.

In the remainder of the century the police force grew rapidly. The conditions of employment improved, although, as this report from the *Daily Telegraph* in 1865 shows, they were hardly satisfactory:

> *The attributes necessary to the making of a thoroughly efficient policeman are that he must be active, industrious, punctual, sober, intelligent, faithful, obedient, courageous, forbearing and incorruptible. He must have an iron constitution, no small power of endurance, the facility of going without his natural rest at stated periods, the eyes of Argus and the stoicism of an ancient philosopher. Can we expect all these virtues, cut and dried, for three and twenty shillings a week?*

Eventually, policemen living in many areas were provided with accommodation and a modest but steady living wage. Their work came under the direct supervision of local councillors, giving local communities a degree of control and sense of pride in their police. Women first joined the force in the 1920s.

The ranks of the police are further increased by the appointment of **Special Constables**. These are unpaid volunteers who assist the police in their work. Special constables were first given statutory authority by the Special Constables Act 1831. This provided that in time of 'Tumult, Riot and Felony', any two Justices of the Peace of a parish or township were given power to appoint

'Householders or other [suitable] persons . . . residing [there] to act as Special Constables . . . for the Preservation of the Public Peace'.

We still have special constables, one of the best known being Nigel Mansell, the motor racing champion, who is a member of the Devon and Cornwall Police Force. In 1914, at the beginning of the First World War, the great English composer Sir Edward Elgar, who was then 56 years old, enlisted as a special constable in Hampstead, North London. A friend records him *'perambulating the streets, firmly grasping his truncheon and looking for German spies'*. Perhaps the most notorious special constable was John Christie, a murderer who was executed in 1953, and who almost certainly swore away the life of an innocent man, Timothy Evans, at the Central Criminal Court (Old Bailey), by giving false evidence against him. The cases of Evans and Christie feature in Chapter 25.

The police have always had wide powers of arrest and search. One of the most sensational arrests in the past century, that of Dr Crippen, which still captures the imagination, took place on 31 July 1910. It was the first arrest in which the 'wireless' (radio) was used.

The arrest of Dr Crippen

In January 1910, an American doctor, Hawley Harvey Crippen, lived with his wife, Cora, at 39 Hilldrop Crescent, North London. She was a failed music hall performer with the stage name Belle Elmore. Dr Crippen had been having an affair with a young woman called Ethel Le Neve. He could not bear the thought of his wife standing in the way of their happiness. He poisoned her and dismembered her body, hiding it beneath the floorboards of his home.

After the murder, Crippen and Ethel (disguised as a young boy) fled the country. They caught the SS *Montrose* for Quebec, Canada. The crime and Crippen's disappearance resulted in massive publicity, and because of the wireless, as it was then called, Captain Kendall of the *Montrose* learned of this while his ship was at sea. He became convinced that Crippen and Le Neve were on board, and telegraphed his suspicions through to Inspector Walter Dew of New Scotland Yard, who together with a police sergeant set sail for Canada from Liverpool aboard the SS *Laurentic*.

The *Laurentic* overtook the *Montrose*, and on 31 July the police boarded this ship and arrested Crippen and Le Neve. They were returned to England and sent for trial at the Old Bailey. Crippen was tried first. After a trial lasting five days, on 22 October the jury retired at 2.15 p.m. They returned to court with their verdict at 2.42 p.m. Crippen was found guilty of murder and sentenced to death. Still protesting his innocence, he was executed on 23 November. Ethel Le Neve was later acquitted of assisting Crippen's escape.

THE MODERN FORCE

There are now 43 police authorities in the United Kingdom. Each is responsible for policing in its area. In 1992 a National Criminal Intelligence Service was set up to gather information sent in from all over the country. The facilities provided by this agency are available to all the police forces. The Police National Computer, which stores a vast amount of information about crime and criminals, is another important instrument in the fight against crime.

The headquarters of the Metropolitan Force has for many years been at New Scotland Yard. At one time it occupied a private house in Whitehall Place, the back of which opened on to a courtyard. This had been the site of a residence owned by the Kings of Scotland, and the courtyard became known as Scotland Yard. When a new police station was built which had to be entered from the yard, it was called New Scotland Yard. Now the police headquarters is a huge building, which also houses the 'Black Museum'. This museum, which contains gruesome exhibits from many notorious trials, is also used to train new recruits in the many ways in which lethal weapons may be disguised.

The police now have the use of advanced modern equipment. This ranges from 'souped-up' motorbikes and squad cars to helicopters. It includes the most advanced surveillance aids, and instantaneous access to the Police National Computer and the facilities of the Forensic Science Service. This service runs highly sophisticated laboratories where forensic (legal) scientists carry out the scientific examination of exhibits.

Many police officers are highly trained and dedicated experts. Specially selected officers are permitted to carry firearms when dealing with dangerous criminals. Police officers are trained in many other skills. The following is a list of just a few of the specialist branches of the force:

- *Crime prevention.* All forces have a department of officers trained to give advice on how citizens may best protect themselves and their property against criminals. They often visit schools and make presentations to children. They also work in co-operation with members of local Neighbourhood Watch Committees.

- *Community relations.* The job of Community Liaison Officers is to improve relations between the police and the different parts of the community they serve, including young people in the area. This includes race relations work. In many areas of the country the police have 'schools involvement programmes', where School Liaison Officers visit schools to talk about subjects as diverse as citizenship, 'crime busting', drugs, and 'personal safety'—which covers such issues as bullying, peer group pressure, racial harassment, and dealing with the attentions of strangers.

- *Dog handling.* These officers are specially skilled in training and handling police dogs, whose duties may range from protection against violent criminals to assisting as 'sniffer dogs' in the investigation of crime. This, of course, includes assisting the drugs squad and HM Customs to detect the presence of dangerous drugs, and the anti-terrorist squad to detect explosives. In July 1997, the Metropolitan Police Dog Section celebrated its fiftieth anniversary.

- *Mounted police.* Even in these modern times the police still make use of horses as a particularly effective means of crowd control, although some forces are considering disbanding the units for reasons of expense. Police horses must be at least 16 hands high. They undergo a period of intensive training to learn to cope with noisy traffic and hostile crowds, and take for granted pistol shots and missiles—even petrol bombs.

- *Scenes of crimes and forensic science.* Scenes of Crimes Officers (SOCOs), as their name implies, are expert in visiting the scenes of crimes and searching for clues. They take fingerprints or the castings of shoe-prints, and remove any item of interest which will require laboratory examination. Police officers are also trained to work in the laboratories. For instance, they may become expert in firearms and the comparison of ammunition, or fingerprints.

- *Drugs Squad.* These officers must become expert in the identification of a whole range of prohibited dangerous drugs and substances—from heroin to cannabis, ecstasy to glue-sniffing. They must become familiar with the 'drugs scene' and the various types of people who become involved in it. Many officers turn out to be excellent actors—working in the drugs scene as undercover officers. At one end of the scale they will be trying to catch the major international drugs smugglers and dealers; at the other, they must handle the distressing cases of those who have become addicted to the most dangerous drugs, and have turned to crime to pay for them.

- *Murder Squad and Flying Squad.* These branches of the force deal with the most serious investigations into murder and other violent crime, such as armed robbery. The Flying Squad gets its name from the ex-Royal Flying Corps vehicles which it once used. Often, too little credit is given to its officers, whose work may place them in real danger, and who show great bravery when dealing with armed criminals.

- *Criminal Investigation Department (CID).* CID officers wear plain-clothes and specialise in detective work. They are frequently called in to interview suspects who have been arrested by uniformed officers.

The above list of police specialities is by no means complete. Police officers are also specially trained to investigate cases of child abuse, or fraud. London has its own section of River Police, and everyone has heard of 'police frogmen'. The police also have a Special Branch, which deals with crimes of terrorism, and are involved in the work of **Interpol**, the International Criminal Police Organisation set up in 1923 to fight crime worldwide. Over 170 countries around the world are members of Interpol and co-operate in its work.

*

The powers of the police are set out in a number of Acts of Parliament. The police have four main powers, to:

- *Stop and search.* The police may stop and search a suspect if they have reasonable grounds for believing that certain offences have been committed, such as theft, the possession of stolen goods, offensive weapons, knives, or other bladed articles, or the unlawful taking of a vehicle.

- *Arrest.* The police may arrest without a warrant (issued by a magistrate) anyone suspected of committing an 'arrestable' offence. 'Arrestable' offences are the more serious offences. The police may arrest with a warrant in other cases.

- *Detain.* The police may detain a suspect while they carry out their investigations. This includes the power to question the suspect. The police now have the power, on the authority of a senior officer, to take 'non-intimate' samples from a suspect, for example of hair or saliva; or 'intimate' samples such as dental impressions, or samples of pubic hair, blood, or urine. These will be analysed by scientists who may be able to identify the suspect as having been involved in a crime.

- *Enter and search premises.* This includes the power to seize evidence. This power is normally dependant upon a magistrate issuing a warrant, but the police may enter premises without a warrant, where, for example, they have reasonable cause to believe that someone is committing an arrestable offence, or to save life or limb, or to prevent serious damage to property. The police may also ask a Crown Court judge for an order allowing them to inspect bank accounts or telephone accounts.

These powers are very great, and they are given to the police as part of their overall responsibility to enforce the law, but they are all governed by the law, and are subject to strict control by rules and regulations. If the police exceed their powers, the person who has been wronged may take action in the courts against the officers concerned and the police force to which they belong. The officers may be disciplined, even prosecuted if their behaviour amounts to a criminal offence, and their force may be ordered to pay compensation.

POLICE INTERVIEWS

One of the important powers of the police, which has caused much difficulty and controversy, is the power to question or interview persons suspected of crime. In some cases, the prosecution's case against a defendant includes evidence that he confessed to the crime. This has on occasion led to the courts deciding that certain defendants have made 'false confessions'—admitting to offences which they have not committed.

We may wonder how this could come about, but there is no doubt that people questioned about even the most serious offences, including murder, have sometimes admitted to committing the crime, and yet it has later been proved that they were innocent. This problem of confessions being obtained by oppression, or from weak or frightened people who are easily 'suggestible' (react to questioning by readily agreeing to suggestions put to them), has been taken very seriously. There are now many rules relating to police interviews, and a great deal has been done to try to make sure that these are conducted fairly, and that anything said by the suspect after his arrest is accurately recorded.

THE POLICE AND CRIMINAL EVIDENCE ACT

The most important of these changes have been made by the Police and Criminal Evidence Act 1984 (known as PACE). This Act provides numerous laws to protect people who are being interviewed by the police, and it is responsible for detailed codes of practice that govern the manner in which these interviews should take place.

All suspects being interviewed now have the right to the advice of solicitors and to have them present at their interviews. Children under the age of 16 must be accompanied by a parent or some other 'responsible adult' concerned for their welfare. All interviews should now be tape-recorded, and copies of the tapes provided to the defence, so that the defendant and his lawyers will be able to check what the defendant said, and demonstrate any unfairness to the jury. These rules and codes of practice have done much to remove the serious disquiet which resulted from a number of sensational cases, where it had been possible to prove later that confessions which defendants had made to crimes were, in fact, untrue.

If lawyers representing a defendant believe that any action of the police investigating a case has been wrong or unfair, and that the result of that might affect the fairness of the defendant's trial, they will try to have the evidence in question ruled **inadmissible** (removed from the case altogether). Sections 76 and 77 of PACE 1984 attempt to ensure that any confessions to the police are made freely and are genuine; section 76 deals with the oppression of suspects; and section 77 protects the mentally handicapped.

TRAINING

The police are now a highly organised force. First, the new recruits must attend an 18-week residential foundation course. This period of intensive assessment and training will involve learning basic policing skills, and include physical training and self-defence, first aid, and a study of the law relating to the police. Just as important is the training in how to understand and communicate with people in a wide range of situations.

Every new constable, on appointment to the force, must make a solemn 'attestation' (as we will see, part of the attestation is echoed in the oath which judges must take on their appointment). It reads:

> I solemnly and sincerely declare and affirm that I will well and truly serve our Sovereign Lady the Queen in the Office of Constable without favour or affection, malice or ill-will, and that I will to the best of my power, cause the peace to be kept and preserved, and prevent all offences against persons and properties of Her Majesty's subjects, and that while I continue to hold the said office I will, to the best of my skill and knowledge, discharge all the duties thereof faithfully according to law.

The new police constable must then begin his or her career working 'on the beat'—patrolling the streets—and will do this for the rest of a probationary period, which is usually two years. New recruits are told: '*working the local streets with experienced colleagues, you'll learn how to relate to people, judge situations and act accordingly. With the support and constructive criticism of your colleagues, you'll gain experience of all types of police work and all aspects of our role within the community*'. The career structure in the police force allows men and women the opportunity to be promoted from constable to sergeant, then through the various grades of inspector and superintendent, right up to the ranks of Deputy Chief Constable and Chief Constable. In London, the head of the force is called the Metropolitan Commissioner. He heads a force which now has more than 25,000 police officers—one-fifth of all the officers in England and Wales.

*

Each police force is supervised by a Police Authority. In England and Wales these consist of local councillors, magistrates, and other independent members. An independent body, the Police Complaints Authority, currently deals with complaints against the police although this is to be replaced by a new, independent, *Police Complaints Commission.*

Ever since the first police force was founded, the police have come under criticism—for denying civil liberties, for failing to catch criminals, or for catching the wrong people. They have also been roundly criticised for discriminating against members of ethnic minorities. We will see something of how these problems may affect the community in Chapter 20. In some cases these criticisms have proved to be justified, and there have been a small number of extremely serious cases in which police officers, who have been paid to enforce the law, have been found to have broken it. These cases, which have resulted in serious injustice, have had a profound effect upon the whole criminal justice system and, of course, the police and the manner in which they carry out their duties. They have also resulted in very significant changes in the law, some being made on the direct recommendation of the *Law Commission.*

Criticisms of the police should be seen in proper perspective. Complaints against the police are normally carefully investigated, but few of them are found to be true; the problem is sorting out the good ones from the bad. It is easy for a criminal, who is upset at being caught and fearful of the consequences, to make a false complaint. It is also easy to dismiss a genuine complaint, which has been made by a man with a bad record, or a genuine complaint of racial discrimination.

The police perform many duties fundamental to the well-being of society but which are unlikely to make them popular. Some find it hard to accept that for every bad police officer, there are many good ones dedicated to the community in which they serve. Few would wish to face and disarm a dangerous criminal, or enter the home of someone who has been murdered, or handle the case of a child who has been badly abused, or attend the scene of a horrific road accident to unravel its causes. It is worth remembering that the police regularly receive commendations and awards for outstanding bravery and service to the community—from tackling and arresting armed criminals, to carrying out difficult and dangerous undercover operations; from rescuing the victims of serious crime, to saving the lives of those threatening to commit suicide.

The British people tend to have a love–hate relationship with their police. This is, perhaps, inevitable having regard to their role as chief law enforcers in the country. This role is, however, a crucial one, and the police force is as necessary and important an element in the administration of justice as any other that we will be examining in this book.

7

Our Law Upholders—the Judiciary

'Above all things, integrity is their portion and proper virtue.'

Francis Bacon, speaking about the judges. He was Lord Chancellor from 1618 to 1620, when he was dismissed from office, fined, and imprisoned in the Tower of London for taking bribes.

*

The courts, and the judges who preside over them, are responsible for upholding the law. We have learned that one fundamental idea of justice is the upholding of rights, and the punishment of wrongs, by the law. Only the judges can do this, and they have been doing it for a long time. In July 2000, in a speech given in Westminster Hall, Lord Woolf, Lord Chief Justice said:

> *Our legal system promotes and upholds the rule of law. We can draw a direct line from the Magna Carta to today. Our legal system has flourished without the support of a written constitution. In medieval times the source of law and order was the King. Our robes are still a visible link with that time. Since the thirteenth century judges have been travelling up and down the country upholding the law.*

The judges as a whole are called the **judiciary** and one of their most important characteristics is that they are *independent*. This means that in whatever type of case they try, whether it is a criminal or a civil case, they must have no personal interest in the result, or connection with the parties to it. They must listen to both sides of the case with equal attention and without prejudice. No one should be able to influence their decision. Only then can they judge the case fairly.

In Chapter 4 we saw that the judiciary is one of the great branches of the constitution. In 1996 Lord Bingham, then Lord Chief Justice, began a lecture on judicial independence with a six-word phrase which will be well known to lovers of Jane Austen: *'It is a truth universally acknowledged that the constitution of a modern democracy governed by the rule of law must effectively guarantee judicial independence.'*

Over the years there have been many notable examples of judges who have stood up to the power of the throne or the State and acted independently. One such judge was Sir Edward Coke (pronounced 'Cook'). A somewhat improbable hero, he was a ruthless operator, disliked intensely by most people who came into contact with him. As His Majesty's Attorney-General in the reign of James I, Coke had been a shamefully unfair prosecutor. As His Majesty's Chief Justice, first of the Common Pleas and then of the King's Bench, and at considerable personal danger, he became a fearless champion of the common law against the might of the King. The case of John Wilkes is the story of two more great judges, Lord Camden and Lord Mansfield, who risked the displeasure of the King and defied his wishes. This case was a milestone in establishing the right of free speech.

The case of John Wilkes

In 1763, John Wilkes wrote a scathing attack on a speech delivered by King George III when he opened Parliament. It was published in a weekly paper which Wilkes himself had founded, called *The North Briton*. First the printers of the paper were arrested on the orders of the King and then Wilkes himself. A writ of *habeas corpus* was immediately issued by the Chief Justice of the Common Pleas, Sir Charles Pratt (later Lord Camden), to have Wilkes brought before the court. Pratt ordered him to be released.

Wilkes became a popular hero, and the following year he was elected Lord Mayor of London, but he soon got into further trouble. This time he fled the country. He was tried in his absence and outlawed. This meant that all his property in this country was forfeit, and he was bound to be imprisoned if he returned.

Wilkes did return to England, and he was imprisoned. Again, a writ of *habeas corpus* brought him before the court — this time before Lord Mansfield, who was Chief Justice of the King's Bench. In reversing the sentence of outlawry and ordering Wilkes's freedom, Lord Mansfield said, '*I will not do that which my conscience tells me is wrong upon this occasion; to gain the huzzas [cheers] of thousands, or the daily praise of all the papers which come from the press. I will not avoid doing what I think is right; though it should draw upon me the whole artillery of libels [abuse]; all that falsehood and malice can invent . . .*'.

To this day, when judges are appointed they must swear an oath to '*do right to all manner of persons without fear or favour, affection or ill will*'. They therefore promise to uphold the law and never to be biased—to do what they believe to be right, regardless of who is involved in the case. That is why, as Lord Bingham explained in a case heard in 1999, '*Justice is portrayed as blind, not because she ignores the facts and circumstances of individual cases, but because she shuts her eyes to all considerations extraneous to the particular case*'.

The responsibility of a judge to be independent of outside pressures was given eloquent modern expression in March 1998 by the American judge,

Hiller B. Zobel, who presided over the trial of the English nanny Louise Woodward, for murder: *'Elected officials may consider popular urging and sway to public opinion polls. Judges must follow their duty, heedless of editorials, letters, telegrams, picketers, threats, petitions, panellists and talk shows. In this country we do not administer justice by plebiscite [popular vote].'*

Not only must judges never actually be biased, they must also never allow themselves to be put in a position where they might be accused of bias. A good illustration of this is the law relating to corruption. *Corruption* is the crime of giving or taking bribes. As long ago as 1215, in Magna Carta, King John promised, *'To no one we will sell, to no one we will refuse or delay right or justice'*. This meant that the King would never corrupt the legal process in his own interests.

Cases in which this royal promise was broken abound, with a succession of Kings and Queens influencing the outcome of State Trials (cases said to involve the security of the State) with the spoken or unspoken threat of terror. Cases of judicial corruption, where a judge has actually taken a bribe offered by one of the parties to litigation, are, however, almost unheard of in our many centuries of legal history. Perhaps the most infamous stain on this record is the corruption of Lord Chancellor Bacon.

The prosecution of Francis Bacon

Francis Bacon (1561–1626) was an exceptionally talented man — a gifted writer and philosopher, he was also a great lawyer; but he was a deeply flawed character. Immensely vain and ambitious, and eager to court favour with those who could advance his career, he was relentless in his use of flattery. In this he was more successful with King James I than with Queen Elizabeth I. Eventually, in 1618, he became James's Lord Chancellor.

Two years later, Chancellor Bacon was called upon to decide two cases. One involved a litigant (party to the case) called Awbrey; the other a man called Egerton. Each of them gave Bacon a bribe: Awbrey gave him £100; Egerton gave him a silver jug and bowl and 400 gold sovereigns. In both cases Bacon actually decided the case against the person who gave the bribe (no, he was not paid more by the other side!). Nevertheless, he was still charged with corruption, for he had received gifts knowing that they were being given corruptly.

Bacon was tried by his fellow peers in Parliament (since the *Magna Carta* laid down that a man must be tried by his equals, it followed that a peer had to be tried by other peers — a privilege given to peers right up to the twentieth century, when it was abolished). In due course he confessed his crimes and pleaded for mercy. He was ordered to pay a huge fine, imprisoned in the Tower of London, and disqualified from holding public office for life. It was not long before Bacon was released from prison; but he had few friends and he died in poverty and disgrace.

Bacon was tireless in his ambition. After his trial he tried hard to climb back into favour. When he failed, this noted philosopher accepted his fate 'philosophically', saying: '*I was the justest judge that was in England these fifty years, but it was the justest sentence in Parliament these two hundred years*'.

It follows that a judge should not try a case if he is associated with either party, or if he has received any sort of favour from them, even if there could be no question of that influencing his decision. He should refuse to try the case even if both sides know about the connection, and do not object to him trying it. This is because not only do the parties in the case have an interest in justice being done, but also the public at large—everyone in the country—has an interest in justice being done. Everyone must feel reassured, and be able to *see*, that a judge is dealing with the case impartially.

In 1924, Lord Chief Justice Hewart stated this principle in these memorable words: '*It is not merely of some importance, but of fundamental importance that justice should not only be done, but should manifestly and undoubtedly be seen to be done.*' The theme of judicial independence is enshrined in the European Convention on Human Rights. Article 6 states: '*everyone is entitled to a fair and public hearing by an independent and impartial tribunal established by law*'. We have recently witnessed a highly dramatic illustration of this important principle of justice in action:

The case of General Pinochet—Part 1

General Augusto Pinochet was the Head of State in Chile in the years 1972–90. In September 1998 he visited England and in October was admitted to hospital for surgery. The Spanish authorities applied for a warrant for his arrest and extradition to Spain on charges that between 1973 and 1990 he was responsible for 'genocide, torture and terrorism'. This allegation included the torture and disappearance of a number of Spanish citizens in Chile. General Pinochet applied for his release from detention on the grounds that as a former Head of State he was immune from prosecution for things which he was alleged to have done in that capacity.

In November the case came before the House of Lords, when the court permitted the human rights group, Amnesty International, to be represented at the hearing. Amnesty's lawyers supported the argument that the General had no immunity from extradition. On 25 November, the House of Lords, in a landmark ruling, by a majority of 3–2, decided that General Pinochet could have no immunity in respect of acts of torture and hostage taking carried out on his instructions during his time in office.

One of the Law Lords who sat in judgment in the case was Lord Hoffmann. He was the last of the five Law Lords to give judgment, and his speech was decisive in the majority decision against General Pinochet; but he had failed to disclose to the parties that he was a Director of Amnesty International. General Pinochet's lawyers petitioned the court to say that as this may at least have given the appearance of the judge being biased, its ruling should be set aside and the case heard afresh.

Five new Law Lords unanimously agreed. They said that Lord Hoffmann should have disqualified himself from hearing the case. Justice may have been done but it had not been 'seen to be done' — the links between Lord Hoffmann and Amnesty International *'were so strong that public confidence in the administration of justice would be shaken'* if they had not overturned the ruling. Accordingly, a different set of Law Lords had to hear the case all over again — an event unique in our legal history. We will learn what happened in this extraordinary case in Chapter 24.

We must never become too grand and self-satisfied about the law and the courts. The legal system is after all run by human beings for human beings, and all human beings are fallible. Judges can and do make mistakes. This is why we have appeal courts, where even more judges must decide whether the original decisions should stand, or be altered or reversed. Sometimes the decisions of the (three) judges of the Court of Appeal are reversed by the (five) judges of the House of Lords.

The use of Latin in the courts is now discouraged, but it has been known for a judge, pompously stressing the independence of the judiciary — or a barrister, hoping to assist an unworthy client — to quote the Latin saying, *'Fiat justicia, ruat coelum'* ('Let justice be done though the heavens should fall'). This is all very well, but it does come from a story of the most appalling injustice:

Piso's justice

Piso was a Roman statesman who lived in the time of Jesus. When he was governor of Syria, he sentenced a soldier to death for the murder of a man named Gaius. The soldier had denied any knowledge of Gaius' disappearance. Just as the centurion, who had been ordered to execute the soldier, was about to kill him, Gaius was found. He was alive and well. The relieved centurion called the execution off — but their joy was short-lived.

When Piso learned what had happened, he sentenced all three men to death — the soldier because he had already been sentenced to die, the centurion for disobeying the order to execute him, and Gaius because he had caused the deaths of two innocent men!

Piso is said to have excused this wicked deed with the words *'Fiat justicia, ruat coelum'*. If the heavens do fall when some kinds of justice are done, they must surely have fallen at this judgment. Still, these words have been handed down over the years as a statement of how the courts should always do justice according to law, no matter the consequences. Lord Camden himself used this very phrase when giving judgment in the case of John Wilkes. (It so happens that *'Fiat justicia'* were the terrible last words of command given to light the fires which consumed the 'heretics' of Tudor England.)

Of course judges do try to ensure that justice is done. As we have seen, in some situations it is easier to look at it another way, and say that they try to avoid doing injustice. They must always do their best to give an independent and fair judgment according to law, even though the judgment may be unpopular. Just as important, and sometimes as difficult, they must by the *manner* in which they try cases also give the *appearance* that they are doing justice. That is why it has been said that every time a judge tries a case, he is himself on trial.

The value and importance of an independent judiciary, and the reasons for our high-minded expectations of judges, were spelled out in a speech by Lord Justice Igor Judge, shortly after his appointment in 2003 to the office of the Deputy Chief Justice:

> *The principle of judicial independence benefits the judge sitting in judgment. The judge does what he or she believes to be right, according to law, undistracted and uninhibited. But the overwhelming beneficiary of the principle is the community. If the judge is subjected to any pressure, his judgment is flawed, and justice is tarnished. When judges speak out in defence of the principle, they are not seeking to uphold some minor piece of flummery or privilege, which goes with their office. They are speaking out in defence of our community's entitlement to have its disputes, particularly those with the government of the day, and the institutions of the community, heard and decided by a judge who is independent of them all . . . Among our tasks we have to ensure that the rule of law applies to everyone equally, not only when the consequences of the decision will be greeted with acclaim, but also, and not one jot less so, indeed, even more so, when the decision will be greeted with intense public hostility.*

The judges are there to uphold the law. This means that it is ultimately their responsibility to ensure that the law in force at the time is obeyed. It is the judges who must interpret the law—if there is a dispute about what the law actually is, they must decide it. It is the judges who decide whether the law has been broken; and they must decide, or preside over courts where juries must decide, whether the people brought before them have broken the law. Lastly, the judges must decide what should happen when the law has been broken.

Parliament has great power, for it is our chief law maker. The police may also be very powerful, for they have the right to enforce the law and arrest anyone suspected of breaking it; but anyone who is arrested must quickly be brought before a court, where only the judges have the awesome power to take away a man's liberty by sending him to prison. It is the judges in their courts who must *uphold the law*.

8

The Legal Profession

'The first thing we do, let's kill all the lawyers.'
William Shakespeare, *King Henry VI, Part 2*, Dick to Jack Cade.

'That whether you're an honest man or whether you're a thief,
Depends on whose solicitor has given me my brief.'
W. S. Gilbert, *Utopia Limited.*

※

In most countries there is only one legal profession. This means that all the lawyers have roughly the same professional education leading to the same legal qualifications, and they are permitted to do all the legal work that has to be done. In England the system is different. Here the profession is divided into two types of lawyers, called **Solicitors** and **Barristers**. Solicitors and barristers are both qualified lawyers, but they have a different legal training; they take different examinations to qualify, and once they have qualified they usually do different types of legal work. This is why it is said that there are two 'branches' of the legal profession.

Lawyers may be either solicitors or barristers. They cannot be both at the same time, but it is possible for a solicitor to become a barrister, and for a barrister to become a solicitor. Lord Widgery was Lord Chief Justice of England in the 1970s. He started his career in the law as a solicitor. He then became a barrister, and eventually the most senior judge in the land.

We will look more closely at the work of solicitors and barristers in Chapters 9 and 10. The legal profession as such has never been popular, and no doubt Shakespeare always got a rousing cheer from his audiences when Dick spoke the words quoted above to the rebel Jack Cade. Indeed, the first thing revolutionaries usually do on seizing power is to overthrow the legal system, blaming it for their ills, and swiftly condemning supporters of the old order in 'trials' of their own devising: *Revenge is Justice!* Lawyers are possibly unpopular for another and more mundane reason. People who lose their cases often blame their lawyers, and resent paying their fees; people who win often believe that as justice was on their side they would have won anyway, and resent paying their fees.

Nevertheless, anyone who has been involved in legal matters or who has been to court will quickly appreciate how difficult and unwise it is for people to conduct their own cases: hence the saying that a man who represents himself 'has a fool for a client'. Anyone who values freedom and individual rights will know that throughout our history lawyers have fought for and gained civil rights in the courts. The careers of successful barristers have been followed like those of film stars, and judges who have confirmed those freedoms, some-times against great opposition, have been popular and revered.

Although lawyers may be at 'daggers drawn' during a case, there are rules of behaviour—codes of professional conduct—which provide that when in court they must always be courteous to one another. Whenever lawyers of any kind appear together in court, they always refer to one another as '*my learned friend*'. The other side of this coin is that however close lawyers may be as personal friends, they must never allow their friendship to get in the way of doing their duty on behalf of their clients. They will never tell one another the professional secrets of their side of the case, and they must always try as hard as they can, whether their professional opponents are people they like or dislike.

Anyone who seeks the advice and help of a solicitor or a barrister is known as a **client**. Solicitors and barristers must do the best they can for their clients; but first and foremost they have a 'duty to the Court' to behave honourably, and not do anything that they *know* will mislead the court and harm the interests of justice. What does this mean? How can lawyers representing opposite sides in a case all be acting honourably in the best interests of just-ice? Surely at least one team of lawyers must believe, or at least suspect, that their client's case is wrong?

'*But what do you think of supporting a cause you know to be bad?*', asked the young barrister James Boswell of his friend Dr Samuel Johnson (writer, author of the great *Dictionary of the English Language*, and a man with a genius for argument). Dr Johnson replied, '*Sir, you do not know it to be good or bad until the Judge determines it . . . An argument which does not convince yourself may convince the Judge; and if it does convince him, why, then, Sir, you are wrong and he is right! It is his business to judge; and you are not to be confident that a cause is bad, but to say all you can for your client, and then hear the judge's opinion.*'

This short extract from Boswell's *Life of Samuel Johnson*, first published as long ago as 1791, shows that this is a question that has troubled people for many years. In 1969, Mr Justice Megarry (later Vice-Chancellor of the Chancery Division) said in the course of giving a judgment: '*As everybody who has anything to do with the law knows, the path of the law is strewn with examples of open and shut cases which, somehow, were not; of unanswerable charges which, in the event, were completely answered; of inexplicable conduct which was fully explained; of fixed and unalterable determinations that, by discussion, suffered a change.'*

Not everybody, however, has had anything to do with the law, and lawyers who represent defendants in criminal cases are often asked: 'How can you defend somebody if you *know* he is guilty?' Here is a rather fuller answer, as it applies today:

> Anyone who is charged with a crime and who denies being involved in it must have a fair trial. If a lawyer is asked to defend that person, he must use all his knowledge and skill to present his client's case in the best possible light. This is so even if the lawyer feels that the defence is not a good one, and that it is unlikely to succeed. In the past many people have had what seemed to be poor, even hopeless defences, but they turned out to be true.
>
> Lawyers are there to represent people, not to judge them. If they were to refuse to represent them, or not try their best just because they did not like them or their point of view, they would be judging them. That is why a lawyer who is available to represent a defendant should never refuse to do so simply because he does not approve of him, or because he does not believe in his case.
>
> A lawyer must not make up a fictional defence for a client out of his own head, or defend someone who tells him that he has committed the crime and is guilty of it. He may plead for a lenient sentence on his behalf, but he must not argue that he is not guilty. That would be dishonest, and a lawyer's first duty is to *the court* to conduct his cases honestly. If a person accused of crime admits it to his lawyer, the lawyer does then know he is guilty, and he must advise him to plead guilty. If he refuses to do so, the lawyer becomes what is known as 'professionally embarrassed', and must have nothing more to do with the case.

Just as judges are expected to be independent, and to do the right thing, so too are members of the legal profession. This means that they should be determined and courageous in putting forward their client's case. Many important advances in the civil liberties of the citizen are due to lawyers having conducted their cases fearlessly, however great the pressure. There have been some modern examples of this, with lawyers fighting for justice in the face of what at first must have seemed to be overwhelming opposition:

- We have already seen that there are now strict rules relating to the interviews of suspects by the police.

- In a criminal trial it is the duty of the prosecution to disclose to the defence anything in their possession which may assist the defence.

- In cases where the prosecution depends upon the identification of the criminal by eye-witnesses, the judge must warn the jury that it is always possible for identifications to be mistaken and that the jury must consider that type of evidence with special care.

Each of these rules is now regarded as extremely important. Each is an outstanding example of a situation where the development of the law is almost entirely due to the tireless work of lawyers who have believed that defendants have suffered injustice, and who have dedicated themselves to proving it, and having the injustice put right.

FEES

The payment received by lawyers for their work is called their **fees**. The legal fees in any court case are called the **costs** of the case. The fees earned by the vast majority of lawyers do not approach the high fees that are sometimes referred to in the press. Many young lawyers find it difficult to earn a living wage.

Whenever clients can afford to pay their costs, they pay them ('privately'). This is so whether they are individuals, or companies which need to have legal work done for them. If the legal work involves **litigation**, which means fighting a case in court, and they win, they will normally be entitled to an order that the other side should pay their costs; but if they lose, they will usually be ordered to pay the costs of the winning side.

In many cases litigants cannot afford to pay the fees of their lawyers. They may apply for *legal aid*, which means that if they qualify for it the State will pay either their full legal fees or at least part of them. For instance, anyone who is arrested and charged with a serious criminal offence who cannot afford to pay for his defence will be entitled to ask for legal aid. If he is taken into custody (kept at a police station) the police must offer to arrange for his representation immediately. Legal aid may also be granted in some civil cases, although it is a matter of great concern that the scope of legal aid to fund civil litigation has been considerably reduced. The legal aid scheme was introduced in 1948. At that time Lord Goddard was Lord Chief Justice of England. Legal aid is now recognised to be one of the most important social advances of the last century, and it undoubtedly provides many lawyers with their main source of income. In his Foreword to Timothy Daniell's fascinating book, *A Literary Excursion to the Inns of Court*, Lord Goddard refers to the introduction of the legal aid scheme, and says: *'How far that has been of advantage to the Bar may be doubted'*. Even a Lord Chief Justice can sometimes be very wrong!

Many people who have legal problems do not know what to do at all, or are worried about going to a solicitor for advice in case they should be asked to pay legal fees which they cannot afford. They can receive free advice at their local Citizen's Advice Bureau or Law Centre. These offices do excellent work. Many public-spirited citizens, including qualified lawyers—even law students—help in giving free advice. If the case is sufficiently serious and may mean going to court, they will advise how to approach solicitors and, if possible, apply for legal aid.

- One of the most important of these legal services is given by the *Free Representation Unit* (FRU). This unit was established in 1987, with the twin objects of providing a free legal service to local communities and enhancing the education of students in the school of law at the University of Central England. The cases dealt with by the FRU have included matters of employment, contract, welfare benefits, and compensation for criminal injuries.

- In 1999, a new scheme was launched by the College of Law, the largest training institution for lawyers in the country. It is sponsored by a number of large firms of solicitors, and thousands of law students, as part of their training, work in a network of free legal advice clinics, helping people with their legal problems. The first clinic was set up in Chancery Lane, London, with students helping members of the public with disputes about jobs, housing, small claims, and negligence claims. Similar clinics have now been set up in Guildford, Chester, and York.

- Some academic institutions now have 'Law Offices' where qualified solicitors employed outside the profession (such as university lecturers) may give advice on behalf of members of the public. The University of Northumbria has a Law Student Office, and conducts a 'live client' programme, where students, under qualified supervision, work on real-life cases. In 2001, they scored a notable success for justice. They researched the case of Alex Allen, who had been convicted of robbery and sentenced to eight years' imprisonment. They prepared a submission for the *Criminal Cases Review Commission*, which revealed that his trial might have been flawed. The case was referred to the Court of Appeal, where Allen's conviction was quashed.

Now a new system of payment of fees has been approved for civil cases. The idea has been imported from America. Under this system, lawyers may agree to take on a case for no fee at all, *on condition* that if the client wins the case and is awarded **damages** (money compensation), they will receive their fees. In some cases, where a great amount of work has been done, this may also include an extra 'success' fee. This scheme is called the **conditional fees scheme**, because the lawyer's payment is conditional on him winning the case.

This scheme is now an important part of the civil justice system, particularly in claims for damages for personal injuries. It has been argued that it is good for **claimants** (people who bring cases in the civil courts) because it means that many claimants who would not otherwise be able to afford to take a case to court will now have access to justice. There is also an argument that it may be unfair to **defendants** (those against whom actions are brought in the civil courts), the fear being that lawyers who work for claimants under these conditions will try so hard to win their cases that they may be tempted to break the important rules of their profession—that they must behave honourably, and not influence the evidence which their clients or their witnesses give.

*

PRIVILEGES

THE PRIVILEGE GIVEN TO CLIENTS

There is a special and very important privilege that has been given to clients. This has been developed over many years, and belongs to them as a matter of public policy, in order to ensure the proper and efficient running of the justice system. This is that a lawyer must not reveal what he or she has been told by the client in the course of preparing a case, without the client's consent. This is a privilege given to the clients who are represented by lawyers; it is not given to the lawyers, who have no choice in the matter.

If, therefore, a client admits to his solicitor and barrister that he has committed the crime with which he is charged, it is their duty to advise him that he should plead guilty, but they cannot go to the police and tell them that their client has confessed. If the police approach them and ask for information, they cannot (without the client's permission) reveal anything—even if the client has confessed to murder. In a case heard in 1996 Lord Chief Justice Taylor stated that legal professional privilege was a fundamental human right. He expressed the great importance of the principle in these terms:

> The principle . . . is that a man must be able to consult his lawyers in confidence, since otherwise he might hold back half the truth. The client must be sure that what he tells his lawyer in confidence will never be revealed without his consent. Legal professional privilege is thus much more than an ordinary rule of evidence limited in its application

to the facts of a particular case. It is a fundamental condition on which the adminis-
tration of justice as a whole rests.

Lawyers are the only professionals to be in this special situation. If someone confesses a crime to his doctor, or priest, or a newspaper reporter, there is no legal privilege. A judge would not wish them to break any understanding of confidentiality, but if he considers it essential in the interests of justice he will do so; and they must then reveal the information which they have received. This is because they now have a legal responsibility to obey the judge's order. If they refuse they may be fined or sent to prison for **contempt of court** (disobeying a court order).

THE PRIVILEGE GIVEN TO LAWYERS

Until recently lawyers too enjoyed an important privilege—an 'immunity from suit'—meaning that they could not be sued (taken to court) by their clients for negligence in respect of their conduct of a case in court. They were privileged from legal action only in respect of work done in court; if a lawyer performed his 'out of court' work negligently, giving bad legal advice, preparing a defective contract, or delaying the start of a claim for so long that the court will not allow it to proceed, the client can take him to court and claim compensation.

The reason for the rule of privilege in respect of conduct in court was the belief that if lawyers could be sued by their clients they would be inhibited in doing their work, and this would make it very difficult for them to fulfil their duty to the court to behave honourably. They might be frightened to ask anything, in case they got the wrong answer, or call witnesses, in case they gave the wrong evidence—and almost every client who lost his case in court would claim that had it been conducted differently, he would have won.

In a case decided by the House of Lords in July 2000, this old law was changed, but the change is a very limited one. The court made it clear that just because a client was dissatisfied with his lawyers, this would not give him the right to sue. Lord Hoffmann grappled with the problem of lawyers having two loyalties, one to the court, the other to their clients. He expressed it as follows:

> *Lawyers conducting litigation have a divided loyalty. They have a duty to their clients,*
> *but they may not win by whatever means. They also owe a duty to the court and the*
> *administration of justice. They may not mislead the court or allow the judge to take*
> *what they know to be a bad point in their favour . . . they may not waste time on*
> *irrelevancies even if the client thinks they are important. Sometimes the performance*
> *of these duties may annoy the client. So, it was said, the possibility of a claim for*
> *negligence might inhibit the lawyer from acting in accordance with his overriding duty*
> *to the court. That would be prejudicial to the administration of justice.*

The House of Lords took all of these matters into account, and decided that in practice it would only be in a very plain case of neglect that a client could ever be successful. For example, in a criminal case a defendant could only bring an action against his lawyers where the Court of Appeal has set aside his conviction because he was so badly represented at his trial.

The problem of being sued for 'professional negligence' is one that greatly worries professional men and women, and it gives rise to some of the ethical problems that are of such concern. It seems obviously right that if a doctor neglects a patient, or gives the wrong type of treatment, the patient should be able to claim compensation; but it is easy for a patient who has not made a good recovery to claim that his or her doctor has been negligent, and this claim might cause immense anguish, and be difficult to defend. In America claims against doctors are so common, and awards of damages so high, that some doctors are even afraid to stop at the scene of a road accident, and help the injured, for fear that they may be taken to court.

9

Solicitors

> 'The law the lawyers know about
> Is property and land;
> But why the leaves are on the trees,
> And why the waves disturb the seas,
> Why honey is the food of bees,
> Why horses have such tender knees,
> Why winters come when rivers freeze,
> Why Faith is more than what one sees,
> And Hope survives the worst disease,
> And Charity is more than these,
>   They do not understand.'
>
> H. D. C. Pepler, *The Devil's Devices.*

※

Solicitors are there to provide members of the public—their **clients**—with skilled advice and representation in all legal matters. The work of solicitors dates back to the fifteenth century. It is believed that the name is derived from people who were paid to petition or **solicit** on behalf of their clients in the old Court of Chancery. It was not until 1873 that solicitors officially became known as **Solicitors of the Supreme Court**.

Solicitors may work on their own in small 'one-man' or 'one-woman' practices, or as partners with other solicitors. A solicitor's practice is called a **firm of solicitors**. There are a great many firms, and they range from small country practices employing perhaps one or two solicitors to large city practices employing scores, even hundreds, of **partners** (solicitors entitled to a say in how the firm is managed, and to a share in its profits) and **associate solicitors** (salaried employees without these rights).

Anyone who wishes to take legal advice or have legal work done will usually go to a solicitor's office, where he will see the solicitor and tell him what he requires. This is called giving a solicitor **instructions**. Many solicitors deal with a range of legal work. We have already referred to some of the main areas of the law, but here is an idea of some of the types of work they do:

- *Litigation*: preparing cases to be tried in the civil or criminal courts.

- *Commercial*: giving legal advice in the field of business, and drawing up contracts (legal agreements between two or more persons for the sale of any type of property or services. This could be anything from the sale of an entire multi-national business to a corner shop, or the 'sale' of a footballer by one club to another).

- *Conveyancing*: making all the legal arrangements for the buying and selling of land, and houses or other buildings.

- *Employment*: assisting employees and employers in cases involving allegations of unfair dismissal, or claims for redundancy payments.

- *Family*: such as divorce and child care.

- *Immigration*: representing foreign nationals, or those without any national status at all, who are claiming asylum in this country, or permission to stay or work.

- *Licensing*: arranging to apply for licences that have to be granted by the courts or other bodies (such as licences for pubs and clubs).

- *Probate*: making wills for clients who, when they die, wish to leave their property to certain persons or charities; and making sure that their wishes are carried out.

At one time most solicitors were general practitioners who would refer to experts in particular fields of law. Many still are, and we will look at the so-called 'family solicitor' below; but the shape of the profession has greatly changed, and more and more solicitors specialise in only one or two fields of law, for example, doing nothing but criminal work, family work, or conveyancing. Some of the largest firms specialise in commercial work. A few of these have branch offices in major cities throughout the world—employing literally hundreds of solicitors—who will act for great corporations, even national governments. They will advise on English and international law, and prepare and complete the legal work for large business transactions.

The profession of a solicitor has developed over the past few years. Solicitors act as legal advisers, but they are also the side of the legal profession whose job it is to provide detailed records of a case as it progresses. The public comes into contact with solicitors more than with any other people who work in the law, and this gives them a unique insight into how decisions of the courts and the work of other law professionals affect our lives.

As *advisers*, solicitors must be able to explain what the law is and how a particular set of circumstances is affected by the law. It is essential that solicitors should have a good knowledge of the law, but also good sound common sense. Sometimes in urgent cases the advice must be given immediately without the benefit of a long time for reflection, and it will be acted upon without hesitation. That advice may be scrutinised subsequently at leisure by the courts, and may make the difference to the success and failure of the case. In these cases common sense and experience are important qualities.

As *recorders*, solicitors will be expected to create or organise a record of what happens in a case, so that the whole case may be understood by those who need to do so. In particular, barristers and judges may need to know precisely what happened since the case began, so they can do their work of presenting, or deciding, a case properly. The recording process starts when the solicitor first meets the client. At this stage he or she will provide the client with important information about what can and cannot be done for the client, and how much it will cost. As the case develops, the solicitor must keep a note of all important meetings and telephone conversations relating to the case, and ensure that all case documents are properly organised. This process is also essential when handling clients' property and money. Solicitors are sometimes trusted to handle very large sums of money and very valuable property. A person may have worked a lifetime to build up an asset, and will then entrust its sale or transfer into the hands of a solicitor.

Perhaps the best-known solicitor is still the 'family solicitor'. He or she provides a general legal service to their local community. They are sometimes thought of as 'country solicitors', and many family solicitors do have their offices in country towns. Still, 'family', or 'high street' solicitors abound in great cities.

THE FAMILY OR 'HIGH STREET' SOLICITOR

One of the most valued professionals, like the family doctor, the family or high street solicitor is 'on call' to deal with almost every aspect of legal life. He or she may be in practice on their own, or as a member of a small firm. The practice will have its individual clients (for crime, personal injury claims, family matters, employment and social security problems), but business will also come from other professionals who are constantly dealing with members of the public, such as estate agents (conveyancing) bank managers (arranging small business loans), and accountants (tax). The work can therefore be very varied. It seems that before long the term 'High Street' solicitor might take on a new meaning. In July 2003, the newly appointed Lord Chancellor, Lord Falconer of Thoroton, was reported as saying that he would give his approval to proposals which may one day see solicitors employed by, and giving advice in the setting of, supermarkets.

In his book, *English Courts of Law*, Professor H. G. Hanbury pays touching tribute to the work of the family solicitor:

> *A good solicitor becomes far more than an animated book of reference to his client; in nine cases out of ten he becomes his intimate personal friend, who can be trusted not only to respect confidence and implicitly carry out instructions, but to give much unobtrusive advice of a nature beneficial to his client and all his family. Countless must be the times when a wise and level-headed solicitor has restrained a client from being impelled by the surge of temporary resentment or caprice to do injustice by a foolish will or settlement; countless also are those in which he has saved his client's fortunes by dissuading him from imprudent investment or profitless litigation. They are the courtiers of the passage of life.*

This somewhat idealised picture of family solicitors seems to imply that they will have ideal clients. They may be fortunate enough to have some, but not every client has a family fortune to protect or bequeath. Nevertheless, many solicitors throughout the country can still claim to answer this description.

SOLICITORS AS ADVOCATES

In the course of their litigation work, solicitors will often appear in court as **advocates**, 'pleading the causes' of their clients. This means that they will actually go into court and present and argue cases on their clients' behalf. In the main, solicitors present cases in the lower courts, in particular the magistrates' courts and the county courts. This can be a very busy and hectic life, requiring quick thinking and the ability to master the facts of a situation, or indeed a whole case, at great speed—and then to move on with equal speed to another one.

After hundreds of years, times are now changing. Specially qualified **solicitor advocates** are allowed to appear in the Crown Court and High Court; and it may not be long before solicitors will be will be given the same **rights of audience** (rights to be heard in court) as barristers. Then they too will be allowed to appear in any court in the land. In April 1997 the then Lord Chancellor, Lord Mackay of Clashfern, made the first appointment of some distinguished solicitors to become **Queen's Counsel** (QCs: see Chapter 10). As we shall see, the rank of Queen's Counsel is currently under threat of abolition, but when it comes to their appointment, the Lord Chancellor invites applications *'from barristers and solicitors who hold, and are entitled to exercise, full rights of audience in the High Court or Crown Court'*.

When they appear in the magistrates' courts, solicitors wear ordinary lounge suits or, if women, dark-coloured suits or dresses. Women are now permitted to wear trouser suits in court. When solicitors conduct cases in the higher courts they must 'appear robed'. In their case, this means that they must wear gowns, but they do not wear wigs.

SOLICITORS AND BARRISTERS

Solicitors have direct contact with their clients. In most cases, barristers do not. The solicitor's relationship with a client is therefore usually more personal. In almost all cases, a client who needs the services of a barrister must go first to a solicitor, who will then instruct, or **brief** the barrister. This means that the solicitor will choose the barrister who is right for the case, and help to prepare the case for court. In simple cases the solicitor will usually leave the barrister to get on with the case in court on his own; in more difficult cases, the solicitor will sit behind the barrister in court and assist in the presentation of the case.

LEGAL EXECUTIVES

The staff who work in solicitors' offices will include secretaries and clerks. Clerks may now receive special training to do work requiring particular skills, and take examinations to qualify as **legal executives**. In *The Summer of a Dormouse*, the barrister and author John Mortimer, whom we shall meet again in the next chapter, recalls, *'In the days when I knocked about in the Probate, Divorce and Admiralty Division, they [legal executives] were known as "managing clerks", and had no legal qualifications except common sense, a lifetime's experience and a deeper knowledge of the mysterious process of issuing writs and filing documents than the solicitors who employed them'*.

All that, or at least a good deal of it, has now changed. Once qualified, as Fellows of the Institute of Legal Executives, legal executives now have limited rights of audience to appear as advocates before District Judges in the county courts and certain tribunals. By a **Practice Direction** (statement of guidance given by the courts on practice and procedure) issued in December 1998, the Lord Chancellor directed that when appearing in open court legal executives should wear the same robes as solicitors.

Those who work in solicitors' offices now have career opportunities they never had before. It is not unknown for young school leavers who begin work in a solicitors' firm doing simple office jobs, to gradually climb their way up the ladder to become legal executives, and in due course—after attending the necessary courses and passing the necessary examinations—to qualify as solicitors.

THE LAW SOCIETY

The professional body that governs the solicitors' branch of the legal profession is the *Law Society*. The Law Society is responsible for the training of solicitors. In order to become practising solicitors, men and women must first receive the necessary education and training. They will then be 'admitted to the Rolls', which means that their names will be entered on the *roll* (list) of solicitors permitted to practise. They must also have in force a *practising certificate* issued by the Law Society. In July 2002, over 89,000 solicitors throughout the country held practising certificates, and were therefore qualified to practise.

The Law Society is the professional body that has the duty to ensure that solicitors do their work properly. The Society makes important rules as to how solicitors should look after their clients' money and assets, and carries out spot-checks and audits to ensure that solicitors are complying with these rules. It also has disciplinary powers. If a client makes a complaint against a solicitor, it will be investigated and dealt with by an independent body, which may recommend that action be taken against the solicitor by the Law Society.

TRAINING

Anyone wishing to become a solicitor must first have suitable academic qualifications. This usually (but not always) means having good A levels and a university degree. A law degree is not essential, but anyone with a degree in law will receive exemptions from certain examinations, and move quickly to the legal practice course (see below). A student who does not go to university at all, or who does not graduate in law and wishes to take a 'conversion course', must sit the Common Professional Examination (CPE) or obtain a Diploma in Law. The CPE and diploma examinations will involve attending courses—the CPE course lasts one year (full time) or two years (part time).

Everyone who does not have some special exemption and who wishes to qualify as a solicitor must also take a **legal practice course**, and must then enter into a two-year **training contract** with a firm of solicitors.

- *Legal practice courses* are now available in many places throughout the country. They usually take one year (full time) or two years (part time). The object of these courses is to equip trainee solicitors with the knowledge and skills to work in a solicitor's office. They will include course-work, and the assessment of practical skills and written examinations.

- *Training contracts* involve work in a solicitor's office. The trainee solicitor will be expected to gain experience in at least three, but usually five, different areas of the law. Trainees will have the opportunity to handle their own cases, see clients, and carry out the responsibilities of a solicitor under supervision. They must also attend a professional skills course, which lasts up to twenty days, and includes such subjects as accounts, professional conduct, and advocacy. Trainee solicitors on training contracts must be paid.

10

Barristers

'In my youth,' said his father, 'I took to the law
And argued each case with my wife;
And the muscular strength which it gave to my jaw
Has lasted the rest of my life.'

Lewis Carroll, *Alice's Adventures in Wonderland.*

*

The full title of a barrister is **Barrister-at-Law**. Barristers are also known as **counsel**. The term 'barristers' derives from the fact that when they qualify they are 'called to the Bar', an expression which dates from the days when each courtroom was fitted with a rail or *bar* dividing the area actually used by the court from the general public. Only barristers were allowed to step up to the bar to plead their clients' cases.

Although solicitors and barristers are all members of the legal profession, there are many important differences between them. Here are some of the main ones:

- Barristers are mainly litigation or 'courtroom lawyers' who actually conduct cases in court. Unlike solicitors, they have **rights of audience** (rights to appear) in any court in the land, and so barristers are those lawyers who appear in the more difficult cases in the Crown Court, the High Court, and the various courts of appeal.

- Although many barristers do a variety of work, a growing number now specialise in just one or two aspects of litigation. This means that they may do only criminal cases, or one or more of the many types of civil case. A small number of specialist barristers do not go into court at all and spend their professional lives advising, and writing *opinions* at the request of solicitors, in cases that involve difficult and complicated areas of the law.

- Clients who need to go to court cannot go to see a barrister directly. They can only arrange to be represented by a barrister or to take his advice by first going to a solicitor. The solicitor will then instruct or 'brief' the barrister to help the client. Just as solicitors may one day have rights of audience in all the courts, it is thought that one day it may become possible for clients to go straight to barristers.

- Unlike solicitors, barristers cannot work in partnership with one another. All professional barristers are self-employed, although normally a number of barristers will as a matter of convenience share offices, which are known as **barristers' chambers**, and have their work organised by the same manager, who is called a *barrister's clerk*. A barrister's clerk arranges court appearances and meetings between clients, solicitors, and barristers (these meetings are known as **conferences**). He or she also negotiates the barristers' fees.

- Another well-known and very obvious difference is the robes barristers wear. In the magistrates' courts and tribunals, such as the Employment Tribunals, they wear their business suits, like solicitors. In all other courts they wear wigs and gowns.

INNS OF COURT

Students who wish to become barristers must first become members of one of the four **Inns of Court**. These are in London. They are called *Middle Temple, Inner Temple, Lincoln's Inn, and Gray's Inn*. In order to become a barrister, a student must pass all the necessary law exams; but he or she must also attend 'qualifying sessions', which include 'dining in Hall' and other educational activities. Dining in Hall literally means eating a number of dinners in the Great Hall of their Inn of Court. This tradition dates from the days when students received their legal education by attending lectures which were given while they were dining in Hall.

The four Inns of Court are all within a short distance of one another in London and form the heart of 'legal London'. The Inner and Middle Temples occupy a stretch of land between Fleet Street and the Thames, which to this day is regarded as one of the most beautiful and tranquil areas in the city. Lincoln's Inn is off Chancery Lane; Gray's Inn is bounded by Gray's Inn Road and High Holborn.

Each Inn has its own hall, common rooms, library, and church. It is run by a number of Masters of the Bench, or **benchers**, who are senior barristers and judges who belong to the Inn and who are elected to govern it. They are called benchers because they sit on the high table or *bench* in the Inn's Great Hall. The head of each Inn, who acts as chairman of the benchers, is called the *Treasurer* and holds the office for one year. The Inns also elect 'honorary benchers'—members of the Royal Family and distinguished men and women from around the world. Even women benchers are called Masters of the Bench, although it is, perhaps, not difficult to understand this is preferable to the alternative.

The historic buildings and beautifully kept gardens of the Inns give them the atmosphere of old university colleges, but the buildings are not occupied by students. Here we find many *sets* of barristers' chambers—the offices where they prepare their cases, and see their solicitors and clients in conference. The upper floors of these buildings contain private apartments, where some judges and senior barristers live. Although the Inns of Court are in London, one should bear in mind that many barristers have their chambers '*on circuit*' (see below), and there are thriving sets of chambers throughout the country.

The Inns have a long and colourful history. For centuries they have been the training institutions and professional societies for barristers, but this was not their only function. During the sixteenth and seventeenth centuries it was fashionable for a gentleman's education to include a period at one of the Inns, whether or not he was 'intended for the law'. This is why we find, for instance, that during the short period 1640–2 no fewer than 300 Members of Parliament had attended one of the Inns of Court.

The Inner and Middle Temples share a wonderful old church called Temple Church. This 'Round Church' was completed in 1185. It was the place of worship of the Knights of the Temple—the English branch of the crusading 'Knights Templar', who took their name from the Temple of Solomon in Jerusalem. These Inns also have beautiful gardens, where, according to Shakespeare (*Henry IV, Part I*), nobles plucked the red and white roses of the Houses of Lancaster and York when they formed the alliances of the Wars of the Roses (1455–85). Temple Bar was a stone arch, which crossed Fleet Street. It marked one of the boundaries of the medieval city of London. At one time it was nicknamed the *City Golgotha* (place of the skull) because it was one of the chief sites where the heads of traitors were exhibited. For many years this arch has lain in decay, but soon it will be restored to a new home in the City of London.

The Temple is a haven of peace and quiet, and yet it is literally only yards away from the bustle of London. Its beauty has inspired many authors. Charles Dickens became a member of the Middle Temple in 1838. In *Martin Chuzzlewit* he waxed lyrical about Fountain Court, one of its beautiful squares: '*Brilliantly the Temple Fountain sparkled in the sun, and laughingly its liquid music played, and merrily the idle drops of water danced and danced, and peeping out in sport among the trees, plunged lightly down to hide themselves.'*

Another great nineteenth-century novelist, Anthony Trollope, who died in 1882, the year of the opening of the 'new' Royal Courts of Justice, published in 1855 *The Warden*, the first of his 'Barsetshire' novels. In it, this description of the Temple suggests that the new courts were being spoken of a full thirty years before they were built:

> *Washed by the rich tide which now passes from the towers of Caesar [the Tower of London] to Barry's halls of eloquence [the Houses of Parliament]; and again back, with new offerings of a city's tribute, from the palaces of peers to the mart of merchants, stand those quiet walls which Law has delighted to honour by its presence. What a world within a world is the Temple! how quiet are its 'entangled walks', as some one has lately called them, and yet how close to the densest concourse of humanity! how gravely respectable its sober alleys, though removed but by a single step from the profanity of the Strand and the low iniquity of Fleet Street! . . . rumour tells us of some huge building that is to appear in these latitudes dedicated to the law, subversive of the courts of Westminster, and antagonistic to the Rolls and Lincoln's Inn; but nothing yet threatens the silent beauty of the Temple: it is the mediaeval court of the metropolis.*

Each of the Inns has its own special attractions. Here is a glimpse of one of them:

Middle Temple

The earliest records of Middle Temple date back to 1501. Its Hall is particularly magnificent, and famous—for it was here on 2 February 1602 that Shakespeare's play *Twelfth Night* was first performed in the presence of Queen Elizabeth I. One of its outstanding features is the great wooden double hammer-beam ceiling, now over four hundred years old. Middle Temple Hall also has two historic tables—the long 'high' table, made from Elizabeth I's gift of a great oak tree, which was floated down the Thames from Windsor Park, and a small serving table made from a hatch cover of Sir Francis Drake's ship, the *Golden Hind*, which circumnavigated the globe in 1590.

Middle Temple claims among its past members many great lawyers, but also others not normally associated with the law. They include Sir Francis Drake and Sir Walter Raleigh. In 1930, before they both became great leaders of their peoples, Winston Churchill scathingly described Mahatma Gandhi as 'a seditious Middle Temple lawyer, now posing as a fakir of a type well-known in the East'. Many famous writers—John Evelyn (the diarist), Henry Fielding (also a well-known magistrate), Richard Sheridan, William Thackeray, Charles Dickens, and John Buchan—also 'dined in Hall'. (Unfortunately, the Inn cannot boast among its list of writers the celebrated contemporary dramatist and novelist Sir John Mortimer QC. He is a member of Inner Temple.)

The Inns of Court are not ancient monuments, of interest only to historians and tourists. They remain very much at the centre of the working lives of judges, barristers, and students. Rather like the school year, the legal year is divided into three terms: the first (Autumn) term is Michaelmas, named in honour of the Archangel Michael, whose day is 29 September; next, Hilary (Easter), named in honour of St Hilary whose day is 14 January; and lastly Trinity (Summer), named after the Holy trinity of Father, Son, and Holy Ghost (Trinity Sunday is the Sunday after Whit Sunday). These terms form the basis of the High Court calendar of court sittings, although the courts now have so much work to do that many sit well outside them. Each day of the three legal terms, the Inns provide lunch for hundreds of lawyers. Each evening, benchers, barristers, and students, many of whom have come from all parts of the world to train for the Bar, put on their gowns and dine in Hall.

One of the finest days in the life of any law student is the day of his or her 'Call to the Bar'. This is the ceremony that takes place in Hall, at which newly qualified barristers are formally *admitted* and welcomed into the profession by the Treasurer of their Inn. When barristers first qualify they are known as 'junior counsel'. They may carry their robes around in a special 'blue bag', an outsize shoe-bag made of blue damask and embroidered with their initials in large white letters. Eventually, if their work is judged to be of a sufficiently high standard, they will be presented with an equally grand 'red bag'. This is a sign that they are making good progress at the Bar. The initials on these bags are no smaller; but blue and red bags are (and look like) relics from a bygone era. As a fashion item they have become as 'old-hat' as the bowlers which at one time set off the black-jacket and striped-trousers uniform of the Bar. Now, fewer and fewer bags are slung over shoulders, barristers preferring the anonymity of their holdalls.

QUEEN'S COUNSEL

After some years' experience, a junior counsel who establishes a large practice, and produces work of a particularly high standard, may be appointed by the Lord Chancellor to be '*One of Her Majesty's Counsel Learned in the Law*', known for short as **Queen's Counsel** (QC). These barristers are now no longer 'junior counsel', but 'leading counsel'. Their gowns are no longer made of ordinary cloth or 'stuff', but of silk. This is why becoming a QC is referred to as '*taking silk*'. The rank of QC dates back many years, and at one time the title meant what it said. Queen Elizabeth I was the first monarch to retain lawyers of distinction as her Counsel, to ensure that they did not act against the interests of the Crown. The first QC to receive his royal patent of authority was Francis Bacon, later Lord Chancellor (see Chapter 7). QCs are now expected to handle the most serious or difficult cases. Despite their title, they may appear on behalf of any person, and conduct cases for or against the Crown. They are usually assisted in court by a junior counsel. Only a QC may present a junior with a red bag.

By the end of 2002, there were 10,742 practising barristers in England and Wales, of whom 1,145 were QCs; but the rank of QC is currently under serious threat. The 'QC system' provides many advantages in terms of the quality of representation it gives, but it is surrounded by ancient practices and traditions, and is expensive for litigants. In 2003, the Lord Chancellor, announcing a period of consultation about the future of the system, said, *'Over the last four centuries, the QC system has become a well-established part of our legal structure. But the legal system must meet the needs of the public.'* Criticisms of the present system have been led by the Office of Fair Trading, which has also questioned whether the Government (in the form of the Lord Chancellor, a political figure) should *'have responsibility for conferring on selected practitioners in a profession a title that manifestly enhances their earning power and competitive position relative to others'*. The Government is to decide whether the QC system *'is objectively in the public interest and whether it commands public confidence'*.

CIRCUITS

All barristers who practise in the courts in England and Wales are currently members of one of the six legal **circuits** into which the country is divided. These are the geographical areas around which the High Court judges still travel as they try the most important cases around the country. The boundaries of the circuits have recently been changed, and are now shown in the map of England and Wales presented in Figure 10.1.

These days barristers usually have their chambers and do most of their work on their own circuits, but they are free to work in any part of the country. Each of the circuits elects a 'Leader', a senior QC who helps to oversee the standards of the profession 'on circuit'; and each of the circuits has its own traditions and enjoys its own 'circuit life'. Some barristers do a great deal of travelling, appearing in courts throughout their own circuits; sometimes on other circuits, or even abroad. Almost all of them will at some time visit London to appear in one of the appeal courts.

The Bar (barrister's profession) is governed by the *Inns of Court* and the *Bar Council*. We have seen that each of the Inns has a body of governors known as benchers. They, and members of the profession elected to serve on the Bar Council, have much the same responsibility for the training and professional conduct of barristers as has the Law Society for the training and good

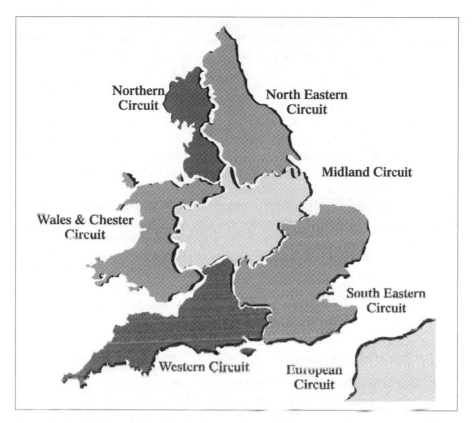

Figure 10.1 The circuits
Source: Bar Council. Reproduced with permission.

behaviour of solicitors. All practising barristers must belong to one of the Inns. If they fall below the high standards of professional conduct laid down for the Bar, they will be disciplined by their Inn.

ADVOCACY

Of all the types of work done by barristers, the best known is that of **advocacy**—their work in court. The art of advocacy is the art of persuasion. Like the skills of a fine musician, it involves natural talent, much hard work (in marshalling and mastering facts), and immense thought and care in the manner of their presentation. Good advocates must be a great deal more than 'good talkers'. They will be sensitive to what is or is not likely to result in effective presentation. They must be able to think on their feet, adapting easily and quickly to the audience they are trying to persuade—whether it be judges or magistrates sitting alone, or a jury—and also to the changing fortunes of the case.

Inevitably, distinguished advocates have from time to time been asked for the secrets of their success; understandably, they have usually made light of them. When Sir John Karslake, Attorney-General in late Victorian times, was asked what were the three things necessary for success at the Bar he replied, *'The first tact, the second tact and the third, tact'*; the great advocate Sir Edward Clark, Solicitor-General in the 1920s, had no doubt that they were, *'To be very poor, very ambitious and very much in love'*.

The history of the Bar is the story of many great advocates. Indeed, in the days before films and television, the most eminent lawyers, including Sir Edward, were often the 'stars' of the day. Their careers were as well known to the public as those of the stars of the entertainment world are now, because court cases were in one sense the prime source of entertainment. One outstanding difference is that they often had the responsibility of defending people whose very lives were at stake. Perhaps it was this element of high drama that made their work so compelling. In days gone by the style of advocacy was very different from that of today. This is how one great advocate of his age, Norman Birkett, gave expression to his admiration for another, Edward Marshall Hall:

> He brought with him a strange magnetic quality that made itself felt in every part of the court. The spectators stirred with excitement and a faint murmur ran from floor to gallery. When he addressed the judge, it was seen that to his great good looks there had been added perhaps the greatest gift of all in the armoury of an advocate, a most beautiful speaking voice.

The 'great' Sir Patrick Hastings, who was idolised in his heyday (1930s and 1940s), would make the most impassioned speeches, weeping openly as he addressed juries; and in doing so he often managed to get them to weep with him. In his wonderfully entertaining autobiography, *Clinging to the Wreckage*, John Mortimer describes his own style as a barrister as *'distressingly flamboyant'*; but styles change, and these days courtroom displays of theatricality and emotion would more likely be received with an embarrassed laugh.

There is another important ingredient in the art of advocacy: the fearless presentation of cases. In fact, one of the fundamental principles of advocacy, set out in the Barrister's *Code of Conduct*, is that *'A practising barrister must promote and protect fearlessly and by all proper and lawful means his . . . client's best interests without regard to his own interests or to any consequences to himself or to any other person'*. Where the State has acted in an oppressive and overbearing manner, some barristers were, and still are, greatly admired for their courage in speaking up for the common man. This championing of the individual against the might of the State has always been seen as one of the most highly prized attributes of an independent Bar.

- The legal profession has always been seen as a training ground for a career in politics. In the 1980s the Prime Minister, Margaret Thatcher, and her Foreign Secretary, Geoffrey Howe, were both qualified barristers. In the mid-1990s all three great Offices of State in the Conservative government were held by QCs—the Foreign Secretary (Malcolm Rifkind QC), the Chancellor of the Exchequer (Kenneth Clarke QC), and the Home Secretary (Michael Howard QC). A number of MPs in the present Labour Government are also barristers, including the Prime Minister, Tony Blair. Michael Howard QC is now the Leader of the Opposition.

ATTORNEY-GENERAL AND SOLICITOR-GENERAL

Two of the most important lawyers in the country are the **Law Officers**. They are the **Attorney-General** and his deputy, the **Solicitor-General**. These are ancient offices. The office of Attorney in its present form dates from the sixteenth century, and the days when Kings and Queens appointed lawyers of distinction to advise them and conduct their cases in court.

The law officers are now appointed by the Prime Minister, and are the chief legal advisers to the Government. There has been no more important expression of this in recent times than that of the advice to the Government in March 2003 of the Attorney-General Lord Goldsmith QC, that it would be justified in declaring war on Iraq. His legal opinion to this effect was summarised in a nine-point statement, justifying the use of force by reference to a combination of Resolutions of the United Nations, which Saddam Hussein was said to have broken. Advice of this kind is normally kept confidential, but the Attorney-General decided that this statement should be published 'in view of the enormous amount of public interest and importance of the issue'.

The Attorney-General and Solicitor-General have other important responsibilities. Prosecutions for certain offences, including terrorist offences and corruption, cannot be commenced without their consent. The Attorney-General must also decide whether any criminal case should be referred to the Court of Appeal on the grounds that the sentence passed on the defendant was too lenient. If this court agrees, it may increase the sentence. By tradition, whenever the security of the State is involved—when, for example, a person is charged with high treason—the case is prosecuted personally by the Attorney-General. Also by tradition, the Attorney-General is the 'Leader of the Bar' (the leading barrister in the profession). Until recently, the Solicitor-General was always a barrister, but Harriet Harman is the first solicitor, and the first woman, to hold this office.

The Attorney-General is also responsible for appointing two heads of the prosecution service: the first is the *Director of Public Prosecutions* (DPP), who is the Head of the *Crown Prosecution Service*, the department responsible for conducting most prosecutions in England and Wales. The second is the *Director of the Serious Fraud Office*, the department responsible for investigating and prosecuting the most serious and complicated fraud cases. By statute they carry out their duties *'under the superintendence of the Attorney-General'*.

TRAINING

Barristers, like solicitors, have to obtain the necessary academic qualifications and undergo a period of practical training. We will recall that all students reading for the Bar have to join one of the four Inns of Court, and eat their dinners—in *Barchester Towers*, Trollope was to call it *'eating for the Bar'*! The academic qualifications are now similar to those required of a solicitor, but the actual subjects which the student barrister will study and the vocational training will be different. It will involve attending the **Bar Vocational Course** and then after qualifying as a barrister, doing at least twelve months' **pupillage**.

- *Bar Vocational Course.* This is a practical course, intended to prepare student barristers for life at the Bar, and help them to get the best out of their pupillage. The idea of the course is to teach the young barrister seven basic skills: *advocacy* (presenting and arguing a case in court), *conference skills* (how to deal with clients in conference), *drafting* (preparing legal documents), *fact management* (gathering together and presenting facts), *legal research* (where to look to find the answers to legal problems, and how to research them), *negotiation* (how to obtain the best advantage for a client in out-of-court discussions), and *opinion writing* (learning how to write legal opinions for solicitors and clients).

- *Pupillage.* This is an apprenticeship, normally for 12 months, with an experienced barrister in a set of barristers' chambers. Often the year is split into two parts, with the young barrister spending six months with one 'pupil master' and six months with another, in order to gain a wider experience. The second six months may now be spent gaining experience in any 'approved legal environment', for example, the Crown Prosecution Service. During the first six months a young barrister is not allowed to appear in court on his or her own. During the second six months he or she may do so in 'appropriate cases' (meaning less serious cases).

At one time pupils had to pay their pupil masters for their apprenticeship, but no longer. Now they may receive payment in the form of scholarships from chambers. The Bar Council has decreed that from January 2003 all pupils must receive a minimum of £10,000. This may involve a chambers' grant of £5,000 for the first six months, and include what they earn during the second six months.

After completing a pupillage, the new barrister is now ready to apply to become a **tenant** in a set of chambers. These days the many applications for pupillage are usually sifted by members of chambers' 'pupillage committees', who will go on to interview the applicants. Applications by pupils to become fully-fledged tenants will normally be considered by a full meeting of chambers. The Bar is at present an over-populated profession, and it can be very difficult for a young barrister to be accepted as a tenant. If successful, the new tenant will now use these chambers as a base, and will be 'clerked' (have his or her career managed) from them. Tenants also have to make a contribution towards the expenses of running the chambers.

THE ROYAL COURTS OF JUSTICE.

11

The Work of the Courts—Part 1
The Courts

'The function of a trial judge is to be quick, courteous and wrong. That is not to say that the Court of Appeal should be slow, rude and right; for that would be to usurp the function of the House of Lords.'
Lord Asquith of Bishopsgate.

*

There are many different types of court, each with its own particular function and responsibilities. In some courts judges sit (try cases) alone. In others they sit with juries. Figure 11.1 is a simple way of showing how our court system is arranged—from the highest court in the land, the House of Lords, to the magistrates' courts and tribunals. By tradition, the names of some courts begin with capital letters; others do not.

The new **Department for Constitutional Affairs** (formerly the Lord Chancellor's Department) is responsible for the organisation and smooth running of the courts, although much of the day-to-day running of the courts is to be carried out by a new **Unified Courts Administration**. This agency will carry out the administrative and support tasks for the Court of Appeal, High Court, Crown Court, and county courts. Its head or Chief Executive is responsible to the Secretary of State for Constitutional Affairs (who is also, at this time, still the Lord Chancellor). For the purposes of administering the courts, the country is divided into 42 local areas within seven main Regions. These Regions generally follow the geographical pattern of the six Circuits, except that London is an additional Region of its own. As to the courts themselves, the courts and their main functions are shown in the chart of the court system presented in Figure 11.1.

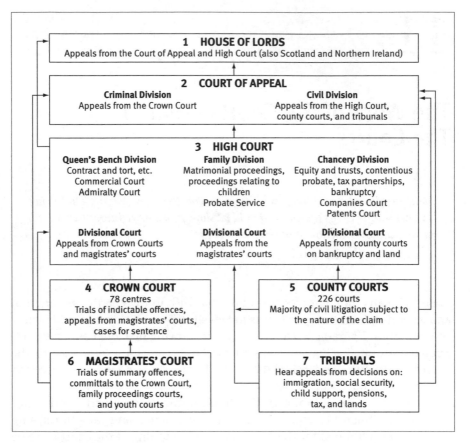

Figure 11.1 The court system
Source: Department for Constitutional Affairs, *Court Service Report for 2000–2001*. Reproduced with permission.
Note: The arrows indicate the system of appeals from court to court.

We will now look at each of the courts in turn, using the same numbers for them as appear in Figure 11.1.

1 THE HOUSE OF LORDS

The story of two of our most senior courts, the House of Lords and the Privy Council, is a tale of two committees. The **House of Lords** is more correctly called the Appellate Committee of the House of Lords. It officially sits as a committee of the House of Lords and is the final court of appeal in England,

Wales, and Northern Ireland in both civil and criminal matters, and from the Court of Session in Scotland on civil matters. It will only deal with cases of real public importance. It is not possible for *anyone* to take his or her case to the House of Lords. Only those cases in which 'leave to appeal' (special permission) has been given, either by the Court of Appeal or by the House of Lords itself, will be heard there.

The judges who sit in the House of Lords are the 12 **Lords of Appeal in Ordinary**. They are commonly known as the **Law Lords**. The extraordinary term 'In Ordinary' simply means that they receive their salary from the ordinary Consolidated Fund (the Exchequer account at the Bank of England into which all revenues are paid); they are not paid by the House of Lords itself. Certain other distinguished judges, for example the Lord Chief Justice and the Master of the Rolls, may also sit in 'the Lords'. All the Law Lords are Life Peers, created from the ranks of judges. They may sit and vote in the House of Lords like any other peer, but unlike those peers who support one political party or another, by tradition they do not become involved in politics, and will only concern themselves 'in the House' with legislation which relates to legal matters. Law Lords might therefore speak in a debate concerning the future mode of criminal trials, or punishment, but not in a debate concerning foreign policy

Normally, each appeal is heard by five Law Lords, although in some, rare instances cases are heard by a panel of seven. Their court is a large room in the House of Lords section of the Parliament building. Their judgments are called **Speeches**, and are delivered 'in the Chamber of the House'. This means that the Law Lords do not announce their decisions in court, but go into the main chamber of the House of Lords to do so. The Law Lords may reach their decisions by a majority, and it is not unusual for the court to decide its cases by a majority of 3–2.

The House of Lords is the highest court in the land. It is the final court of appeal and hears appeals in both civil and criminal cases. Its judges also sit in the Judicial Committee of the Privy Council, which is the final court of appeal for the Isle of Man, Channel Islands, Commonwealth countries, and certain independent Commonwealth States.

The **Judicial Committee of the Privy Council** was established by statute in 1833 to hear appeals from '*any dominion or dependency of the Crown in any matter, civil or criminal*'. It is therefore a relic of the colonial days of the British Empire, when it sat as the supreme court of appeal for all the colonies and dominions. Although it is called a committee the Privy Council sits as a court, and hears a strange mixture of cases. It still tries appeals from some of the 'dependent' territories. For example, although it no longer hears cases from Canada, India, and Australia, it still hears cases from New Zealand, Jamaica, and Trinidad and Tobago. It is also the final court of appeal from the ecclesiastical courts and prize courts (which decide cases arising from the capture of ships in time of war); and it hears appeals from professional bodies, who have the power to strike members off their registers, such as the British Medical Council.

The members of the Judicial Committee include holders or past holders of the office of Lord Chancellor, and past and present Law Lords. Other senior judges have also been co-opted to sit in this court, as have distinguished judges from abroad. In February 2001 Dame Sian Elias, Chief Justice of New Zealand, became the first woman to sit in the Privy Council, when she was invited to spend two weeks as a member of the court.

As we shall see, the rulings of the House of Lords are always **binding** (must be followed by the lower courts). The rulings of the Privy Council are normally not binding on other courts, but they are of strong **persuasive authority** (the rulings do not have to be followed, but should be given attention and great respect when courts are deciding what the law is).

A NEW SUPREME COURT

On 12 June 2003, as part of its programme of constitutional reforms, the Government announced its intention to create a new Supreme Court to replace the Appellate Committee of the House of Lords. Lord Chancellor Falconer said the object of the creation of this 'new free-standing Supreme Court' will be to 'separate the highest appeal court from the second house of Parliament, and remove the Lords of Appeal in Ordinary from the legislature . . . the proposed new Court will be a United Kingdom body legally separate from the England and Wales courts since it will also be the Supreme Court of both Scotland and Northern Ireland'.

The main reasons for the establishment of this court are constitutional, and based upon the need for a clear separation of powers. A Consultation Paper prepared by the Department for Constitutional Affairs refers to:

> questions about whether there is sufficient transparency of independence from the executive and legislature to give people the assurance to which they are entitled about the independence of the judiciary. The considerable growth of judicial review in recent years has inevitably brought the judges into the political eye. It is essential that our systems do all that they can to minimise the danger that judges' decisions could be perceived to be politically motivated. The Human Rights Act 1998, itself the product of a changing climate of opinion, has made people more sensitive to the issues and more aware of the anomaly of the position whereby the highest court in the land is situated within one of the chambers of Parliament.

It has also been suggested that the new court will take over the work of both the Appellate Committee and the Judicial Committee of the Privy Council. Government proposals include the removal of the court from its present site to a new building, the renaming of the Law Lords (possibly to Justices, or Lord Justices, of the Supreme Court) and converting the position of the Senior Law Lord into that of the President of the Court. Care would be taken to ensure that, unlike the members of the US Supreme Court, the members of the Supreme Court of the UK could not be appointed on political lines.

2 THE COURT OF APPEAL

The **Court of Appeal** hears most of the important civil and criminal appeals from courts in England and Wales. Very few cases go on appeal from the Court of Appeal to the House of Lords. The Court of Appeal has two main functions: to hear appeals in *civil cases* from the High Court and county courts, and to hear appeals in *criminal cases* from the Crown Court. The courts of the Court of Appeal are situated in London, in the Royal Courts of Justice, the great building designed by George Street, which was the subject of the Introduction to this book.

APPEALS IN CIVIL CASES

The Appeal Court judges who deal with civil cases are the Master of the Rolls and 37 **Lords Justices of Appeal**. The female judges of the court are known as **Lady Justices of Appeal**. The appeals in civil cases will each be heard by three Lord (or Lady) Justices sitting together, although there are circumstances in which two Lords Justices may sit alone, or with a High Court Judge. They usually deliver unanimous judgments—in which they all agree—but they may reach their decisions by a majority of 2–1. When they do so, the judge who is in the minority will give a **dissenting** (disagreeing) judgment, explaining why he does not agree with the others. Sometimes, if the case then goes on appeal to the House of Lords, these dissenting judgments are preferred by the Law Lords.

APPEALS IN CRIMINAL CASES

Appeals in criminal cases are heard by the Criminal Division of the court. This was created in its present form in 1966. Again, these cases will normally be heard by three judges sitting together. This court will be presided over by the Lord Chief Justice or a Lord Justice of Appeal, but he will not usually sit with two other Lords Justices, but with two High Court Judges of the Queen's Bench Division. A change in the law has permitted the Lord Chief Justice to recommend experienced Circuit Judges to sit in the Court of Appeal.

The most important criminal appeals are likely to be heard by the Lord Chief Justice, or his deputy, the Vice-President of the Criminal Division, sitting with two judges of the High Court. The decisions in criminal appeals are always given as the decision of all three judges. This means that if one judge disagrees with the others, he must follow their decision; he will not give a dissenting judgment.

The Court of Appeal also functions as a Courts-Martial Appeal Court. In this capacity it deals with appeals from the various Courts-Martial of the Army, Navy, and Air Force.

3 THE HIGH COURT OF JUSTICE

There are three divisions of the **High Court of Justice**—the Queen's Bench Division, Chancery Division, and Family Division. In the next chapter we will look more closely at the types of case which they try.

The Queen's Bench Division consists of about 80 High Court Judges, and is headed by the Lord Chief Justice. The judges of this Division try criminal and civil cases. The Chancery Division consists of about 20 High Court Judges and is headed by the Vice-Chancellor. The Family Division consists of about 20 High Court Judges, headed by the President of the Family Division.

The judges who sit in these divisions of the High Court try cases **at first instance** (their courts are those in which the proceedings are commenced, and which actually hear the first trial, unlike the **appellate courts**, which only deal with cases on appeal). The judges of the Queen's Bench Division and the Family Division in particular work a rota, trying cases in London, but also travelling throughout the country to the major court centres on each of the circuits, to try cases there. This practice of going out on circuit is a living relic of a system which dates back to the twelfth century (see Chapter 3).

It therefore follows that a High Court Judge in the Queen's Bench Division is likely to find the year divided up into periods when he or she will be in London, or say, Leeds, Manchester, Cardiff, or Winchester trying either serious criminal cases or important civil cases, or sitting in the Court of Appeal, assisting the Lords Justices to hear criminal appeals. It is a busy and exacting life. (No, there is no danger of a High Court Judge hearing an appeal from one of his *own* judgments! Justice must be *seen* to be done.)

4 THE CROWN COURT

There are about eighty **Crown Court** centres throughout the country. In some of these as many as 10 to 15 courts may be trying criminal cases. These courts hear all the criminal cases involving trial by judge and jury.

High Court Judges usually (but not always) try the most serious criminal cases. Circuit Judges may be specially approved to try cases involving certain types of serious criminal offences, such as murder, rape, child abuse, and fraud. All the remaining *indictable offences* (which are heard by judge and jury) are tried by Circuit Judges and part-time Crown Court judges called Recorders.

5 THE COUNTY COURT

County courts were introduced in 1846 to enable civil claims for small amounts to be heard quickly and cheaply. They still meet that need, and a large majority of civil actions are heard by the judges of the county court, who are now Circuit Judges and District Judges. They almost always sit alone— without juries—and they deal with a great variety of civil work. They will be permitted to try family cases only if they have been specially trained and approved for that work. Recorders also sit as part-time judges in the county court.

There are more than 220 'districts' in England and Wales, in which a county court is held at least once a month. In some large cities, the county court building may contain several courts, which are in operation full time.

6 MAGISTRATES' COURTS

The vast majority of all criminal cases are dealt with in the magistrates' courts by **magistrates**, who are also known as **Justices of the Peace** (JPs). The office of Justice of the Peace is one of the oldest in the country, and could date back to 1195, when King Richard I made a royal proclamation that 'knights of the peace' should assist the sheriff in the keeping of law and order. By 1361, in the reign of Edward III, the office was well established, but it was by a statute of that date that the title 'Justice of the Peace' was first created.

In some major cities, where the court building may house a number of magistrates' courts, qualified lawyers may be appointed to sit as full-time **District Judges (magistrates' courts)**. They sit alone and usually deal with the more complicated cases. Until recently they were called 'Stipendiary Magistrates' because they are paid a *stipend*—an old word meaning a salary.

There are over 600 magistrates' courthouses in the country and over 30,000 JPs. They try the huge number of criminal cases which are brought for relatively 'petty' (trivial) crimes such as motoring offences, petty theft, causing criminal damage, drunkenness, and minor offences of violence and other breaches of public order. The men and women who become JPs are ordinary members of the community, They have no legal qualifications, although they must undergo a period of training. JPs are unpaid. Anyone who wishes to become a JP may apply to the Lord Chancellor. They must be supported by references, and will be interviewed to determine their suitability.

Members of the public sit as magistrates as an act of public duty. They must be able to show that they are respectable people who have had some experience of life, and that they have a genuine interest in their fellow citizens—for these are the qualities which are likely to make them good judges. In a speech delivered in July 1999 Lord Bingham strongly defended the work done by magistrates, describing them as a *'democratic jewel beyond price'*. He said:

> *Above all justices are chosen for their qualities of fairness, judgment and common sense, alert to the needs and concerns of the communities they serve and enabling local issues to be determined by local people. And in the eyes of the public, they have one great advantage: that they are free of the habits of thought, speech and bearing which characterise professional lawyers and which most people find to a greater or lesser extent repellent.*

JPs not only hear criminal cases concerning adults; they play an important role as judges in the youth courts. They also hear certain civil cases, and sit in Family Courts. Here they deal with some of the adoption cases, and a variety of problems that arise following the break-up of families. If, however, any of these cases are of special difficulty, they will be sent up to the county court or the High Court, to be heard by Circuit or High Court Judges.

7 TRIBUNALS

Tribunals are independent judicial bodies set up by Parliament to hear appeals from decisions made in certain types of cases by civil servants and others. They are presided over by chairmen and women (who are usually legally qualified). They normally sit quite informally. Nevertheless, they have to make a variety of important decisions affecting the lives of ordinary citizens. There are more than 60 different types of tribunal. These are a few of them:

- *Agricultural land tribunals* have been set up in different parts of the country. There are seven which cover England, and one for Wales. They settle disputes between the landlords and tenants of farms, for example disputes relating to the drainage of water between neighbouring landowners.

- *Employment tribunals* deal with matters of employment law involving many aspects of disputes between employers and employees, including redundancy, dismissal, and racial and sexual discrimination at work.

- *Immigration appeal tribunals* hear appeals from the decisions of the immigration authorities relating to the refusal of leave to foreigners to remain in this country, or the making of deportation orders in cases where it is considered that the further stay of foreigners is against the public good.

- *Mental health review tribunals* are responsible for reviewing cases of patients who have suffered from mental illness, and who have been compulsorily detained in hospital. They have the power to discharge a patient from hospital; they may recommend that the patient should have a period of leave away from the hospital, or they make other orders affecting the welfare of these patients.

In addition there are tribunals which make decisions affecting the *finances* of members of the public:

- Decisions as to whether people are entitled to social security or child support payments.

- Decisions in relation to the payment of pensions.

- Decisions concerning the liability of individuals and companies to pay tax.

- Decisions as to what property owners should pay by way of rates.

There are literally thousands of tribunals around the country. Some professional bodies have their own tribunals, which deal with matters of professional discipline, and have power to suspend or 'strike off' members whose conduct falls short of the standards expected of them. Tribunals do not necessarily have to allow legal representation, but they must always follow the basic *rules of natural justice*—they must not be biased, must give reasonable notice of any hearing and the nature of any complaint, and must allow those involved a proper opportunity to be heard. If they do not obey these rules, their decisions may be challenged in the High Court.

8 CORONER'S COURT

The office of **coroner** is one of the oldest in England, dating back to the early twelfth century. The coroner was a royal officer—the word means 'the Crown officer'. In *Hamlet*, Shakespeare referred to him as the *crowner*. Originally, coroners' special duty was to safeguard the King's rights in relation to land and property. This meant they were required to enquire into events likely to result in forfeiture of property to the Crown. These might be investigating the finding of treasure trove, or apparently unnatural deaths, for the property of anyone convicted of murder might be forfeit to the Crown.

These days, coroners are mainly concerned to investigate causes of death. A coroner must be a barrister, solicitor, or registered medical practitioner (doctor) of not less than five years' standing. His duty is to hold an inquiry, known as an **inquest**, into the cause of death of anyone who appears to have died by violent or unnatural means, or who has died in prison. He must also hold an inquest if a doctor refuses to issue a death certificate because the cause of death is unknown.

Every district throughout the land has a coroner. Whenever it is necessary to hold an inquest the coroner must always view the body. If it appears that the deceased suffered a violent death, or where death is unexplained, or it is suspected that it may be due to drink or drugs, he must also order an autopsy. In cases of difficulty, where, for example, the circumstances of death may point to someone being to blame, a jury will be sworn to give a verdict as to the cause of death. It must decide whether death was caused by 'misadventure'—an accident or mischance—or was the result of unlawful killing. For many years juries also had the unpleasant task of viewing the body, but not since 1926. At one time coroners could actually charge people with murder or manslaughter, and have them committed to the local assize court for trial. They no longer have that power, but if the coroner's court reaches a verdict of 'unlawful killing', this will be reported to the police, who will be expected to investigate the case thoroughly.

The ancient role of the coroner is under review. There are plans to provide better training for coroners in how to conduct the more difficult inquests, where feelings run high, and how best to relate to the families of those who have died.

COURT AND JUSTICES' CLERKS

All courts have clerks. The clerk of the court sits just in front of the judge's bench and assists in the administration of the court. He or she is responsible for the smooth running of the court, and for keeping a record of its decisions. In criminal cases in the Crown Court the clerk of the court must sign the indictment (the formal document charging the defendant with an offence), and it will be the clerk of the court who will ask the jury if they have reached verdicts, and 'take' their verdicts (asking them whether they find the defendant guilty or not guilty).

In the magistrates' court the clerk is called the 'justices' clerk'. In this court he or she is a particularly important figure, for not only are clerks responsible for the management and smooth running of the court proceedings; they must also must give the magistrates legal advice as and when this is required. They may not take part in the actual decision making of the magistrates, but must be able to advise them of their powers of sentence, or advise whether evidence that is given before them is properly admissible. In a large court centre, justices' clerks have assistants to help them cope with all the courts.

∗

BINDING PRECEDENT—'STARE DECISIS'

We have had a look at the courts from the highest in the land to the lowest. We have also seen that English law has been developed over many years by courts following the decisions of other courts. This works in practice with the principle of **binding precedent**. This principle, which dictates that one court is *bound* to follow previous decisions of other courts, is also known by the Latin phrase **stare decisis**—'To stand by decisions'. It has been described as a 'sacred principle' of English law. In practice it works as follows: when a court is faced with a set of facts, it may be bound to decide the case by applying principles of law decided in a previous case with a similar set of facts. The previous case is said to be a 'binding authority' or precedent for the legal principle involved.

The court does not have to accept and follow everything that the previous court said—only the principle going to the heart of the decision. In 1880, Lord Jessel, the Master of the Rolls (whom we met in Chapter 1 at the opening of the Royal Courts of Justice), said '*The only use of authorities or decided cases is the establishment of some principle which the judge can follow in deciding the case before him*'.

- Decisions of the House of Lords are binding upon every court in the land, except the House of Lords itself. This means that every other court is bound to follow its decisions. The House of Lords must consider carefully its previous decisions, but need not follow them.

- Decisions of the Court of Appeal (Civil Division), which deals with appeals in civil cases, are binding on all lower courts and on itself. It must therefore follow its own decisions.

- Decisions of the Court of Appeal (Criminal Division), which deals with criminal cases, are binding on all lower courts. However, although it will normally follow its own decisions, it is not bound to do so if that would cause injustice.

- Decisions of judges sitting at first instance trying cases in the High Court are binding on all *inferior* courts, but not on other judges of the High Court.

- Decisions made by all other judges—Crown Court judges (Circuit Judges and Recorders), county court judges, and magistrates—cannot become binding precedents.

Judges faced with difficult decisions are not confined to reading cases already decided by other judges. Over the centuries great **jurists** (writers on the law) have written major works, which have been **cited** (referred to) in the courts. The principles set out in these books are not binding authority, but if the author is a respected lawyer and the book has earned a suitable reputation it may be treated as *persuasive* authority. This means the writings are entitled to the respectful consideration of the court, which may follow them if it thinks it right to do so.

In years gone by two of the most influential of these works were *Coke's Institutes of the laws of England*, written between 1628 and 1644 by Sir Edward Coke after he had been removed from the office of Chief Justice, and *Commentaries on the Laws of England*, written between 1765 and 1769 by Sir William Blackstone. Blackstone was a failed barrister, but he became Professor of English Law at Oxford University and following the success of his *Commentaries* was appointed a judge of the Court of Common Pleas. Blackstone's work was revered for over one hundred years as the definitive statement of the structure and principles of the common law. Today, practitioners and judges have access to a large number of law reports and distinguished law books. Many of these are transferred to CD-ROM, or can be accessed via the Internet. Leading judgments delivered in the higher courts are now available on the World Wide Web.

The OLD BAILEY.

12

The Work of the Courts—Part 2
Criminal and Civil Cases

'The Criminal justice system exists to help protect us from crime, and to ensure that criminals are punished. The Civil justice system is there to help people resolve their disputes fairly and peacefully.'
Lord Irvine of Lairg, Lord Chancellor, *Modernising Justice*, 1998.

'I must say that, as a litigant, I should dread a lawsuit beyond almost anything else short of sickness and death.'
Judge Learned Hand, American judge.

※

We have already seen enough to realise that the courts have to deal with a huge variety of cases. These involve many different areas of the law, and when we looked at the solicitors' and barristers' professions we saw that many of them specialise in one field or another. For simplicity, all cases which come to court may be divided into **criminal** cases and **civil** cases.

There are certain very important differences between criminal and civil cases. When in later chapters we come to look at how cases used to be tried and how they are tried now, we will be concentrating upon *criminal* trials; but we should not forget that *civil* cases form a major part of our law, and that a number of important courts deal only with civil cases.

We looked at the structure of the court system in Chapter 11. Figure 11.1 (see page 116) showed the different levels of our courts, and it will be helpful to keep this in mind when reading on.

✳

CRIMINAL CASES

Before trial a defendant will be charged with an offence, and then he will be remanded either **in custody** or **on bail**. A remand *in custody* means that he will be detained in prison or a young offender institution pending his trial. A remand *on bail* means that he will remain free, but bail may be 'unconditional', or 'conditional'—the court will impose certain conditions, such as residence at a particular address, reporting to the police, or surrendering a passport. Bail should only be refused if there are good reasons to believe that the defendant will abscond, commit further offences, or interfere with (intimidate) witnesses connected with his case.

Almost all criminal cases are those in which the **State** prosecutes someone who is alleged to have committed a crime. This means that the prosecution is conducted on behalf of society as a whole, and not by an individual. There are rare cases in which private prosecutions (commenced by individual citizens) have been brought, and some have been successful, but in this chapter we will concentrate on the usual case, which is brought by the State in the name of the Crown (Queen).

In all criminal cases the person accused is called the **defendant**, and his or her trial will result in a **verdict** (decision) of either **guilty** or **not guilty**. If the verdict is 'guilty', the defendant has been **convicted**. He will now have a criminal record for that crime, and will be **sentenced** (punished) by the court. If the verdict is 'not guilty' the defendant has been **acquitted**. There will be no record, and, of course, he will be allowed to leave court without punishment.

In a criminal trial the **prosecution** brings the case against a defendant, and the prosecution must prove the case against him so that the court is sure that he is guilty. The duty to *prove* the case is called the **burden of proof**. The duty to *make the jury sure* of guilt, is called the **standard of proof**. A defendant never has to prove his innocence. If the court is not sure of guilt (this used to be called proving the case beyond reasonable doubt) he must be acquitted.

Crimes that are less serious, when the court can only impose a limited punishment, will usually be tried in the magistrates' court by a bench of two or three magistrates, or a single legally qualified District Judge. They sit without a jury. All serious criminal charges are tried by a judge and jury. There are literally hundreds of different criminal offences. Almost all of them are created by statute. Whenever Parliament makes something a crime, it also says what the maximum penalty (punishment) for that crime should be. There are still a few offences, originally created by the common law, which are 'punishable at common law' (there is no set maximum sentence), but these are becoming increasingly rare.

When two or more persons *agree* to commit any crime, they are guilty of a criminal **conspiracy** to commit it. The offence of conspiracy is committed as soon as they have made their criminal agreement. So, if two people agree to commit murder, and their plotting is overheard by someone who informs the police, the police do not have to wait until the plotters kill their victim! They may be arrested immediately and charged with 'conspiracy to commit murder'.

The Gunpowder Plot

Perhaps the best-known conspiracy in our history is the *Gunpowder Plot.* Judges still sometimes refer to it in court when explaining to juries what is meant by a conspiracy. In 1605, Guy Fawkes and his associates plotted to blow up the Houses of Parliament. Their plan or 'criminal agreement' was to murder King James I and MPs in attendance at the Opening of Parliament.

On the night of 4 November 1605, following an anonymous 'tip-off', Guy Fawkes was arrested in the cellar beneath the House, where he was guarding the explosives (gunpowder). The conspirators' plan was therefore discovered, and they were caught before they had caused any harm at all. Nevertheless, they were convicted of 'conspiracy to commit high treason', and were executed, because all conspiracies to commit crimes are liable to be punished in the same way as the crimes themselves.

Nearly 400 years later, 4 November is still known as *Mischief Night* and 5 November as *Bonfire Night,* when we commemorate the capture of the conspirators by 'burning the Guy', and setting off fireworks (explosives).

INDICTABLE AND SUMMARY OFFENCES

All criminal offences are (with certain exceptions, see below) either **indictable** offences or **summary** offences. Indictable offences are the more serious offences, which must be tried in the Crown Court by a judge and jury. Summary offences are less serious offences, tried by magistrates.

INDICTABLE OFFENCES

Offences that a defendant in the Crown Court is alleged to have committed are set out in a document known as an **indictment.** This lists the charges against him, which must be set out in sufficient detail to enable him to know what he is said to have done. An indictment must be signed by a court clerk. It will contain only charges for offences which may be tried in the Crown Court by a judge and jury. All serious crimes such as murder, wounding, rape, robbery, and causing death by dangerous driving are indictable offences which can only be tried in the Crown Court. Figure 12.1 (page 132) is an illustration of an indictment charging a man with robbery.

Appeals from convictions in the Crown Court go to the Court of Appeal (Criminal Division). At this point the defendant becomes known as the **appellant.** If appeals in criminal cases involve difficult points of law of real public importance they may go further to the House of Lords. These appeal courts will not re-try cases themselves, although the Court of Appeal may sometimes agree to hear further evidence to help it decide if the conviction is

---

INDICTMENT

The West London Crown Court

Statement of Offence

Robbery, contrary to section 8 of the Theft Act 1968

Particulars of Offence

John Smith, on the 1st day of January 2004, robbed Jane Brown of a gold necklace, a handbag, and £20 in money.

Figure 12.1 An indictment

safe. The appeal courts will decide if the original trial was conducted properly. If it was, the appeal will be **dismissed** (unsuccessful), and the conviction will stand. If they decide that for whatever reason the appellant was wrongly convicted or there is doubt about whether he was rightly convicted, the conviction would be regarded as unsafe, and the appeal will be **allowed** (successful). In this case the Court of Appeal will **quash** (cancel) the conviction altogether, or order a re-trial.

Until recently the prosecution was never allowed to appeal against a jury verdict of 'not guilty'. If a defendant is acquitted by a jury, he can normally never be tried again for the same offence—even if he later *admits* that he committed it. This is the historic principle against 'double jeopardy' and we will learn more about this principle, and how it is being altered, in Chapter 17.

SUMMARY OFFENCES

Summary offences are less serious crimes, which Parliament has said must be tried by magistrates. They are called summary offences, because they are tried *summarily*, which means speedily by the most convenient court, and with the minimum of formality. Almost all motoring offences are summary offences, as are offences involving minor thefts and assaults, criminal damage, prostitution, and drunk and disorderly behaviour in a public place.

Whenever a summary offence is charged it is set out in writing in a document called an **information**. This document must be 'laid before' (presented to) the magistrates' court, and a copy is sent to the defendant. Figure 12.2 is an illustration of an information containing a charge of assault.

INFORMATION

West London Magistrates' Court

To

Jane Brown
14 Tower Green, London

Charge:
At 3.30 p.m. on 2 January 2004, assaulted John Smith, thereby occasioning him actual bodily harm.

Contrary to section 47 of the Offences against the Person Act 1861

Figure 12.2 An information

Magistrates do have the power to send people to prison, but this power is very limited, the maximum sentence for any one offence being six months. (Under the Criminal Justice Act 2003, this power will in due course be increased to 12 months.)

Usually a person charged with a summary offence will have to appear before the magistrates in person, but Parliament has decreed that many minor road traffic cases may be dealt with differently. In these cases the defendant may be given the option of pleading guilty by post. If he does, he will not have to appear in court at all, and the magistrates will simply sentence him in his absence—invariably to pay a fine. A sentence of imprisonment or disqualification may be passed only in a defendant's presence.

Persons convicted by the magistrates may appeal to the Crown Court, when a Circuit Judge or Recorder will sit with two magistrates *to hear the whole case afresh*. A defendant may also appeal to the Crown Court against his sentence.

- If the *only* point in the appeal from a decision of the magistrates concerns a technical *matter of law*, the appeal will go straight to a special court of the Queen's Bench Division, called the **Divisional Court**. The prosecution, too, may appeal if they consider that the court has made a mistake *in the law*. (This is another very rare case when a verdict of not guilty may be reversed on appeal.)

'EITHER-WAY' OFFENCES

There are certain offences that may be tried either in the magistrates' court or by the Crown Court. Because they can be dealt with in either court they have been nicknamed 'either-way' offences. Offences of burglary and handling (receiving) stolen goods are good examples of these. In these cases a defendant may choose to be tried by a judge and jury in the Crown Court. He may feel that he will have a better chance of being acquitted if his case is heard by a jury. Equally, the magistrates may choose to send the case to the Crown Court if they consider it is so serious that they do not have sufficient powers to deal with it properly. New procedures under the Criminal Justice Act 2003 are designed to enable cases to be dealt with at the level of court appropriate to their seriousness, and to ensure they reach court as quickly as possible. This will mean that a defendant's right to elect jury trial in many less serious cases will be curtailed.

THE 'REASONABLE MAN'—CRIME

Normally, a defendant's conduct will be judged by his own state of mind at the time. If a defendant is charged with murder, it will therefore be for the jury to decide whether it was the defendant's act which killed his victim *and* whether he intended to kill or cause really serious bodily harm (in either case, under our law the defendant would be guilty of murder). There are cases where the jury will also be expected to decide whether the defendant's behaviour was reasonable in the circumstances. These cases usually arise when the defendant admits doing the act alleged against him, but puts up a **defence**. Here are three examples:

- *'I admit taking some stationery from work, but I didn't think I was acting dishonestly, because everyone in the office, including the boss, was doing it.'* Here it may be necessary for a jury to decide if the defendant knew that what he was doing was dishonest by the ordinary standards of reasonable and honest people.

- *'I admit striking the victim with a baseball bat, but he was attacking me with a knife, and I was acting in lawful self-defence.'* Here it may be necessary for the jury to decide whether what the defendant claims to have done in self-defence was reasonable in all the circumstances. If it was, then he may be found not guilty. If it was not, he may be found guilty.

- *'I admit to killing the victim, but I should be convicted of manslaughter and not murder because I was provoked into losing my self-control and acting as I did.'*

Here the jury may find the defendant guilty of manslaughter only if they believe that the defendant was being provoked by his victim, and that any person in his circumstances might reasonably have been expected to behave in the same way.

YOUNG PERSONS

Under the Crime and Disorder Act 1998, any child over the age of ten years may now be convicted of crime. As we shall see in Chapter 21, this represents a change in the law, but there are still strict rules as to how young offenders should be tried and punished.

ENFORCING ORDERS IN CRIMINAL CASES

Enforcing an order means making sure that it is obeyed. In criminal cases, a defendant who is convicted but not sent to prison (or, in the case of a young person, to detention), may be fined or made the subject of a community penalty (in short, placed on probation or ordered to perform community service). What happens if he refuses to pay the fine, or attend appointments with his probation officer, or perform the community service? The court may then enforce its order, directing that if he does not obey it, he must serve a period in custody **in default**. In cases of a fine there is a sliding scale. If the fine is no more than £200 the court may order that in default of paying it (within a set time) the defendant will go to prison for seven days. If the fine exceeds £1 million, the period in default could be as high as ten years.

*

CIVIL CASES

Most civil **claims** (proceedings) concern disputes between individuals or companies who are asking the court to provide some kind of legal **remedy**— to put right, or compensate them for some harm which has been done to them. Money compensation is known as **damages**. Civil claims are usually private matters—the State is not involved.

THE CIVIL PROCEDURE RULES

Since April 1999 the whole process of civil litigation has undergone a major change, as a result of recommendations made by Lord Woolf, then Master of the Rolls (now Lord Chief Justice). Civil litigation had become very expensive, with the costs of going to court far too high and out of proportion to the amount at stake in the case. It had also become very slow, with the hearing of cases sometimes being delayed, even deliberately delayed by one of the parties, for many years. Lord Woolf's recommendations were designed to tackle these evils, and resulted in a new procedural framework for the conduct of civil cases known as the **Civil Procedure Rules** ('CPR').

Before the CPR, it was largely up to the parties themselves, and their legal advisers, to progress the case at their own pace, to decide what issues they wanted to have heard, and to call whatever evidence they wished at the trial. Now, under the CPR, it is for the judges to manage cases. In particular, they must set timetables to bring cases on for trial as quickly as possible; they must control and try to simplify the issues that have to be decided; and they must put strict limits on the evidence which may be called at the trial.

Under the CPR the court has '*an overriding objective to deal with cases justly*'. This includes:

- Ensuring that the parties are on 'an equal footing' (treated alike).

- Saving expense.

- Dealing with cases in ways which are proportionate to the amount of money involved in the case, the complexity of the issues, and the financial position of each party.

- Ensuring that the case is dealt with promptly and fairly.

- Allotting to the case an appropriate share of the court's resources, taking into account the resources needed for other cases.

One important area in which judges are now expected to manage cases is that of expert witnesses. In the past, some cases were far more costly than they needed to be because the parties brought in expert witnesses—such as medical specialists, engineers, and other professional people—to give evidence in great detail and at great expense about technical questions said to arise in the case. Now courts must restrict expert evidence to what is reasonably required to decide the case. Also, they can order that, instead of each party having its own expert, a single 'joint expert' can investigate and report on a technical problem on behalf of all the parties.

The CPR introduce new, up-to-date expressions. The person making a claim (formerly 'bringing an action') is now called a **claimant**, instead of the *plaintiff* (as he was known for hundreds of years). The person against whom the claim is brought is still called the **defendant**. Until 1999, many claims began with the issue of a formal legal document known as a *writ*. Now proceedings are commenced with a **claim form**, stating the nature of the claim and the remedy that the claimant is seeking. The claim form must be served upon the defendant, and that activates a number of options:

- If a defendant wishes to defend the claim he too must file a document with the court setting out his answer to the claim. If he also wishes to make a cross-claim against the claimant, he may do this by filing a document called a **counterclaim**.

- If a defendant does not reply to the claim, the claimant may obtain a **default judgment**—and the court will award judgment in his favour without the need of going to trial.

- If a defendant states that he wishes to defend the claim, but it appears that he has no real defence to it, again the court may decide the claim without a trial by giving **summary judgment** in his favour.

- The court may also give summary judgment against the claimant himself, if it appears that his claim has no reasonable prospect of succeeding.

During the court's 'case management' of a civil action, all civil cases are allocated to one of three 'tracks':

- The **small claims track** is normally for claims of up to £5,000 in value. Claims on this track are usually dealt with swiftly and informally by a District Judge.

- The **fast track**. This is normally for cases in which the amount involved does not exceed £15,000, and the trial is not likely to last longer than one day. Cases on this track are usually heard by a District Judge or Circuit Judge.

- The **multi-track**. This is for all other claims. Cases on this track, which include all the most complicated and valuable claims, are usually heard by a Circuit Judge or a High Court Judge.

The CPR also contain various provisions designed to encourage the parties to settle their differences by negotiation and compromise, rather than pursue them to the bitter end in a contested hearing.

Family cases are rather different, and may involve the court giving **orders** (instructions) which relate to the circumstances in which family members are to live. In family cases the person bringing the case is usually called the **applicant** or **petitioner**, and the person on the other side is called the **respondent**.

In civil cases the claimant or applicant who brings the case has the burden of proving that his or her claim is a good one, but does not have to make the court *sure* about it (as the prosecution must when they bring a criminal case). The standard of proof a claimant has to meet is to show that is *more probable than not* that his or her case is right. This is called proving something **on a balance of probabilities**. This is how the burden of proof in criminal and civil cases may be contrasted:

- The first is a criminal case in which the charge is theft. The prosecution must make the court *sure* that the defendant is guilty. If the court is not sure, it must acquit the defendant, even if it finds that he was probably guilty.

- The second is a civil case in which a female claimant, who has been injured in a road accident, is claiming damages against the male defendant who caused her injury because his driving was negligent (careless). Here, in order to win her case she does not have to make the court sure that the defendant was negligent. She only has to show that he was probably negligent.

It must always be easier to make someone else believe that something is probably so than to make them sure of it. It is therefore easier to prove a civil case than it is to prove a criminal case.

Almost all civil cases are tried by judges alone. Juries do try some civil cases, but this usually only happens when the action concerns the liberty of the subject, or his reputation. An illustration of the first is when a claimant claims compensation against the police for *assault and wrongful imprisonment*. An example of the second is when the claimant claims damages for *defamation of character*—where he alleges that unpleasant and untrue things have been written or said about him that have damaged his reputation.

Jury trials in defamation cases

- Jury trials in cases of defamation (see below) have themselves acquired a bad reputation, because not only do juries have to decide whether the claimant has been defamed, but they also have to decide how much money should be awarded as compensation for the defamation. Jurors have no experience in this area of assessing damages, and from time to time have made some extraordinarily high awards, which have been heavily criticised. For example, when Sonia Sutcliffe, the wife of Peter Sutcliffe (the serial killer known as the 'Yorkshire Ripper') successfully sued the magazine *Private Eye* for defamation of her character—it had been suggested that she might have known something of her husband's activities—a jury awarded her £600,000 damages. This huge award was later reduced on appeal to £60,000.
- Juries now rarely try these cases, and it is thought that one day they will not do so at all. In a case heard in December 1995, concerning an award of damages to the singer Elton John, the Court of Appeal made an important alteration to the common law, stating that judges are now allowed to give guidance to juries to help them assess the proper level of damages.

- In January 2001 the Court of Appeal set aside altogether a jury award of £85,000 damages to the footballer Bruce Grobelaar. The goalkeeper had sued the *Sun* newspaper for defamation after it had accused him of accepting corrupt payments to 'throw matches'; but the Court of Appeal held the jury had reached a 'perverse decision', and reversed the decision. This unprecedented ruling was strongly criticised as undermining the jury system. The case went to the House of Lords. The Law Lords allowed this appeal; they did not disturb the jury's finding that Grobelaar had been defamed, but reduced the damages to a nominal sum of £1.

There are many different types of civil case—so many that it is impossible to deal with them all in this, or any other book. For convenience, we will look at some of the civil work of the High Court, but it should be remembered that only the most serious and difficult cases are tried at this level. The great majority of civil disputes are dealt with by the county courts. A case can be transferred from the county court to the High Court, or vice versa.

Three **divisions** of the High Court hear civil cases. These are the Queen's Bench Division, the Chancery Division, and the Family Division.

THE QUEEN'S BENCH DIVISION

This division of the High Court changes its name depending on whether a king or queen is on the throne. It is headed by the Lord Chief Justice. Civil cases heard in this division include commercial and admiralty cases. Commercial cases involve a number of specialised fields of commercial law. Admiralty cases may concern the sinking of a ship or the collision of ships at sea. The vast majority of cases which come before the civil courts are cases of breach of contract or tort.

BREACH OF CONTRACT

A contract is an agreement between two or more persons (known as **parties**), which they intend to be legally binding. It could be an agreement to buy and sell goods, or provide services—in fact to do anything that is lawful. Many cases come to court where one or both of the parties to a contract claim that the other has broken it. If this happens, a claim will be commenced for **breach of contract**. The court has to decide if either party has acted 'in breach of contract', and if so, what the compensation should be.

There are many rules of contract law. The basic rules are that for a contract to be **enforceable**, which means that the courts will uphold it and give a remedy for its breach, six conditions must be met:

- There must be an offer by one party, and an acceptance by the other. The law lays down when this takes place. For example, X goes into a supermarket to buy some food. The *offer* is made when X goes to the checkout and offers to pay. The supermarket *accepts* when the cashier takes the money.

- The parties must intend that their agreement will be legally binding. X agrees to increase his employee's weekly salary, but does not pay it. This is an enforceable contract. On the other hand, if X agrees to increase his wife's allowance, but does not pay, she may not take him to court. An informal family agreement is not an enforceable contract.

- Each party must agree to give a 'price', or value. This is known as a **consideration**. X promises to sell his car (worth £500) to Y for only £50. This is enforceable, as Y has agreed to pay a price, however small. If X agrees to give his car to Y who offers nothing in return, this is not an enforceable contract.

- Both parties must have the legal capacity or standing to enter into it. Normally, children (persons under the age of 18) cannot enter into legally binding contracts.

- Each party must genuinely consent to the agreement. X agrees to sell his *car* to Y for £1,000. Y mistakenly believes X has agreed to sell his *boat* for £1,000. In this situation there is no contract. Also, a contract induced by fraud (dishonesty) or entered into under duress (fear of violence) is not enforceable.

- The subject matter of the agreement must be legal, and it must be moral. X pays Y to burgle a house, but he does not do so. A prostitute agrees to provide sexual services, but does not do so. 'Contracts' such as these are not enforceable. The first is illegal; the second is immoral.

TORT

The word *tort* comes from the French word meaning 'wrong'. The special wrongs which one person may do to another, resulting in awards of compensation or some other remedy, are called **torts**. Not all wrongs lead to the courts. If someone calls you an unpleasant name, or accidentally injures you while you are playing a sport, you could not take them to court and get damages. The best-known torts are the torts of trespass, negligence, nuisance, and defamation:

Trespass

A person may be sued for damages if he commits a trespass to someone else's land or his goods or his person (body).

People are not allowed on private land without consent. This has given rise to the saying, derived from *Coke's Institutes* (see Chapter 11) that *'An Englishman's home is his castle'*. For example, the law is that the only people who are allowed to come into your home are those who are lawfully there—either at your 'invitation', or because they have been given authority to enter by the courts (such as police entering your home after first obtaining a warrant). Someone who unlawfully invades your property may be sued for trespass. The court may order the trespasser to pay damages. It may also issue an **injunction**—a court order prohibiting him from trespassing again.

Anyone who takes your belongings away without permission may be prosecuted in the criminal courts for theft. You may, however, also bring a civil claim against him *'in trespass'* and for wrongful interference with your goods. If you are successful you will recover your property or, if it has been disposed of, receive damages.

It is also possible to commit trespass to the person. If someone assaults you or keeps you somewhere against your will, you will have a claim for *trespass to the person*. If a police officer arrests you without lawful cause, a claim can be brought against him.

Negligence

Each year thousands of people are killed or injured in road accidents or accidents at work. This frequently happens because somebody has been in breach of their duty to take reasonable care for the safety of others. This means they were *negligent* in some way. If the parties cannot reach agreement and settle the case amongst themselves, the courts have to decide who, if anyone, has been negligent and what the compensation should be. This may be a fairly simple task in some cases, but imagine the difficulties where there has been a multiple 'pile-up' on a motorway involving several buses and cars, and many people have been injured.

Sometimes a judge may decide that both sides have been to blame to some extent, and that the claimant has contributed to his injury by his own negligence. When this happens, the claimant's own negligence is called *contributory negligence*. Then the court will have to apportion blame accordingly:

- The claimant was trapped in a ladies' lavatory because of a faulty lock on the door. The lock was the responsibility of the defendants, who owned and ran the premises. She fell and was injured while attempting to climb out of the cubicle by standing on the toilet-roll holder. The court held that the defendants were mainly to blame, but the claimant was also at fault for 'standing on a revolving object'. Her fault was assessed at 25 per cent, and so the defendants had to pay 75 per cent of the damages awarded by the court.

As we can see from this illustration there are countless situations in which one person may harm another by negligence. These days the courts also hear many cases of *professional negligence* where, for example, it is alleged that doctors, lawyers, or accountants have been negligent in dealing with the cases of their clients.

Nuisance

We all have the right to **enjoy** our property. The legal meaning of this word is that we have the right to keep it without its value to us being disturbed or spoiled. A person who does spoil another's enjoyment of his or her property can be ordered to pay damages. He can also be ordered to stop committing the nuisance—by an *injunction*.

There are numerous ways in which a nuisance can be caused: factory or farm premises may create nuisances by giving off a terrible smell, or polluting air or rivers; neighbours cause a nuisance when they make an unreasonable noise. People who have played their stereo equipment so loudly and at such unreasonable hours that it has disturbed and upset their neighbours have been found to have committed a nuisance.

- In January 1998 James Evans was before a Cardiff court. It was alleged that he had been listening to his Spice Girl discs for up to 16 hours a day, with the volume so loud that the words could be heard in houses on the other side of the street. An environmental health officer gave evidence that he visited the next-door flat at 2.15 a.m. and heard the group so clearly that he could write down the lyrics. Evans was banned from making any further noise.

In most cases involving allegations of *negligence* or *nuisance*, the court will be concerned to judge whether the claimant has proved that the defendant has in some way behaved *unreasonably* and that this conduct has been of sufficient seriousness to justify a remedy in the form of compensation or some other court action. This could be by failing to take reasonable care for the safety of others or their property (negligence) or in causing an unreasonable situation to exist which prevents their normal enjoyment of everyday life or property (nuisance). In the case of James Evans, when the court heard that he had already disobeyed earlier orders not to disturb his neighbours, he was fined and his powerful sound system was confiscated.

Defamation

The tort of defamation concerns damage to reputation. The law says that anyone is entitled to be protected from having untrue and damaging things written (**libel**) or spoken (**slander**) about him. Libel is regarded as more serious than slander, because things that are written are obviously more permanent than things that are said. Things that are broadcast on radio or television and which may therefore reach millions of people are also regarded as libel, not slander.

Not all unpleasant or unkind things can be made the subject of an action for defamation—only those which would tend to lower a person's reputation *'in the estimation of right-thinking members of the community'*. Merely swearing at someone, or 'name calling', cannot form the basis for a claim for defamation. If it could, the queues of litigants would stretch around the country.

There are many important and interesting exceptions to this general rule. As a matter of public policy (in recognition of the importance of uninhibited freedom of speech), all things said in Parliament and in a court of law are privileged. This means that they are free from the danger of a claim for defamation. All 'fair comment' on matters of public interest is allowed. It is therefore permissible for an art critic to criticise the work of an artist in an art exhibition, or a theatre or music critic to criticise a performance. It is accepted that your local newspaper, or you, may say exactly what you think (well, almost exactly what you think) of anyone in your football team who misses two penalties.

There are circumstances in which it is proper for one person to write unpleasant things about another person's character providing this is not motivated by personal malice. Indeed, they may be under duty to do so—for example, employers who are asked to provide *references* for their employees will be expected to give honest opinions about them, and they cannot be taken to court if they are unfavourable. Precisely the same thing applies when, for example, teachers are applying for jobs, or pupils to universities.

THE CHANCERY DIVISION

The work of the Chancery Division now covers a number of highly technical areas of the law. Some of the main aspects of Chancery work include dealing with company law matters, partnership claims (for instance, when business partners fall out), conveyancing, and land law matters (transferring the ownership of land, factories, houses). It is also concerned with probate matters (the administration of the property of persons who have died), patent and copyright actions, and revenue (taxation) cases.

The Chancery Division has always had a special involvement in the administration of **trusts**. A trust is a type of confidential arrangement, which was originally recognised only by the Court of Chancery. Trusts are created when property is given to and held by one person who must look after it on behalf of another. In this case the original owner of property (*settlor*) creates a legally binding trust, giving the property *on trust* to another person (*trustee*) for the benefit of a third person (*beneficiary*). In managing trust property the trustee promises to obey the wishes of the settlor.

Trusts are now quite common. They are sometimes arranged for tax reasons. They are also a way of reassuring the owner of property who wishes to give it to another (for example parents wishing to give property to their children) that it will be looked after carefully, that each of the beneficiaries will be treated fairly, in accordance with their wishes, and that it will not be squandered.

Judges of the Chancery Division and the Commercial Courts of the Queen's Bench Division are also highly experienced in dealing with cases with international connections. This may well happen in the case of trusts or contracts between people or companies of different nationalities. These judges are renowned throughout the commercial world, and it is common for foreign parties to a transaction to agree that in the event of a dispute between them, it should be decided by the English courts. If, therefore, an English company and a Spanish company enter into a contract to supply goods to a Brazilian company, the parties may well agree that in the event of a dispute between them, it should be decided according to the law of England by the English courts.

THE FAMILY DIVISION

Traditionally, the Family Division has been concerned with the hearing of divorce cases, and other matrimonial causes (disputes between husbands and wives). This will include applications for **ancillary relief** (financial orders for the division of family property, or payment of money for the **maintenance** or keep of a spouse or children).

Increasingly, however, the work of the Family Division is concerned with disputes involving the **welfare of children**. These disputes are either *private law* or *public law* disputes.

- *Private law disputes* are mostly between separated parents (both married and unmarried) about questions, such as, with which parent their children should reside, and how much contact (if any) the children should have with the other parent.

- *Public law disputes* usually arise when children are said to have been exposed to significant harm while in the care of their parents. If they have, this is a matter not merely of private concern, but of public concern. In these cases if the court decides that children have suffered or are at risk of suffering significant harm while in their parents' care, it may make a **care order**. This enables a local authority to remove the children temporarily or permanently from their care, or a **supervision order** enabling a local authority to monitor the parents' care for a period. These matters are looked at in greater detail in Chapter 21.

The Family Division also deals with other cases involving children, including **adoption**, where 'new parents' take over a child's care, and **wardship**, where the court itself takes charge of a child's affairs. The court will also decide disputes concerning the removal of a child from one country to another.

Because almost any question involving the welfare of a child can be referred to the Family Division, the judges of this court can be asked to make important and difficult decisions about the medical treatment of children. Sometimes, life and death decisions have to be made: doctors may advise that a child needs to have a surgical operation to save his or her life, but the child's parents may refuse to allow this because it would mean the child having a blood transfusion, to which they are opposed on religious grounds. In such a situation, the court has the power to override the parents' wishes and allow the operation to go ahead. The court may be asked to give permission for treatment to be discontinued to a patient who is 'brain dead', and is being artificially kept alive by a life support machine. One of the most dramatic cases to come before the Family Division in recent years is reported in the Law Reports simply as '*Re A* (Children) *(2000)*'. In fact it is the case of the Mary and Jodie, the 'Siamese twins'.

'*Re A* (Children) *(2000)*' — the case of the Siamese twins

In September 2000, Judges in the Court of Appeal heard an appeal from a decision of Mr Justice Johnson of the Family Division. They were called upon to decide the fate of newly born conjoined (Siamese) twins, who for the purposes of the case were called Mary and Jodie. Under an arrangement with the Maltese health authorities, their mother had come to England for their birth from her home in Gozo, a small island off the coast of Malta. After their birth, it was discovered that Mary had a primitive brain, her heart had failed, and her lungs were tiny and malformed. She was entirely dependent upon Jodie's organs for her 'life support'.

Doctors attending the children recommended that they should be surgically separated. This would save the life of Jodie—who had the prospect of 'a fairly normal, at least not intolerable life'—but would inevitably kill Mary. If they were not allowed to operate, then in a few months' time both children would die. Their parents, both devout Catholics, objected to surgery, believing that it was morally wrong to end the life of one of their children in this way. They loved their daughters dearly and equally, and could not contemplate killing one to save the other. '*They sincerely believed that it was God's will that they be born with the afflictions they have and that they should be left to live their lives joined together as they are for so long as God in his mercy shall ordain it.*'

The Court of Appeal ruled that the surgery should go ahead, and the twins should be separated. Lord Justice Ward said, '*the sad fact is that Mary lives on borrowed time, all of it borrowed from her sister. She is incapable of independent existence.*' He continued:

> One cannot escape the fact that Mary has always been fated for early death: her capacity to live has been fatally compromised. Though Mary has a right to life, she has little right to be alive. She is alive because and only because, to put it bluntly but nonetheless accurately, she sucks the lifeblood of Jodie and her parasitic living will soon be the cause of Jodie ceasing to live. Jodie is entitled to protest that Mary is killing her. Nobody but the doctors can help Jodie. Mary, sadly, is beyond any help. The best interests of the twins is to give the chance of life to the child whose actual bodily condition is capable of accepting the chance to her advantage, even if this has to be at the cost of the sacrifice of a life which is so unnaturally supported. I am therefore left in no doubt at all that the scales of justice come down heavily in Jodie's favour. The least detrimental choice is to allow separation to take place.

The operation to separate the twins did take place. Mary sadly died, but Jodie is alive and well, and much loved by her parents.

THE 'REASONABLE MAN'—CIVIL CASES

There are cases in which the civil law too takes as its test for responsibility whether the parties have behaved reasonably. This applies especially in actions for negligence and nuisance, and also in a particular area of the law of contract: a condition in a contract of employment that an employee will not do similar work for anyone else will only be enforced by the court if it is reasonable.

- A man is employed by a firm as a milkman. It may be a reasonable term of his contract of employment that he should agree not do that type of work for another firm in the same area for two years; but the courts would refuse to enforce a clause in his contract which was unreasonable, such as preventing him from working anywhere in the world as milkman after his employment had ended.

The test of reasonableness does not apply in every civil case. Normally, when two adults enter into a contract, whatever it may be, the court will not decide whether it was a fair contract for both sides. Provided the conditions (set out above under the heading 'Breach of contract') are fulfilled, they will be bound by its terms whether they are reasonable or not. In a family dispute as to who shall have custody of a child, the court will not decide whether the mother has behaved more reasonably than the father in their relationship together. It will decide what will be in the best interests of the child.

YOUNG PERSONS

Young persons under the age of 18 used to be known in the civil courts as 'minors'. They are now called **children**. They are not normally allowed to sue (bring cases before the civil courts), or be sued. They can, however, bring and defend cases in the name of an adult, who is now known as their **litigation friend**. This means that one of their parents or guardians, or some other appropriate adult, must act as their legal representative. In practice the fact that it is a young person who has made a claim or is responsible for a tort will not matter. There are strict rules about children entering into contracts. With a very few exceptions they are not allowed to enter into legally binding contracts.

ENFORCING COURT ORDERS IN CIVIL CASES

We know that if someone breaks the criminal law and commits a crime he or she may be prosecuted and punished. How is an order of the civil courts enforced? How does the law ensure that anyone who is ordered by a court to repay a debt, or pay compensation, or stop committing a trespass or nuisance, will do as the court says?

In the case of an order to pay money, the court may order that the defendant's property should be seized and sold, or there may be an order declaring him bankrupt. More generally, if a person deliberately disobeys any court order either to do something or not to do something, he or she will be guilty of a **contempt of court** and the punishment for contempt is a fine or committal to prison.

- In July 1995 a woman aged 68 came before the court. She had committed a nuisance by regularly throwing very large amounts of bread around her house to feed the birds. Birds had flocked to her home, which was a semi-detached house in a suburban area. This caused serious inconvenience and concern to her neighbours and local authority, because it became a health hazard. Despite several warnings by the court that her behaviour was unlawful, she persisted. Eventually the court granted an injunction ordering her not to do this. Almost immediately she disobeyed this order. This time she was committed to prison for contempt of court. After a few days in prison the woman apologised to the court and promised not to do it again. The court decided that she had now 'purged her contempt' (wiped the slate clean) and she was released.

This is an example of someone who has not committed a crime, but has nevertheless been sent to prison by a civil court for disobeying its orders. In this way the civil court was able to enforce the law.

13

Judges

'The silence awoke Mr Justice Stareleigh, who immediately wrote down
something with a pen without any ink in it, and looked unusually profound,
to impress the jury with the belief that he always thought most deeply with
his eyes shut.'

Charles Dickens, *The Pickwick Papers* — 'The trial of *Bardell* v *Pickwick*'.

*

When we looked at the structure of the courts system, we saw that there were
different courts, each type of court having its own function and responsibilities. There are also several different types of judge. Most judges are full-
time judges, but there are also many part-time judges who, when they are not
sitting as judges, carry on their careers as solicitors or barristers. In Chapter 11
we learned about magistrates, and the important role they play in the justice
system. In this chapter we will be concentrating upon the different types of
professional judges who are appointed to sit in judgment on their fellow
citizens.

In this country almost all the judges are appointed by the Queen on the
advice of the Lord Chancellor. He has a special department known as the
Judicial Appointments Group, which collects information about judicial candidates and 'screens' them to ensure their suitability. There are very few
exceptions to this, but they are extremely important ones. The most senior
judges in the land, including the Lord Chief Justice, the Master of the Rolls,
and the Law Lords, are appointed by the Queen on the advice of the Prime
Minister.

Until June 2003 (see Chapter 5), the Lord Chancellor was the only judge to
be a political appointment. He sat as a judge only during the continuation of
his appointment. He no longer sits as a judge. All other judges are permanent
appointments. As we will see, the Lord Chancellor has announced that there
is to be a new way in which judges are to be appointed.

The American tradition of democracy established the idea that State judges, at least, should be directly elected by the people. In this way, judges will be chosen who are truly representative of the people. In America a judge standing for office may well canvass for votes on the strength of his or her record of being tough with criminals, or support for the death penalty. The British system follows a different line. Unlike many American judges, ours do not stand for election, and their decisions cannot therefore be influenced by the desire to catch votes by popular appeal. The argument is that judges should not have to court popularity in order to be appointed; and that it would be dangerous if, once in office, they could be accused of giving way to pressure on popular causes; and that their judgment in individual cases should never be wrongly influenced by such matters.

We have already discussed the importance of judges being independent. In order to ensure that they are independent, they can be removed from office only if it is proved that they are unfit to be judges—either because of some serious disability, or because they have done something which makes them unfit to sit in judgement on others.

Since the Act of Settlement of 1700, a High Court or Court of Appeal judge can only be dismissed 'upon the address of both Houses of Parliament'. This means that both the House of Commons and the House of Lords must vote their agreement to remove a judge from office. Other judges can be dismissed only by the Lord Chancellor. There have been cases where judges have resigned following misconduct or have been removed from office, but this has happened very rarely.

These days all judges must have gained very considerable experience in the law before they are appointed. The qualifications for appointment are now published in a booklet entitled *Judicial Appointments*. This sets out the basic qualifications for appointments to 'the bench', whether full-time or part-time, and to the numerous tribunals. The Government has now stated its intention that judges should be appointed on the recommendation of a new 15-member *Judicial Appointments Commission*, which will consist of five judges, five lawyers, and five non-lawyers and be independent of any political persuasion.

The judiciary as a whole has often been criticised as being too '*white, male, and middle-class*'. There may be some justification for this criticism, although the problem is largely accounted for by the fact that until the last twenty years most of the barristers, from whom judges tend to be drawn, could be described in that way. Many more women lawyers and lawyers from different ethnic groups are now becoming eligible for appointment to the bench, and recent appointments suggest that the Lord Chancellor is anxious to see that they are.

PART-TIME JUDGES

Part-time judges are solicitors or barristers who are appointed to sit between 20 and 50 days a year as judges. They may sit as Recorders trying criminal cases in the Crown Court or as Deputy High Court Judges or Deputy District Judges trying civil cases in the High Court or county court.

Generally, the men and women who are chosen to sit as part-time judges will be at least 35 years of age. They are in fact normally in their forties. They will have had at least ten years' experience in legal practice. Before any of these judges are allowed to sit, they must go through a period of judicial training (see below).

FULL-TIME JUDGES

There are several different types of full-time judge. These days almost every judge who becomes a full-time judge will first have had experience as a part-time judge, and will have proved that he or she is competent to try cases, and has the right qualities to sit as a judge. The following are the main types of judge. As we look at them it will be helpful to refer to the diagram of the courts in Chapter 11 (see Figure 11.1 on page 116).

HOUSE OF LORDS JUDGES

The top rung of the judicial ladder is the House of Lords. A Lord Justice of Appeal may be appointed to become a Lord of Appeal in Ordinary, sitting in the House of Lords. Judges in the House of Lords are called 'Lord . . .'. There are 12 Law Lords and they always sit in the building of the House of Lords in London. We have seen in Chapter 11 that the Appellate Committee of the House of Lords and the Judicial Committee of the Privy Council will in due course be replaced by a new Supreme Court.

The House of Lords is the final court of appeal, and the most important court in the land. This is the only senior court where judges do not wear robes, although the barristers appearing before them do. The Law Lords also sit as the judges of the Judicial Committee of the Privy Council, which is the final court of appeal from Commonwealth countries, as far away as the Bahamas and New Zealand.

COURT OF APPEAL JUDGES

A High Court Judge of special distinction may be appointed a Lord (or Lady) Justice of Appeal. They sit as appeal judges in the Court of Appeal. By tradition, all judges of this court are also appointed to the rank of Privy Councillor. They are therefore known as 'The Right Honourable Lord or Lady Justice . . .'. Lords and Lady Justices almost always sit at the Royal Courts of Justice in London, although very rarely the Court of Appeal has gone out 'on circuit'.

At the time of writing there are 37 Lords Justices of Appeal. Three of them are now woman. When the first Lady Justice, Dame Elizabeth Butler-Sloss, was appointed, no one knew how to address her, and for a while she was called *Lord* Justice Butler-Sloss! In July 1999 *Lady* Justice Butler-Sloss was appointed President (Head) of the Family Division. She is the first woman to be appointed Head of one of the great Divisions of the courts. In October 2003, when *Lady* Justice Brenda Hale became the first woman to be appointed to the House of Lords, it was announced that she was to become a *Lord* of Appeal in Ordinary.

HIGH COURT JUDGES

A High Court Judge is known as 'The Honourable Mr or Mrs Justice. . . .', and in court they are called 'My lord' or 'My lady'. High Court Judges try most of the difficult and serious civil and criminal cases.

At present there are about 120 High Court Judges, sitting in the three Divisions of the High Court. Many try cases in London, but in addition, at each major court centre throughout the country there will be two or three High Court Judges trying criminal, civil, and family cases in that area. When they go out 'on circuit' (outside London) to try cases they live together in judges' lodgings, which are often large country houses in pleasant surroundings.

CIRCUIT JUDGES

Each of the six circuits has a number of Circuit Judges. These judges do not travel the country as a whole. They remain on their circuits, either working at one court centre or travelling between two or three of the circuit courts. They may sit in the Crown Court and county courts, and will try a large number of the criminal and civil cases which come before the courts in their areas.

There are over 500 Circuit Judges. They are addressed as 'His or Her Honour Judge . . .' and in court they are called 'Your Honour'. If a Circuit Judge was a QC before becoming a judge, he or she keeps the courtesy title 'QC'. We will see an example of this when we come to look at judges' robes.

OTHER JUDGES

There are several other types of judge. District Judges are full-time judges. They deal with the more difficult cases in the magistrates' court or the less serious cases in the county courts. Masters of the Supreme Court deal with many of the technical problems that arise in the early stages of important civil cases. Judge Advocates preside over cases concerning people in the Armed Forces. There are numerous legally qualified chairmen and chairwomen of tribunals of one kind or another.

Whitaker's Almanack is an annual publication, which sets out many facts about the structure of power in the United Kingdom as a whole, and names the persons who exercise that power. The vast array of interesting information in this book includes lists of all the courts and tribunals in England, Wales, Scotland, and Northern Ireland. It also lists the names of the many people who hold judicial office and the salaries they are paid by the State.

THE HEADS OF THE DIVISIONS

When the Lord High Chancellor (his full title) sat as a judge in the House of Lords, he took precedence in that court, and usually gave the leading speech (judgment). In June 2003, on his appointment as Secretary of State for the new Department for Constitutional Affairs, Lord Falconer of Thoroton brought to an end a tradition that has lasted many hundreds of years. He announced that although he would continue to act as Lord Chancellor until a decision had been taken about the future of that Office, the Lord Chancellor would no longer sit as a judge in the House of Lords. Lord Bingham of Cornhill, as the senior permanent Law Lord, is now the most senior judge in the House of Lords. He has the distinction of being the first judge to hold this office and also to have held the offices of Master of the Rolls and Lord Chief Justice.

At present four judges head the great divisions of the Supreme Court, although they will soon be joined by a fifth. The Lord Chief Justice presently heads the Queen's Bench Division and the Criminal Division of the Court of Appeal, but the Constitutional Reform Bill 2004 proposes that he shall also assume the title of 'President of the Courts of England and Wales', and there will be created an entirely new office of 'President of the Queen's Bench Division.' The Master of the Rolls heads the Civil Division of the Court of Appeal; he will also be known as the Head of Civil Justice. The Vice-Chancellor heads the Chancery Division; he will be known as the Chancellor of the Chancery Division (thereby perpetuating for our legal history the ancient title of Chancellor). The President of the Family Division will also receive an additional new title Head of Family Justice. We will look at the two of the most senior of these offices.

THE LORD CHIEF JUSTICE OF ENGLAND

It is almost certain that the title of Lord Chief Justice of England was first taken by Sir Edward Coke. As Attorney-General in the reigns of Elizabeth I and James I, we have already met him in this book, and will do so again. He went on to become Chief Justice of the Common Pleas and then Chief Justice of the King's Bench. Coke appears to have invented the title Lord Chief Justice of England for himself. When he was dismissed from office in 1616, the Earl of Suffolk told him, '*Amongst other things, the King is not well pleased with the title of the book [which Coke had written] wherein you entitled yourself "Lord Chief Justice of England". Whereas by law you can challenge [claim to be] no more than Lord Chief Justice of the Kings Bench.*'

In fact the title Lord Chief Justice of England was *officially* conferred on the head of the Queen's Bench Division 240 years after Lord Coke's death, by the Supreme Court of Judicature Act 1873. We have seen that Coke was also a jurist—as a legal expert, he wrote a number of books or 'commentaries' on the law which he called *Institutes*. Future generations of lawyers regarded them as classic expositions of the law.

Another great judge and jurist was Sir Matthew Hale. In 1666, when Chief Baron of the Exchequer, he presided over the court of 'Fire Judges'. This special court was set up to decide property disputes following the Great Fire of London, which in September of that year consumed almost 80 per cent of the City, including St Paul's Cathedral. In 1671, Hale too became Chief Justice of the King's Bench. His work, *Pleas of the Crown*, was for many years the standard text on criminal and other Crown proceedings.

Over the years there have been many notable holders of the office of Lord Chief Justice—towering figures who have had a real influence upon the development of the common law, in particular in the field of criminal law. The Prime Minister recommends the appointment of the Lord Chief Justice, although this may soon be changed. Indeed, for many years this was a political appointment, the holder of the office usually having served in the Government as Attorney-General.

- Sir Rufus Isaacs (1865–1935) was a remarkable example of a political appointment. In 1910 he became Solicitor-General, then Attorney-General. He was the first Attorney-General to become a member of the Cabinet. On his appointment as Lord Chief Justice he was elevated to the House of Lords, taking the title Lord Reading. He then went on to become British Ambassador to the United States, Viceroy of India, and finally Foreign Secretary.

- The earliest non-political appointment to the office of Lord Chief Justice was that of Mr Justice A. T. Lawrence. In 1917, when he was aged 77, he was appointed Lord Chief Justice as a stop-gap, because the Attorney-General, Sir Gordon Hewart, was unable to take up the appointment as Chief Justice at the time. He agreed to accept the office on this basis. It is reliably reported that when Hewart himself became available to take up the appointment, Lord Chief Justice Lawrence first learned of his resignation when he read it in *The Times*!

The appointment of Lord Chief Justice is no longer a political one. This position is now given to the Law Lord or Lord Justice who is considered best qualified to hold the office. Senior judges also preside over major public inquiries. The present Lord Chief Justice is Lord Woolf of Barnes. His predecessor but one was Lord Taylor of Gosforth, who as a Lord Justice presided over the Hillsborough Inquiry, which made such an impact on the safety of football grounds. Lord Woolf also conducted a major inquiry. In the 1980s, following the Strangeways Prison riot, he conducted a review of the prison service, acknowledged to be a landmark in prison reform. More recently, he conducted a review of the civil justice system (see Chapter 12), recommending ways in which civil cases can be tried more efficiently and with less expense. In 2003, another Law Lord, Lord Brian Hutton, who was Lord Chief Justice of Northern Ireland, conducted one of the most dramatic of these inquiries, into the death of Mr David Kelly, the weapons expert who had commented upon the state of weapons in Iraq before the war with that country.

The Lord Chief Justice, who is assisted by his Deputy, is the senior permanent judge in the country. His new title 'President of the Courts of England and Wales' will give him overall responsibility for the work of the Court of Appeal, the High Court, the Crown Court and the magistrates' courts. He will also be responsible for the swearing-in, training and good conduct of the judiciary. The Lord Chief Justice's traditional role of special involvement in criminal justice will be seen by the fact that he, or his nominee, will also be given the title 'Head of Criminal Justice'. For example, at present he gives judgments in many of the most important criminal appeals, and he is responsible for setting the standards of sentencing in criminal cases for judges throughout the country. This includes hearing appeals initiated by the Attorney-General against sentences which are thought to be too lenient. He is also consulted by the Home Secretary when any changes in the criminal law are proposed. In cases where defendants are sentenced to life imprisonment, he must advise on how long they should serve before they become eligible for parole.

THE MASTER OF THE ROLLS

The office of Master of the Rolls originates from the appointment of a guardian responsible for the safe-keeping of all charters, patents, and records of the most important judgments and decisions of the courts which were entered upon the Parchment Rolls. At first this official was called the Clerk or Curator of the Rolls, but a time came when he also became responsible for supervising all the records of the Court of Chancery, including a register of all the writs issued under the Great Seal of the Lord Chancellor. Eventually, he became the chief clerk or *Master* who advised the Lord Chancellor in the Court of Chancery, and then the Chancellor's deputy judge of that court. His combined duties as clerk and judge (*Master*) and keeper of records (*Rolls*) led to the title *Master of the Rolls*.

The office of Master of the Rolls has evolved over hundreds of years. Since 1881, he has been a member of the Court of Appeal. He is now the leading judge dealing with the civil work of that court, and as such he will often preside over the most difficult and sensitive civil cases that come before it. He still has the historic responsibility of being in charge of documents of national importance, for he is the Chairman of the Advisory Council on Public Records and Chairman of the Royal Commission on Historical Manuscripts. He is also responsible for supervising the admission of solicitors to practice, and appoints members of the Solicitors' Disciplinary Tribunal. The present Master of the Rolls is Lord Phillips of Worth Matravers. In 1999, he presided over the public inquiry into the causes of the health problem BSE. When he was first appointed he said, '*I am not quite sure what the Rolls were of which I was Master. I had, as have many people, a vague idea that they were or included the roll of solicitors. That is not the case.*' One of the best-known holders of this office in recent times was Lord 'Tom' Denning.

Lord Denning

When Lord Denning was appointed Master of the Rolls he was already a Law Lord. In his book *A Family Story* he describes the circumstances of his appointment in this matter-of-fact way:

> In 1962 Lord Evershed, the Master of the Rolls, resigned and became himself a Lord of Appeal in Ordinary. Who was to succeed him? We all wondered. Then at lunch one day in the Lords, the Lord Chancellor, Lord Kilmuir, (when the others had left the table) said to me: 'I hear that you would like to be Master of the Rolls yourself. Is that so?' Now I had mentioned this to no one—unless it were to Lord Parker—in 1957—five years before. I said at once that I would. It was the opportunity I wanted.

Lord Denning was a progressive and adventurous judge; a 'judicial activist', he had a passion for doing justice in the individual case, and was unafraid of breaking new legal ground to achieve it. During his career as a judge, which spanned 38 years, including a remarkable 20 years as Master of the Rolls, he was responsible for many important developments in the civil law. These included major advances in the law of contract, fundamental reforms in the law of divorce (for example, giving deserted wives their full and fair share of family property), and a range of cases which corrected abuses of power by the State.

In his later years Lord Denning disappointed some of his admirers by making controversial and reactionary remarks about the criminal law, but it was as a great civil judge that he secured his reputation. In January 1999 he celebrated his one-hundredth birthday, when tributes were paid to him from around the world. Lord Woolf described his legacy to the law as 'unrivalled . . . he put the Court of Appeal's civil division on the map. Until his time it was the great criminal cases that caught the public imagination. With him, for the first time, it was civil cases, because he was protecting the little man against the big battalions.' Lord Denning died shortly afterwards. He was by common consent a great judge; but he is by no means the only judge in modern times who might lay claim to have made a lasting contribution to the development of English law.

DECIDING FACTS

Judges are expected to get the law right, but like juries, judges also constantly have to make **findings** (decisions) about the facts of a case—what actually happened. How can they, or indeed anyone, tell if someone is telling the truth or lies, or giving accurate or inaccurate evidence? Of course, a witness may be caught telling lies, but in his book, *The Judge*, Lord Devlin, a former Law Lord, describes how hard it can be to decide between two different versions of events: *'In difficult cases [the judge] cannot be right every time; certainly he will not convince the losing party that he is right. The object of the process is not, however, to force the contender to submit to superior reasoning. It is to provide a civilised method of resolving disputes. It is . . . to remove a sense of injustice.'*

Lord Devlin went on to quote with admiration extracts from a lecture given by Mr Justice MacKenna, in which he explained how he made findings of fact in a civil case. He said that he did not attempt to judge from the witness's demeanour whether he is telling the truth:

> He speaks hesitantly. Is that the mark of a cautious man, whose statements are for that reason to be respected, or is he taking time to fabricate? Is the emphatic witness putting on an act to deceive me, or is he speaking from the fullness of his heart, knowing that he is right? Is he likely to be more truthful if he looks me straight in the face than if he casts his eyes on the ground perhaps from shyness or natural timidity? Instead, I start with the undisputed facts which both sides accept and I add to them such other facts as seem very likely to be true, as for example those recorded in contemporary documents or spoken to by independent witnesses like the policeman giving evidence in a running down case [road accident] about marks on the road . . . I

judge a witness as unreliable if his evidence is, in any serious respect, inconsistent with these undisputed or indisputable facts, or of course if he contradicts himself on important points . . . When I have done my best to separate the true facts from the false by these more or less objective tests, I say which story seems to me the more probable, the Claimant's or the Defendant's.

JUDICIAL ASSISTANTS

Some Judicial Assistants are appointed to assist Law Lords or Lords Justices in their work. These appointments are usually made for one, two, or three law terms. Assistants will be newly qualified lawyers (barristers or solicitors), who have completed at least one year of their pupillage or traineeship, and will be expected to have attained a high standard in their examinations.

'JUDGES AND SCHOOLS'

For many years judges around the country have welcomed school children (over the age of 14) to visit their courts. They have also met children to talk about the justice system, and conducted *moots* (mock trials) in which the children take part. The *Judges and Schools* project, which is led by the Lord Chief Justice, is intended to build on that work, and to encourage and expand the number of school visits to courts—both to see how cases are tried and to meet judges.

TRAINING FOR JUDGES

All new judges now receive training and most experienced judges have to attend 'refresher courses' from time to time. All of this training is organised by a special office within the Department for Constitutional Affairs called the *Judicial Studies Board* (JSB).

The JSB organises separate training courses for judges who will be asked to try criminal, civil, and family cases. These courses may last up to a week and will include lectures and practical exercises. One aspect of training is that of *racial awareness*, designed to give judges a greater insight into the differences and problems of different cultures, and help them guard against discrimination. Another special course deals with sexual offences and child abuse.

Experienced judges attend JSB courses as 'tutor judges' to assist in the training of new judges, and to discuss the day-to-day problems that are likely to arise in the courts. The course for new Recorders includes tackling difficult sentencing problems, and taking part in a mock trial in which they are trained to deal with some of the tricky points of law that may arise in a case. They also learn how best to cope with the many things that can go wrong. Judges who try criminal cases also visit prisons and young offender institutions. Trainee judges will be expected to sit as observers in court with experienced judges. The JSB produces much useful information for judges, which is designed to bring them up to date with recent developments in the law, and help them to do their work efficiently and well.

14

Legal Robes

'If judges really wish to preserve their anonymity by wearing robes, why not wear yashmaks?'

Lord Taylor of Gosforth, Lord Chief Justice of England, 1991–6.

*

One of the strongest mental pictures conjured up by the mere mention of British courts is of the lawyers wearing their wigs and gowns. The butt of almost every cartoonist, the judge is invariably seen as a bad-tempered, gnarled old man wearing a long wig down to his shoulders. He has a wooden gavel in his hand, ready to bang for 'order', and he is always saying something that suggests he is either a fool or a hypocrite or totally out of touch with real life—or all three! The barristers are also made to look absurd. No matter who else is shown in the drawing, and however they may be dressed, they always look a little saner than the lawyers.

There can be no doubt that judges do sometimes deserve criticism. They do occasionally say foolish things in court, or show that they are out of touch with what may be going on, invariably in an area of life with which they are unfamiliar. Normally they do their best to avoid these problems, and will accept criticism with good grace. Good judges will profit from it.

Judges and barristers can do little to alter the *impression* that they are remote from the ordinary experiences of everyday life in the twenty-first century, simply because they are made to dress as if they belong to the seventeenth and eighteenth centuries. This may or may not be a good thing. The legal profession is one of immense power and importance, and it draws much of its strength from its great traditions. One of these traditions is the wearing of legal robes, and many distinguished people believe that it should be preserved. What is this extraordinary costume?

*

Judges and barristers wear **court dress**. This is commonly known as their **robes**. It includes wigs, gowns, and white bands—two strips of white linen that hang down at the collar. The robes worn in court by judges and barristers are different: in fact, a judge does wear a wig and a *robe*, which is a closed garment (now done up by a system of 'hooks and eyes'). A barrister wears a wig and a *gown*, which is an open garment. Solicitors who appear in the higher courts wear bands and gowns, but not wigs.

WIGS

Before wigs were worn in court, judges and barristers did wear some form of headgear. In early Tudor times it was a black flat bonnet or cap. Then came the square cap. Right up to the abolition of capital punishment in 1969, judges wore a form of this black cap, on top of their wigs, when passing sentence of death. In the sixteenth and seventeenth centuries judges and lawyers all wore round black skullcaps.

The wearing of wigs became fashionable in the late seventeenth century, in the reign of Charles II. It was largely influenced by the dress of the contemporary French court. The word *wig is* itself short for *periwig*, derived from the French word *perruque* (a wig). This was the time of the 'Sun King' of France, Louis XIV, who built the magnificent palace at Versailles; and beginning in Versailles the trend for wearing wigs quickly spread throughout Europe.

Louis XIV's courtiers were exceptionally fashion conscious. They tried to surpass one another with the size of their wigs. This fad also reached the English royal court. In the reign of Queen Anne (1702–14) wigs reached preposterous sizes. Wigs worn by men covered the back and shoulders and cascaded down over the chest. Ladies eager to outshine one another wore wigs so high that they had to be supported on frames. Wigs were then so popular that the fashion quickly spread across the Atlantic to the American colonies. Even to this day a person who is of particular importance, or thinks he is, is sometimes called a 'Bigwig'.

By 1680, most judges and barristers wore wigs in court. In doing so they too were simply following the fashion of the day. At first wigs were made of human hair. Many people in debt would sell their own hair to the wig maker, and there was a macabre trade in the hair of the dead. Wigs could be disgusting. In October 1663, Samuel Pepys felt obliged to invest in a good one. In his diary he describes going to '*one or two Perriwig shops about the Temple (having been much displeased with what we saw—a head of greasy and old woman's haire) and there I think I shall fit myself of one very handsomely made'*. As time wore on, wigs came to be made of horsehair. Wig making was an important trade, and fine wigs were expensive. The father of Jonathan Wild, the notorious 'thief-taker' we met in Chapter 6, was a wig maker in Wolverhampton. Wig thieves became common, and were known as 'Wool-pullers'; some of them became expert at cutting holes in the backs of coaches, and putting their hands inside to grab the wigs of unsuspecting passengers.

Fashions, by nature, come and go. Wigs were so costly that they came to be regarded as a symbol of class distinction. In the late eighteenth century Georgiana, Duchess of Devonshire, revived the style of big wigs. In her hands, or rather on her head, wigs climbed up to three feet high, and ladies travelling to and from social engagements had to sit on the floors of their carriages to accomodate them. By the end of George III's reign (1760–1820), few people other than members of the professions—lawyers, doctors, soldiers, and clergymen—wore wigs. When Queen Victoria came to the throne (1837), they were worn only by lawyers, coachmen, and those bishops who sat in the House of Lords. Bishops stopped wearing wigs in the Lords in 1880, and so we are now down to lawyers and coachmen!

The wigs we see in court today are made of grey horsehair, and are of different styles for judges and barristers, although one recently retired judge, His Honour Mota Singh QC, instead looked magnificent in his turban. A judge's wig is called a 'bob-wig'. It has 'frizzed' sides, unlike the barrister's wig which has side-curls. The cost of a judge's wig is about £800 and that of a barrister about £375. The long full-bottomed wig, worn on ceremonial occasions by judges and QCs, costs about £1,750. Ede and Ravenscroft of Chancery Lane, London, are reputed to be the oldest firm of bespoke tailors in the world. They have supplied full-bottomed wigs to every Lord Chancellor since 1697, when one cost six guineas (£6. 6s.). The purchase of judges' wigs and robes is subsidised by the State, but sometimes wigs are handed down from one generation of judges to another.

The wearing of wigs today is not confined to the courts of England and Wales. They are also worn in court in Scotland, and both Northern Ireland and the Republic of Ireland. They are still worn as far afield as Australia and New Zealand, Hong Kong, and the Falkland Islands. They are also worn in countries with some of the hottest climates in the world, including Jamaica, Barbados, the Bahamas, Ghana, Nigeria, Malawi, Uganda, and the Seychelles. Louis XIV has much to answer for.

ROBES AND GOWNS

SOLICITORS AND BARRISTERS

Solicitors wear plain black gowns, which have flat, square collars at the back and long- hanging sleeves. They are similar in overall style to gowns worn by QCs, except that the QC's gown is made of silk. Junior barristers also wear black gowns, but they are different in style, having small gathered pleats at the shoulders and baggy wide sleeves. Whereas solicitors and junior barristers wear ordinary suits under their gowns, QCs wear a special *court coat* and waist-coat. The court coat is a tailcoat and is similar to the jacket worn by a man wearing 'tails', except that it has no collar and is studded with (over 50) small, black, cloth-covered buttons.

JUDGES

Judges' robes vary considerably.

High Court judges have several different sets of robes—depending on whether they are trying civil or criminal cases, and whether it is summer or winter. Their most familiar robes are the scarlet robes worn when they try criminal cases, but a full set of the High Court judge's robes makes daunting reading. It includes: '*Full-bottomed wig, small bench wig, scarlet cloth and fur robe mantle and hood, black cloth and fur robe, scarlet cloth and silk robe mantle and hood, purple cloth and silk robe, scarlet tippet [sash], black silk scarf, silk girdle [belt], black silk gown, robe case, wig case and black cloth cap [for death sentences!].*'

Judges who sit in the Court of Appeal, like QCs, wear plain black gowns over their court dress. The Law Lords sitting in the House of Lords and the Privy Council do not wear special robes at all—simply ordinary suits. One Law Lord, Lord Millett, wrote to *The Times*: '*English judges are an eccentric lot. When I had a full head of hair I wore a wig. Now I have no hair, I have dispensed with my wig.*' The ceremonial robe of the Lords Justices and the Law Lords is a magnificent con-coction of black and gold—a splendid black cloth woven with a flowered design (damask), heavily embroidered with gold lace. This is not the half of it—the ceremonial dress of *all* the judges and QCs includes full-bottomed wigs (shoulder length) lace jabots (collar ruffs), black knee-breeches (worn with black stockings or tights), and patent black leather shoes with silver buckles.

To the ceremonial dress of the Lord Chief Justice is added the 'Collar of SS'. This is his great chain of office. Made of solid gold, it is worn on State occa-sions. It weighs 1.5 kilos (almost four pounds), and consists of a number of links in the shape of Ss, together with other links in the shape of garter knots and roses, and two in the shape of a portcullis (castle gate). The Ss were a badge of the Royal House of Lancaster; the roses and portcullis was a Tudor badge. In times gone by, this chain was worn by the Chief Justices of the three common law courts. After the title Lord Chief Justice of England became official, only the holder of this office has worn it. The present chain was made in 1859.

In her superb biography of Sir Edward Coke, *The Lion and the Throne*, Catherine Drinker Bowen writes of the moment when he was invested with the robes of his office of Chief Justice of the Common Pleas: '*The SS collar, it was called, from the letters ornamenting it, although no one remembered what the letters meant; Coke said "Sapience [wisdom] and Science". Whatever they signified, between the golden links the figure of a spiked portcullis stood out, sharp toothed like Traitors Gate.*' The author goes on to describe Coke's stately procession out of London, when he went out on Assize: '*Trumpeters rode ahead, pikemen behind; the official train numbered fifty or more: clerks in livery, sumpters [animals carrying loads] with pack mules carrying Coke's judicial wardrobe—gowns of violet silk, of scarlet silk and black, faced with changeable taffeta for summer, in winter furred with minniver [a plain white fur]; long hoods of scarlet velvet, satin lined; a square black velvet hat . . .*' and so on!

Circuit Judges wear violet robes. If a Circuit Judge is trying a criminal case the robe is faced with a red tippet (like a sash); if the case is a civil one, a lilac tippet. Circuit judges also wear ceremonial robes on special occasions.

Women lawyers and judges wear versions of these costumes that are strikingly similar to those worn by their male counterparts. They are, however, excused the knee-breeches, and may wear skirts instead. All lawyers and judges who wear robes also wear a pair of white bands or tabs that hang down from the collar. These are after the fashion of clerical robes. They are said to have their origin in representing the two tablets of the law which Moses, the great Jewish lawgiver, prophet, and leader, brought down from the Holy Mount in Sinai.

*

Professor J. H. Baker, one of the most eminent legal historians of our age, begins his book *A History of English Judges' Robes* with these words:

> *Continuity, or at least the appearance of continuity, is a valuable asset to any legal system. People have more faith in a system which has stood the test of time, a system which was good enough for their ancestors. English law has undergone vast and sweeping changes, not least in recent years, but has managed to preserve the appearance of continuity. The robes worn by judges have undoubtedly contributed much to this pleasing illusion, for they have continued unaltered in essentials for six hundred years.*

There is now much debate in the legal profession as to whether judges and barristers should still wear wigs and gowns; or should they, for example, simply wear a gown over their ordinary, everyday clothes? Does the wearing of wigs give the impression that the law and lawyers are out of date with the times; or is it a quaint tradition worth preserving for its own sake, which also has the advantage of providing a degree of anonymity for lawyers and judges, who sometimes have to deal with dangerous criminals? Perhaps the wearing of wigs truly does 'lend dignity to the meanest appearance'—a sentiment captured by Charles Dickens in the *Old Curiosity Shop*: '*Would you care a ha'penny for the Lord Chancellor if you'd know'd him in private without his wig? Certainly not!*' In his novel, *The Small House at Allington*, Trollope also noted the psychology of an imposing costume: '*It is that same majesty that doth hedge a king . . . A bishop in his lawn, a judge on the bench, a chairman in the big-room at the end of long table, or a policeman with his bulls-eye lamp upon his beat, can all make themselves terrible by means of those appendages of majesty which have been vouchsafed to them. But how mean is the policeman in his own home . . . or the judge asleep after dinner in his own slippers.*'

So far, those who wish to keep wigs and gowns have won hands down. In 1992, Lord Taylor of Gosforth, then Lord Chief Justice, expressed some concern that the wearing of wigs and gowns in this day and age could give the wrong impression—that of an outdated legal system. The following year, when a poll was taken in the courts of the opinions of lawyers, jurors, witnesses, *and* defendants a large majority of those canvassed said that they wished to see wigs and gowns retained. (This was hardly the most scientific survey, as these people were not given the chance to see the judges and lawyers in action *without* their wigs!). In 2003, another, even wider, process of consultation took place, with illustrations being given of possible alternatives to the current court dress.

The argument goes on, and perhaps it should. It is one thing for judges and barristers appearing in the ancient courts of the Royal Courts of Justice to wear wigs and gowns. There, legal robes may be in perfect harmony with their surroundings. Today most courts are modern, functional rooms which have been built during the last thirty years. The jurors who try criminal cases may well be wearing T-shirts and jeans. The atmosphere in these courts is very different from that in the Royal Courts of Justice, or some of the other, older courts, which we rightly prize as part of our legal heritage.

In 1963, following a national scandal, Stephen Ward was charged with and convicted of offences of living off immoral earnings. He committed suicide before he was sentenced. In his compelling book, *The Trial of Stephen Ward*, Ludovic Kennedy wrote:

> *The tragedy of our courts is that means have come to count more than ends, form more than content, appearance more than reality. The antique ritual is positively harmful,*

for it drives a wedge between the citizen and the law, outlawing him as a stranger in his own land, making him a hostage to customs which he has had no share in framing. A small reform like the shedding of horsehair would be a step in the right direction; for it would enhance rather than diminish the dignity of the law. Judge and counsel would be seen as human too, and would no longer feel the need to go on acting a part which they mistakenly believe tradition demands of them; wigless, they might think twice about daring to say to a jury 'albeit' when they mean 'although', and 'avocation' when they mean 'job'.

More recently, in his book, *Judges*, the distinguished barrister and law commentator, David Pannick QC, added another eloquent voice to this topic:

The legal process is not a pageant to be admired by tourists for being old and quaint. It is, rather, a vital organ of government to be assessed by reference to its ability to further the goal of justice under the law. The masquerade of the law tends to make judges and barristers objects of ridicule. Judges cannot expect to be taken seriously as they deserve, and cannot hope to be properly respected and understood until they abandon the priestly garments that separate them from ordinary men and women.

Some senior judges have now added powerful support to the criticism of our court dress. In November 1997 Lord Irvine, the Lord Chancellor himself, said: *'Wigs project an image of the Bar and Judiciary which is old fashioned, out of touch and self satisfied'*. In 1999, Sir Richard Scott, then Vice-Chancellor and head of the Chancery Division said, *'The wearing of wigs almost encourages a cruel parody of the judicial process'*. He thought they are *'positively damaging to the image of the civil justice system'*. There have been more recent attacks on the wearing of robes. The Master of the Rolls, Lord Phillips, talking about the elaborate robes worn by a High Court judge, said: *'Because our dress stems from the days when there was no heating, in winter we wear something like Father Christmas to keep warm; then red for crime, black for civil . . . different colours and different weights for the summer and winter, and then a fifth outfit for administrative cases. Instead of the simple black gown of a QC, we have five uniforms. Ridiculous!'* He agreed that wigs should not be worn, at least in civil cases, and favours the European-style of court dress—a black gown and *faullard*, or collar.

Most forms of dress, whether uniform, costume, or just our ordinary everyday clothes, are intended to send out a message of one kind or another. The men and women who serve in the armed forces know the value of their ceremonial dress, but they tend to reserve it for ceremonial occasions. Most people agree that it would be appropriate for the judges and the advocates to wear some form of distinctive dress, but would not a simple robe suffice? The appearance of curly wigs in the setting of a modern court environment may in the eyes of some be quaint, and even endearing; it is undoubtedly ridiculous. To ordinary people who must use the courts it can also be intimidating. It certainly carries on a tradition, but perhaps this too should be reserved for ceremonial occasions.

The court system is presently in a state of great change, and there is one very practical reason why it may not be long before wigs are consigned to legal history. Solicitors are being given greater rights of audience in the higher courts. They are not permitted to wear wigs. It is going to look very odd when it becomes routine for some lawyers to wear wigs in court, while others appearing in the same case do not; and it could lead to defendants and witnesses being confused and discomfited when this happens. Legal robes are very visible. Justice must be *seen* to be done, and this should include the lawyers who appear in court in the same case being seen to dress alike. For this reason, wigs have already been discarded in many civil courts. Only time will tell whether this also happens in courts throughout the land. Barristers will then take pleasure in showing their wide-eyed grand children these weird concoctions of horsehair, and telling them about the days when they actually worked with them on their heads.

There is at least one impression of judges that we have from the cartoonists, which is a total fiction. Judges do not have wooden gavels, and therefore *never* use them to bang for order in their courts!

15

Criminal Trials through the Ages

'Gentlemen, you shall not be dismissed till we have had a verdict that the court will accept; and you shall be locked up, without meat, drink, fire and tobacco; you shall not think thus to abuse the court; we will have a verdict, by the help of God, or you shall starve for it.'

The Recorder of London, to the jury in the trial of William Penn and William Mead, 1670.

器

The history of trials in this country helps us to understand how society has changed over the centuries.

Looking back over the years, we may see our legal history as a story of superstition and ignorance, brutality and cruelty. When we come to look at criminal trials in ancient times we should remember that for many hundreds of years there was no system of education in the country, and the vast majority of people lived in conditions of appalling poverty. There was no lighting, heating, and sanitation, such as we take for granted; no proper roads or means of communication; and of course there was no police force, and little chance of investigating crime. It is therefore hardly surprising that there was a great deal of violent and drunken crime.

People lived in dark, crude, dangerous, and frightening times. As we come to look at the manner in which trials took place over the years, it may be difficult to imagine that any society could seriously believe that justice was being done, but the system of justice in being at any particular time must be seen against the background of these simple, rough, and unprotected conditions. Times change, and we might wonder whether it will be equally difficult for those who live in centuries to come to believe that our present system of justice was a good one.

VERY EARLY TIMES (BEFORE JURIES)

In very early times our laws were strongly influenced by those of two other countries. The first is now Italy: the Romans, who invaded Britain and made it part of the Roman Empire, put into force the Roman criminal law. The second is now France: the Normans, who invaded Britain (from Normandy, France) under William the Conqueror, introduced their criminal law. That is why we find that for centuries afterwards the languages of the Romans (Latin) and the Normans (French) were in regular use both in government and in the courts.

The medieval period of our history, between about AD 1000 and AD 1500, was a very important age in the development of our laws, and the form of criminal trials. It was during this time that the jury system came into being. We will look first at the forms of criminal trial in the time before juries. In doing so, we should understand that for many years the law and religion were not seen as separate, but as closely related to one another. The law was thought to have a mystic significance. The law was 'perfect'; only those who took part in it were fallible. Sir John Fortescue, a great fifteenth-century judge, agreed with the Roman view of judges as 'priests of the law' and declared that '*All judicial sentences [of punishment] are the judgment of God*'. The clergy were among the very few who were literate; and as the religious leaders of the community they naturally playing an important part in some early forms of trial.

INFANGTHIEF

This was hardly a trial at all. It was more a licence to kill. The king granted to certain influential people—usually the lords of townships who were great landowners—the right to inflict immediate punishment on anyone whose behaviour did them harm: the thief caught stealing; the man caught committing adultery—anyone believed to have been caught doing wrong could immediately be put to death, or at least be made to 'buy' his life with the payment of money. This speediest of all methods of doing 'justice' lasted for many years, and probably came to an end in the reign of Edward III (1327–77).

TRIAL BY BATTLE

Trial by battle was introduced by William the Conqueror. It was a simple contest of physical strength. If there was a dispute between two persons, they would have to fight or 'battle' until one of them either surrendered or was killed. The winner was declared to be right.

Trial by combat, or *battle* as it was commonly known, was particularly dramatic when nobles were in conflict. They would range their own private armies to do battle against one another; but this form of trial was also used by less important people. Indeed, it was one way of resolving disputes which survived the centuries, in the unofficial form of 'duelling.'

COMPURGATION

Anyone accused of crime would find that he was heavily dependent upon the opinion of his neighbours, who would know his character and be able to answer the all-important question, 'Can the oath of the defendant be relied upon?' In *compurgation*, all an accused man had to do to prove his innocence was to find a number of his friends to swear an oath that he was an honourable man and was telling the truth. They were commonly known as *oath helpers*. (Note, in these early times anyone accused of crime had to prove that he was innocent, and so, unlike the position today when the prosecution have the duty to prove guilt, the 'burden of proof' was on the defence.) No one really knows why we have 12 jurors today, but it could be that the origin of this stems from the days when a defendant had to produce 12 oath helpers to say that he was telling the truth. Compurgation in criminal cases began to decline in the reign of Henry II. Oath helpers could easily be bribed to ensure the acquittal of a guilty man, and they often did just that.

TRIAL BY ORDEAL

If *compurgation* was a form of trial favourable to a prisoner, *trial by ordeal* was quite the opposite. Once again, an accused man had to prove his innocence, but now he had to do so in the most bizarre and terrifying circumstances.

There were various kinds of trial by ordeal, but they took the same basic form. First, following an accusation of crime against a man, it had to be shown to the local people, who were known as **jurors**, that there was some evidence that he had committed the crime. If the jurors agreed that there was evidence against him, and if he denied the crime, he was required to stand trial *by ordeal* and prove his innocence.

The 'ordeal' was invariably some form of torture, which a defendant could only survive by calling upon God to prove his innocence, by working a miracle in his favour. Because of the strong religious element involved in these trials, as someone had to confirm that God had actually answered this prayer, they were supervised by priests.

- *Ordeal by fire*. The accused person might be made to hold a red-hot weight of iron, or plunge his hand or arm into boiling water. If he suffered no injury, or made a quick and complete recovery, then God had worked a miracle for him and he had proved his innocence. If not, he was condemned as a guilty man.

- *Ordeal by water*. The most common of these trials was ordeal by water. The *water ordeal* was the form of trial in countries throughout Europe. The accused person would be bound and thrown into water. If he was innocent the water would 'receive him' (he would sink); but if he floated to the surface, the water had rejected him and he was guilty. There are different ideas as to whether an 'innocent' person would be rescued before he or she drowned.

In the late Middle Ages the *water ordeal* was often used as a means of trying suspected witches, although the pitiable women who were tried in this way had very little chance of survival. They were 'cross bound'—the right thumb to the left toe and the left thumb to the right toe—and thrown into water. In this way it was almost impossible for them to sink.

In early times it was very important to die 'honourably'. A person guilty of crime could be put to death; but in addition his property would be confiscated by the king, and his family left in penury and disgrace. For this reason it became the habit for some accused persons to refuse even to plead guilty or not guilty. They would remain 'mute' in order to escape a conviction and avoid this additional suffering for their families.

A special form of torture was devised even for this. It was known by the French expression *peine forte et dure* ('punishment strong and hard'). Anyone who refused to 'plead' (say whether he was guilty or not) would be laid on his back and heavy stones were placed on his body. Usually a man subjected to this terrible torture would speak, but if he still refused he would be 'pressed' by more weights until he died. This form of forcing a person into pleading guilty or not guilty was introduced in 1406. It was abolished in 1772. One of last recorded cases of its use was in 1741 at the Cambridge Assizes. There, a prisoner refused to plead to the charge against him, and after unsuccessfully trying the torture of *thumb tying*, he was pressed to death.

*

THE JURY SYSTEM

Originally jurors were always men who lived in the area where a crime had been committed. They had to decide whether a prisoner should stand trial by ordeal. This was done by summoning them to appear before justices to swear an oath to give an honest opinion about whether the prisoner was properly suspected of having committed a crime.

Henry II was particularly interested in getting local people involved in the administration of justice. He believed that those who knew both the accuser and the accused would be best qualified to say whether there was likely to be truth in the **allegation** (accusation).

In 1215, Pope Innocent III declared that trial by ordeal could no longer be said to show God's judgement, and he ordered that priests should not take part in this form of trial. Some other form of trial had to be considered. In that same year, by clause 39 of the Magna Carta, King John agreed that *'No freeman shall be taken, imprisoned, disseised [have his estate confiscated], outlawed, banished or in any way destroyed, nor will we proceed to prosecute him, except by the lawful judgment of his peers and by the law of the land'*. It is to be noted that this privilege was confined to a 'freeman'—one who possessed the freedom of a borough or city, as opposed to a slave. At this time the system of trial by jury as we know it today was unheard of; and so, contrary to popular belief, the Magna Carta does not mark the foundation of our present jury system. Nevertheless these important events paved the way towards it.

Just four years later, in 1219, during the reign of Henry III (1216–1272), the new idea of using ordinary people to help in providing justice became a significant part of our law. It is said that in a small community everyone knows everyone else's business, and practical use was made of this home truth. In their earliest form jurors were dependable local witnesses who, as men of standing in their district, were expected to know about the facts of a case. In criminal cases they were 'local accusers' who might be called upon to identify criminals; in civil cases they might decide local property disputes. Eventually, by a gradual process, it became the jurors of the neighbourhood, and not royal judges, who actually had to decide the fates of those accused of crime with their verdicts of guilty or not guilty.

Judges who travelled the country to do 'the King's Justice' would ask prisoners awaiting trial the question: *'Are you willing to put yourself upon your country?'* This meant that they were now being given the chance not to be tried by ordeal, but to be *judged* by their neighbours. These men were known by the same name—'jurors', and this new form of **jury trial** marked the early beginnings of the jury system as we know it today.

Some legal historians have questioned whether the Magna Carta is truly a statute, as we understand the expression. In a case heard in 1990 the Lord Chief Justice, Lord Lane, ruled that the *'Magna Carta is indeed a statute, with all that entails'*. The rights given by the Magna Carta were endorsed and repeated by Henry III in his statute of 1225. Chapter 29 of this statute ends with another famous expression of our liberties: *'to no one will we [the King] sell, to no one will we deny or delay, right or justice'*.

From this time onwards, right up to the first half of the twentieth century, an accused person would first face the *grand jury*, which would decide if he should be tried at all. If the grand jury decided that he should, a *petit jury* then had to decide if he was actually guilty or not. The number of persons serving on the *grand jury* was often more than 20 (in the USA they still have *grand juries*, with 23 jurors serving on them). In 1367, it was decided that the *petit jury* should consist of 12 *men*. Their decision, or **verdict**, had to be unanimous, that is, all 12 of them had to agree.

For many years jury trials were often very unsatisfactory, and bore little resemblance to the trials we have today. Judges were very powerful, and were often impatient and ruthless with juries who could not agree. Juries were not given food and water. The poet Alexander Pope, in *The Rape of the Lock* (1712), a mock epic which satirised a quarrel between two eminent families over the theft of the lock of hair, had little doubt that many an innocent man was hanged so that jurors might get home to supper:

> *The hungry Judges soon the sentence sign,*
> *And wretches hang that Jury-men may dine.*

Worse still, from the point of view of juries, if the judge had to move on to another town, they might be *carted*, that is literally put in a cart and made to follow the judge on his journey. In days when most people never travelled more than a few miles from their homes, we may imagine how frightening a prospect this must have been for them, and how great was the pressure to decide the case quickly. Judges did not, however, always have everything their own way. At one time judges who tried cases at Northumberland Assizes were given 'dagger money', to buy protection for themselves and their company against Scottish raiders and the vengeful friends and relatives of criminals they had tried.

Trials usually took a very short time. Juries frequently convicted on the basis of confession evidence, and defendants often confessed under torture.

The rack

Perhaps the most notorious instrument of torture used to extract confessions was the rack. This was a horizontal frame with rollers or pulleys at each end. The victim's wrists and ankles were attached to these by ropes. If he did not give the information looked for, his body would be stretched, causing excruciating pain — sometimes to the point where limbs would be dislocated. The rack was normally used only on the highest authority, that of the monarch. We find that Queen Elizabeth I herself signed a warrant on 15 September 1571 addressed to *'our trusty and well beloved councillor Sir Thomas Smith, knight and to our trusty and beloved Doctor Wilson to examine [question] Barker and Bannister'*. (They were two of the Duke of Norfolk's men — he was suspected of treason.) The warrant is addressed to them 'at the Tower' [of London], and reads:

> *And if they shall not seem to you to confess plainly their knowledge of the truth without torture then we warrant to cause them both, or either of them, to be brought to the rack, and first to move them with fear thereof to deal plainly in their answers. And if that shall not move them, then you shall cause them to be put to the rack, and to feel the taste thereof until they shall deal more plainly.*

It was not until 1628 that Sir Thomas Richardson, as Chief Justice of the King's Bench, ruled that the use of the rack to obtain a confession was unlawful.

In the great State Trials for treason or other serious crimes, all but the bravest juries would return the guilty verdicts expected of them. The trials of most defendants who were charged with treason were little more than a formality, a conviction in a matter of minutes being a foregone conclusion.

Treason has always been regarded as the ultimate crime against the Crown (the King or Queen's person). To kill or plot to kill the monarch (known as 'encompassing the King's death') was treason. It was also treason to commit crime against the Crown as the embodiment of the 'nation State'. In practice this meant that any effort or plot to prevent the monarch and his government from carrying out the monarch's policies could be regarded as treasonable.

In cases of treason, especially severe laws and rules of procedure were in force. Deeds could of course be treasonable, but for many years so could words, and it was easy for a clever State prosecutor to learn of a chance remark, have it misheard or misinterpreted and then twist it — or, as we might say today, 'spin' it — into evidence of treason. As if this were not enough, those accused of treason had great obstacles placed in the way of a fair trial. They could not be represented by a lawyer, nor could they call witnesses. Little was left to chance. In his biography *Elizabeth I*, David Starkey describes how, following a rebellion during the reign of her half-sister Mary, Sir James Croft was tried for treason, but as only eight of the 12 jurors were prepared to condemn him, the rest were dismissed and *'four others, more compliant and of inferior quality, were empanelled to secure his conviction'*.

One of the most notorious State Trials was that of the great Elizabethan seaman and adventurer, Sir Walter Raleigh.

The trial of Raleigh

In 1603, at the beginning of the reign of James I, Raleigh was tried for treason. The trial was held at Winchester, because London was then in the grip of plague. Raleigh pleaded not guilty and 'put himself upon his country'. His jury consisted of 12 men, including four knights. They had been specially chosen by the Sheriff (the King's representative in the County) as being 'dependable'. The Attorney-General, Sir Edward Coke, conducted the case for the prosecution.

From beginning to end the trial was monstrously unfair—a shameful travesty of justice. Coke made wild accusations against Raleigh, and added fuel to the flames with deliberately inflammatory language. The case against him was supported by little or no evidence; and he was not given a proper opportunity to present his defence.

The hand-picked jury took only 15 minutes to find Raleigh guilty of treason. He was duly sentenced to death, but after a period of imprisonment in the Tower of London he was, for political reasons, allowed his freedom. After many adventures, and again for political reasons, he was arrested and imprisoned. In 1618, some 15 years after his trial, and after yet more judges had decided that the original death sentence was still in force, he was executed.

Raleigh's jury reached its verdict after only a few minutes, and it was by no means unusual in State Trials for the jury not to retire at all, but to announce their guilty verdict immediately. (We have learned that at the trial of Crippen for capital murder in 1910 the jury convicted him in less than half an hour. When we come to look at some more twentieth-century cases at the end of this book, it will be interesting to note for how long, or rather how short a time, juries were out considering their verdicts in cases which inevitably led to sentence of death.) Trials for treason throughout the ages have a particularly bad reputation, and we should realise that some 'modern' treason trials have also been much criticised.

Nevertheless, as the years went by juries trying criminal cases did become increasingly courageous and independent. They may not have realised it at the time, but by bravely standing up against unfair prosecutions and oppressive judges they had a vitally important effect on the development of our liberties. One of the most important cases in which a jury's courage advanced the cause of freedom was *Bushell's Case*:

Bushell's Case

In 1670, William Penn and William Mead were tried for preaching to an unlawful assembly. They were two devout Christians and peace-loving men who belonged to the Quaker sect, whose members are also known as 'Friends'. (William Penn was later to set sail for America, and the State of Pennsylvania is named after him.) After attending a service in a Friends Meeting House they were accused of breaking a law which made it a crime to attend 'conspiratorial gatherings'.

The trial was a disgrace and it began with a farce. The two men had lost their hats when they were arrested. The Lord Mayor, who was present in court, ordered hats to be put on their heads. Then the judge, who was the Recorder of London, fined each of them for disrespect to the court by wearing them! When William Penn demanded to know what he had done wrong, he was ordered to be locked away in an area at the back of the court.

The evidence against Penn and Mead was worthless, and the judge's summing-up extremely unfair. When the jury refused to find the two men guilty they too were threatened and insulted. They were ordered to be locked up without food and drink; and when on the third day they found the men not guilty, they were all fined.

Eight of the jurors paid their fines, but four, led by Edward Bushell, refused to pay, and spent months in prison. At last the case came before Chief Justice Vaughan, who ruled that juries had the right to *'give their verdict according to their convictions'*, and no jury could ever be punished for its verdict.

Only 18 years later—a tiny fraction of time in our legal history—another jury put its new-found power to such use that it helped to bring down an unpopular king, and led to a landmark reform in our constitutional law:

The Trial of the Seven Bishops

James II was a tyrannical monarch, bent on overthrowing the constitution. In 1688, he had seven bishops, including the Archbishop of Canterbury, prosecuted for 'seditious libel'—the offence of publishing words exciting disaffection against the Crown. For once James was behaving reasonably. It was a time of fierce anti-Catholic feeling, and James, a Catholic himself, had ordered the reading in church of a 'declaration of indulgence', pleading for more tolerance towards Catholics.

James was also set upon abolishing the power of the ecclesiastical courts. The 'crime' which the bishops committed was to petition him against the forced reading of the declaration. James said the petition itself was seditious libel. He had the bishops imprisoned in the Tower. By this time he was so deeply unpopular with Parliament, the Church, and the people that when at last they came to trial, amidst great public rejoicing, the jury found the bishops not guilty.

A plot to oust James was already under way. The jury's verdict was taken as the signal the plotters needed. On the very day of the verdict a written 'invitation' was sent to his son-in-law, William of Orange (then part of the Netherlands), to *'come to England to redress grievances'*—a polite way of inviting rebellion. William accepted, and on 5 November he landed with an English and Dutch army of 15,000 men. They quickly gained a huge following. James fled the country. Parliament declared the throne vacant, and the following February William and Mary (James's daughter) were proclaimed King and Queen. Shortly afterwards (see Chapter 4), major constitutional freedoms were guaranteed in the Bill of Rights 1689.

Since *Bushell's Case*, the vital principle that juries could never be punished for their verdict has been affirmed many times by the judges. In 1784, Lord Chief Justice Mansfield said that a judge could tell a jury how to do right, *'but they had it in their power to do wrong, which is entirely a matter between God and their consciences'*. Not long afterwards these words became particularly meaningful, for at the time of the French Revolution, the English Parliament, terrified that rebellion might spread across the Channel, passed harsh laws forbidding any criticism of the King and State. A number of people were prosecuted for their 'treasonable' writings, but they were usually found not guilty by independent-minded juries who hated these new, repressive laws.

In the first part of the following century another fundamental principle of the English criminal law was established—after two sensational murder trials, and one unpopular jury verdict. This principle concerned the defence of insanity, and the circumstances of these cases bore a remarkable similarity:

The defence of insanity

It was always our ancient common law that a man could not be executed if he was insane. What if he was insane at the time of the act of which he was accused, rather than the time of his execution; and what was meant by insanity?

- In 1812, John Bellingham stood trial at the Old Bailey for murdering Spencer Perceval, the Prime Minister. The law took its course with devastating speed: Bellingham shot Perceval in the lobby of the House of Commons on a Monday at 5.15 p.m. He was tried the same Friday, and executed at 8.00 a.m. the following Monday—less than a week after the killing. His counsel tried to persuade the jury that Bellingham might have been insane. In his summing-up the Lord Chief Justice asked them this question: *'Had the prisoner possessed sufficient understanding to distinguish good from evil, right from wrong?'*

- In 1843 Daniel M'Naughten killed a man named Drummond, who was private secretary to Sir Robert Peel (then Prime Minister)—almost certainly in mistake for Peel himself. His trial for murder aroused great public interest, but the verdict came as a shock, for M'Naughten was acquitted on the grounds that he was insane.

The outcry caused by the M'Naughten verdict led the House of Lords to ask the judges to consider certain specific questions regarding persons said to have 'insane delusions'. The judges' reply, which was expressed in the form of 'Answers' to these questions (and not a judgment of a court), was that:

> *The jury ought to be told in all cases that every man is presumed to be sane ... unless the contrary be proved to their satisfaction; and that, to establish a defence on the ground of insanity, it must be clearly proved that, at the time of the committing of the act, the party accused was labouring under such a defect of reason, from disease of the mind, as not to know the nature and quality of the act he was doing, or, if he did know it, that he did not know what he was doing was wrong.*

These tests, to be applied when deciding if a defendant has a defence on the ground of insanity, became part of the common law, and have been known ever since as *'The M'Naughten Rules'*. Despite much consideration in many later cases, and much critical analysis, they still remain the law both in England and in much of the English-speaking world.

*

There have been many changes in the jury system over the years. For example, as from 1705, jurors no longer had to come from the defendant's home area. (Jury trial was for centuries also an accepted way of trying many civil cases, although the use of juries in most civil cases came to an end with the Common Law Procedure Act 1854.) In the twentieth century, many more important changes were made. Women were permitted to serve on juries. More recently, the law relating to jury challenges has been altered. At one time it was possible for defendants in criminal trials to challenge (excuse from service) up to seven jurors without giving any reason. That number was reduced to two, and now defendants objecting to *any* jurors trying their cases must give some good reason for their objection. This means that, unlike in the USA, where it can sometimes take days or even weeks to 'swear in' 12 jurors, who may first be subjected to personal and undignified questioning about their beliefs, in England a jury is selected at random and is usually 'sworn in' in a few minutes.

Even to this day important refinements are being made to the jury system. In the Criminal Justice Act 1967, Parliament introduced **majority verdicts** (see Chapter 17). Until recently, once juries retired to consider their verdicts, they had to remain under the watchful eye of the **jury bailiff** (usher sworn to guard them against interference) until they had finished. The Criminal Justice and Public Order Act 1994 has altered this law, and once juries have been sent out to consider their verdicts, they no longer have to stay late at court, or be taken to hotels. The judge may now permit them to **separate**—go home and come back to court to carry on their work the next day.

*

Jurors are ordinary men and women who are selected to serve by ballot. So great is the task of managing juries throughout the country that a computerised system of calling them for service is now in operation. Jurors often make a considerable sacrifice by coming to court to perform their important public duty. Some of the cases they try may be harrowing, or may last for many weeks, taking them away from their work. In Northern Ireland, in recent times, judges have sat alone (without juries) to try 'terrorist cases', to counter fear for the safety of jurors, or that under intimidation the criminal justice system would break down. When it seemed that peace was returning to Northern Ireland, one of the first changes under consideration was a return of the jury system in all cases.

There have always been critics of our jury system. It has been suggested that the age limit be raised, because jurors who are only 18 years old are too inexperienced in life to try cases. It has been said that a jury is an unsuitable means of trying long and complex fraud cases. We have seen that the jury system is constantly changing and developing, and no doubt this process will continue.

We may agree that the defendant's right to be tried by jury is a very important symbol of our democracy. The fact that ordinary members of the public should be personally involved in the administration of justice creates public confidence that our system is an open and fair one. The great power given to juries to reach whatever verdict they believe to be right makes them a hallowed part of our constitution. Why should we cherish this power? Could it ever be right for a jury to do wrong (return the wrong verdict)? Of course, this is not intended to mean that in an ordinary case a jury should ever decide to return the wrong verdict just for the sake of it. Jurors themselves swear an oath to *faithfully try the defendant and return a true verdict according to the evidence*. It simply means that juries have the ability in an appropriate case to act as our guardians against unfairness and oppression—that of either an unfair and oppressive law or an unfair and oppressive prosecution, or even an unfairly conducted trial—and it is left to them to decide.

In recent times there have been strong moves to reduce the right to trial by jury. In 2001, Lord Justice Auld in his *Review of the Criminal Courts* proposed that the structure of the criminal courts be changed, and that the right to trial by jury should not be available to people charged with less serious crimes of dishonesty and violence. These proposals, and others like them, have met with fierce resistance from those who believe that any further shrinking of the right of trial by jury would amount to a serious denial of a basic civil liberty. The right of jury trial has already been removed for certain types of crime (for example, driving under the influence of drink and minor cases of causing criminal damage), and some fear that this further step may be just another along the road to the total abolition of juries. There may be strong practical arguments in favour of petty cases being tried in the magistrates' courts, but when it comes to crimes for which substantial sentences of imprisonment may be passed, different considerations apply, and those who claim to understand the real value of the jury system, and the protection it affords, stand firm against them.

There are two ways in which the Government presently proposes to diminish the right to jury trial. Only time will tell whether in due course these will be implemented, and become law. The first is to permit trials on indictment without a jury in certain cases: where a judge decides that there is a real and present danger of jury tampering, or where a case is likely to be so long and complex that it would place an excessive burden on the life of a typical juror. The second is to increase the sentencing powers of magistrates so that they would be able to try many cases which up to now have been tried by a judge and jury.

Lord Devlin and Lord Denning were two of the most distinguished judges of the twentieth century. Both were convinced that juries are 'the grand bulwark' ensuring the protection of our liberties. Lord Devlin in his book *Trial by Jury* wrote:

> *The first object of any tyrant in Whitehall would be to make Parliament utterly subservient to his will; and the next to overthrow or diminish trial by jury, for no tyrant could afford to leave a subject's freedom in the hands of twelve of his countrymen. So that trial by jury is more than an instrument of justice and more than one wheel of the constitution: it is the lamp that shows that freedom lives.*

Many lawyers and legal commentators believe that these resounding and oft-quoted words should be the last ones on the subject, but they are not. There is a strong body of opinion that we should replace parts of the jury system in certain types of case with a system which is less expensive and more efficient. It is true that the jury system has its defects, as does any system. Doubtless, it can be improved upon, and one of the most important improvements we could make is to treat jurors with more respect and consideration. Those who advocate drastic change may not fully understand that our 'adversarial' system of justice, where the parties investigate their own cases and call their own evidence, is geared to trial by jury and not to trial by judge. Trial by judge alone is geared to an 'inquisitorial' system, where it is accepted that judges themselves become involved in investigating crime and calling evidence (for the difference between these systems, see Chapter 17).

It may be that a system of trial by judge alone would be less expensive and more 'efficient', whatever that may mean. The jury system is, however, deeply embedded in our social culture and constitution. It is perhaps the best opportunity any citizen has to identify with and perform his or her public duty; and because it involves the public so directly, generally it has the confidence of the public. It is also an important feature of attempts to secure equality of treatment, and confidence in the justice system of all those from so-called ethnic minorities. After all, there may be very few black or Asian judges, but there are tens of thousands of black and Asian jurors, and jurors are the real judges in Crown Court trials. Trial by jury is a vital and indispensable part of the constitution because, for all its faults, it has the advantage over any other system of being profoundly democratic, social, and fair, and profoundly reassuring.

16

Punishments Through the Ages

'I went out to Charing Cross, to see Major General Harrison hanged, drawn and quartered—which was done there—he looking as cheerfully as any man could in that condition.'
Samuel Pepys, *Diary*, 13 October 1660.

*

When we had a look at the story of trials in this country, we saw some of the terrible things that could happen to those who claimed to be innocent of the charges against them. As for those who confessed (often under torture) or who were found guilty, the punishments that many suffered seem to us to be totally barbaric. Readers who enjoy watching horror films or visiting shows such as the London Dungeon or the Chamber of Horrors at Madame Tussaud's will be interested in the gory details. Those who prefer more delicate pursuits may wish to turn to the next chapter.

It may, however, be of value to learn something of the inhumanities of the past, if only in the hope that by doing so we may ensure that they are never again repeated. These are not just fine words. If we look at legal systems around the world today, we find that terrible things are still happening to people convicted of crime—punishments which take us straight back to the Dark Ages and remind us that, for all our advances in culture and science, much remains to be done to live up to Sir Winston Churchill's warning that *'the measure of a country's civilisation is the way it treats its prisoners'*.

Just as it was important to remember the conditions in which people lived when we looked at trials through the ages, as we look at punishments we must appreciate that, in a sense, life was much cheaper than it is today. Violent punishments were very common, and were accepted as a normal way of life. The average life span was much lower. In medieval England it was just over 30 years; by the late nineteenth century it was still under 50 years. At childbirth, death for both mother and child was always a grave risk, and the rate of infant mortality was very high. Effective medicine was almost unheard of, and if the hangman didn't get you, there was always the prospect that some disease (with which we could now deal quite easily) would.

Human beings have unfortunately proved to be at their most imaginative and inventive when it has come to inflicting punishment upon their fellow men and women. Our own history of punishments has been as savage and inhumane as that of many other nations. It is a story of three main types of punishment: **capital punishment** (the death penalty), **loss of liberty** (imprisonment and transportation), and **corporal punishment** (physical violence such as floggings, whippings, the pillory, and the ducking stool).

CAPITAL PUNISHMENT

In early times a superstitious belief in omens, ghosts, witchcraft, and the like was very common. Many people lived their lives in the grip of superstitions. It was tempting and easy to blame misfortune on somebody else, and harmless, sometimes senile old women were often the targets, being accused of all kinds of witchcraft. 'Witches' were frequently hanged or burnt at the stake. Matthew Hopkins, the 'witch-finder' of Essex, Suffolk, Norfolk, and Hunting-donshire, in one year was responsible for the hanging of 60 'witches' in Essex alone. It was estimated that between 1643 and 1661 over 4,000 people suffered death for witchcraft.

Trial of the Suffolk witches

In 1665, a trial was held which became known as the 'trial of the Suffolk witches'. Two elderly women, Rose Cullender and Amy Dunny, were tried for witchcraft. They had had a quarrel with the parents of some children. These parents then claimed that their children had been bewitched.

The children were declared too young to give evidence, but the sort of nonsense evidence the court received included that of their aunt who swore—although she admitted that she had not seen it herself—that '*a little thing like a bee flew upon the face*' of one of the children who, then '*vomited a nail with a broken head. The bee then brought this nail and forced it into her mouth*'. These wretched old ladies were both convicted of witchcraft, and were hanged.

In the days before newspapers, radio, and television, only a tiny minority of the population could read. If you didn't enjoy mystery plays or morris dancing, trials and public ceremonies of hanging and mutilation were the major form of entertainment. Important executions were used as an excuse for public holidays. Some executioners were given star status, and being an executioner was a highly sought-after occupation—so highly prized that the 'business' was even handed down from father to son.

At one time the gallows were given the name 'Gregorian Tree', after three successive hangmen: Gregory Senior, Gregory Junior, and Gregory Brandon. Gregory Brandon, public executioner, was so highly esteemed that he was granted his own coat of arms. He was the father of Richard Brandon, who was reputed to have executed King Charles I. The executioner Thomas Cheshire was 'wittily' known throughout the country as 'Old Cheese'.

Another famous executioner, in the late seventeenth century, was Jack Ketch. He was known for his bungling of executions and for his 'gallows humour'—the black humour associated with the terrible punishments of the times. In *Pickwick Papers*, Charles Dickens introduces Sam Weller as a boot-cleaner at the Pickwick Club. When we first meet Sam he is refusing to oblige a customer by cleaning his boots out of turn. He tells him, '*No, no, reg'lar rotation, as Jack Ketch said when he tied men up. Sorry to keep you waitin', sir, but I'll attend to you directly.*'

The wages of executioners may seem small. In the reign of James I, the fee was set at 13 pence per hanging, plus two pence for the rope. Noblemen who were beheaded were expected to pay the headsman £7 to £10 for doing a good, clean job, although they were hardly in a position to complain if he failed. The skill of the executioner and the state of his axe or sword mattered. When Sir Walter Raleigh was on the scaffold he asked to inspect the axe. After testing the blade with his thumb, he expressed his satisfaction, saying, '*This is a sharp medicine, but it will cure all diseases*'. Executioners in the 1950s were paid 15 guineas (£15. 15s., now worth over £200) for their 'work'. We might wonder if they did it for the money.

The execution of Lord Ferrers

Money certainly seemed to be of the greatest importance to the executioner of Lord Ferrers. In 1760 Ferrers was tried by his peers in Westminster Hall for murdering his steward, John Johnson. He was convicted despite his attempted defence of insanity. As he pointed out to the court, if a man has to argue his own insanity, he will lose either way—whether he 'argues lucidly or badly'.

Ferrers was the last nobleman to be sentenced to a felon's death—to be hanged in public at Tyburn. The event attracted such record crowds that the cart carrying him to the scaffold took several hours to get there. Even then his ordeal was prolonged, for he had mistakenly given five guineas to the executioner's assistant, and had to watch as the two men argued over who was to get the money before he was dispatched.

Still, it may be that at one time the pay for executioners was quite good, simply because there was so much work about. It is estimated that during the reign of Henry VIII (reigned 1509–47) well over 70,000 executions took place. Many of these have rightly been described as 'judicial murders', with innocent men and women being sentenced to death on trumped-up charges, simply because their presence on earth was inconvenient to the king. Among the many who were beheaded were two of Henry's wives. An executioner specially summoned from Calais was paid £24 to behead his second wife, Anne Boleyn. In her book *The Six Wives of Henry VIII* Antonia Fraser tells of Anne's last moments on Tower Green:

> To watchers it then seemed that 'suddenly the hangman smote off her head at a stroke' with his sword which appeared by magic, unnoticed by anyone including the kneeling woman. In fact the famous 'Sword of Calais' had been concealed in the straw surrounding the block. In order to get Anne to position her head correctly, and stop her looking instinctively backwards, the hangman had called 'Bring me my sword' to someone standing on the steps nearby. Anne Boleyn turned her head. The deed was done.

During the next three hundred years the slaughter continued. One notoriously cruel judge was Judge Jeffreys. In 1683 he was made Chief Justice. In 1685 Charles II died, and James II ascended the throne. James, Duke of Monmouth mounted a rebellion against the new king. Monmouth was unsuccessful, and many who were accused of being his followers were tried at the 'Bloody Assizes' held by Judge Jeffreys in the West Country. There, he sentenced literally hundreds of people to death, and many more to transportation abroad, where they were sold into slavery.

James II was so satisfied with Jeffreys' ruthlessness that he soon afterwards made him Lord Chancellor. The Duke of Monmouth was himself sentenced to death, and had the doubtful honour of being executed by Jack Ketch. It was one of Ketch's worst efforts. This is an account of what actually happened:

> The Duke had given Ketch six guineas to ensure that the blade of the axe was sharp, and to cause him the least possible pain. In fact the blade was not sharp, and the first stroke merely wounded his neck, causing the Duke to look Ketch in the face. This seems to have completely unnerved him, for the second blow was hardly more effective. After the third, Ketch threw down the axe crying 'God damn me I can do no more'. The crowd now started to howl for Ketch's blood, and he was ordered to carry on. Monmouth died only after the fifth stroke of the axe.

Judge Jeffreys was infamous, but not only for his harsh sentences. His reputation for cruelty extended to savouring the spectacle of executions themselves. On the River Thames, between Wapping New Stairs and King Edward's Stairs, stood the site of Execution Dock, where pirates were hanged '*at low water mark, and there to remain until three tides had overflowed them*'. Judge Jeffreys was a regular spectator at these events, watching from the wooden balcony over the tideway in the historic *Prospect of Whitby* tavern (built in 1520, it still stands as a public house). It was to this area of Wapping that Jeffreys escaped following the overthrow of James II. There he was captured, narrowly escaping a lynching. He was imprisoned in the Tower, where he was kept for his own protection, and where he died in 1689.

If beheadings were bungled, hangings were hardly scientific affairs. Due to the short 'drop', death was rarely instantaneous. Many a convict died by strangulation, a sight of prolonged struggling. Callous onlookers would bet on how long the dangling convict would do the 'Newgate Jig' before succumbing. Sometimes the hangman, sometimes even relatives and friends of the condemned man, would go beneath the scaffold and hang onto his legs to hasten death—said to be the origin of the phrase 'hangers-on'. In Chapter 15 we learned of the trial of John Bellingham, for the murder of Spencer Perceval. An eye-witness account of his execution in *The Times*, 19 May 1812, reads '*the clock struck eight, and while it was striking the seventh time, the Clergyman and Bellingham, both fervently praying, the supporters [wooden supports] of the scaffold were struck away and Bellingham dropped. He did not struggle at first, and very little afterwards, the executioners below pulling his legs that he might die quickly.*' It was not until the mid-part of the nineteenth century that the executioner William Marwood 'perfected' the long-drop method, which allowed an extra length of rope and was designed to and did (usually) ensure almost instantaneous death.

As late as the nineteenth century there were, in theory, no fewer than 220 offences for which men and women could be hanged. These included such 'crimes' as '*appearing in disguise on a public road . . . stealing sheep . . . shooting rabbits . . . stealing anything of the value of five shillings or more, and writing letters extorting money*'. Children too could be sentenced to death, and there are many recorded cases of children being publicly hanged. In 1801 a boy aged 13 was executed for housebreaking and stealing a spoon. In 1808 a girl aged seven was publicly hanged at Lynn. Sentences of death were being passed on children as late as 1833. In 1834 Lord Eldon (the ex-Lord Chancellor) boasted that he had '*been His Majesty's advisor for twenty-five years and as far as my knowledge extends, mercy has never been refused in any instance where it ought not to have been withheld*'.

Executions in England have never lacked 'theatre'. In the thirteenth century the English devised the penalty of 'hanging, drawing and quartering'. This was usually reserved for cases of High Treason, although it did not seem difficult for imaginative lawyers to find some way to ensure that anyone who offended the monarch might be found guilty of this crime. The words used by judges when sentencing in these cases express the fate that was to befall the condemned man. He was sentenced to be: '*dragged along the surface of the ground tied to the tail of a horse, and "drawn" to the gallows and there "hanged" by*

the neck until he be half dead, and then cut down; and his entrails be cut out of his
body and burnt by the executioner; then his head is to be cut off, his body divided
into "quarters" to be set up in some open places directed.' When these sentences
were carried out, important landmarks, such as London Bridge, were used as
display areas for heads and limbs as a grim warning to others.

- At the trial of Guy Fawkes and his fellow conspirators in the 'Gunpowder Plot', the
  chief prosecutor, the Attorney-General Sir Edward Coke (whom we met as the prosecutor in the trial of Raleigh), described in gruesome and flowery language his own
  reasons for demanding this terrible punishment. It was inflicted on Thomas Winter,
  Ambrose Rookwood, Robert Keyes, and Guy Fawkes on 31 January 1606. The place of
  execution was Old Palace Yard—directly opposite Parliament House—with
  Rookwood, Keyes, and Fawkes being forced to watch the barbarous fate of the others
  who were executed before them.

- One of the last convicts sentenced to be 'drawn and quartered' was a 70-year-old
  man with a mental illness. On 19 June 1832, King William IV and his royal party
  attended the races at Ascot. There in the crowd was Dennis Collins, described as 'old
  and decrepit, with a wooden leg and the tattered garb of a sailor'. As the King
  stepped forward to acknowledge the cheers of his subjects Collins threw two stones
  at him; one hit him on the face. Collins was immediately set upon and dragged
  before the Chief Magistrate of Westminster, who, as luck would have it, was attending the races that day. The Magistrate held court in a room beneath the grandstand.
  There he committed Collins to Reading Jail and to stand his trial at Abingdon Assizes,
  where a few days later he was convicted of High Treason and sentenced to death by
  'drawing and quartering'. Having regard to his age, mental state and excellent service in the Navy, the sentence was later commuted (reduced) to transportation for
  life.

At various stages of our history, many men and women were killed for their
religious beliefs and so became martyrs for their faith. Sir Thomas More, a
Lord Chancellor in the reign of Henry VIII, was beheaded for insisting that
the Pope and not the King was the Head of the Church. Not long afterwards
the tables were turned. When Henry's Roman Catholic daughter Mary Tudor
came to the throne, Bishops Hugh Latimer and Nicholas Ridley were burnt at
the stake because they refused to acknowledge that the Pope was the Head of
the Church. Shortly afterwards, Archbishop Cranmer met the same fate. The
shocking stories of their deaths, and the deaths of many more who died for
their religion, were told with almost loving attention to detail by John Foxe in
his *Book of Martyrs*. Many superstitions grew out of these gruesome events.
The rope used to hang convicts was used to touch people suffering from illness—to 'cure them'. Worse still, after executions it became the practice (for
payment, of course) to allow members of the crowd to touch the bodies for

this purpose. In the mid-seventeenth century the severed hand of an executed convict—'to be used in the cure of diseases and the prevention of misfortunes'—could command as much as 10 guineas. These events are not accepted by everyone to be mere superstitions. Over 300 years later, it was said that one of these relics actually saved a man's life:

- In July 1995, *The Times* recounted the story of another martyr. In 1679 John Kemble was 'drawn and quartered' for his religious beliefs. In 1970 he was canonised by Pope Paul VI. It seems that when Kemble was executed one of his hands was hacked from his body and was thrown to the crowd. It was caught by a woman, kept by her, and has been preserved as a religious relic ever since. Reputed to have been used as the instrument of a number of healing miracles, it is said in the report to have been laid on the head of a Benedictine monk who had suffered a stroke. He had been in a coma and was not expected to live, but within a few days of being touched by St John Kemble's 'hand' he had recovered, and was walking and talking.

It would seem that in each age, as the treatment of criminals reached a climax of harshness and brutality, society somehow reacted against it and developed a way of relieving the terrible barbarities. In the twelfth century it became the practice for any member of the clergy charged with an offence to be tried by the Church courts. These courts did not pass sentence of death. This privilege was then extended to employees of the clergy, and in the fourteenth century it was given to anyone who could read the opening words of the first verse of Psalm 51. The reasoning behind this appears to have been that at this time hardly anyone could read, and the ability to do so was associated with 'holiness'.

This method of escape from execution became known as **benefit of the clergy**, and the verse became known as the 'neck verse', because many people—even those who could not read—learned it off by heart, and in that way saved their necks. The verse which saved so many lives reads: '*Have mercy upon me, O God, according to Thy loving kindness; according unto the multitude of Thy tender mercies blot out my transgressions*'. These are not easy words for an illiterate and uneducated person to remember, but many students will acknowledge a surprising ability to learn things when feeling that one's 'life is at stake'. The *neck verse* was not available to everyone. It could not save those convicted of treason, or other very serious crimes, and from 1490 anyone who used it to escape death was branded on the thumb, and could not use it again.

- One employee of a clergyman who definitely did not 'benefit' from his position was Richard Roose. He was a cook who in 1530 was found guilty of trying to poison his employer—John Fisher, Bishop of Rochester. He had added some powder to his master's soup, which was said to have killed some beggars being fed at the Bishop's residence, and to have made the Bishop himself ill. Roose was ordered (in the spelling of the time) to be '*boyled to deathe withoute havynge any advauntage of his clargie*'.

(Bishop Fisher was himself executed five years later, like Thomas More before him, for refusing to acknowledge Henry VIII as the Head of the Church of England.)

- As late as 1765 Lord Byron, a great-uncle of the poet, was tried in the House of Lords for murder. He was found not guilty, but convicted of manslaughter. When asked why sentence for that offence should not be passed he claimed benefit of clergy, and escaped scot-free.

Benefit of the clergy was finally abolished in 1827, but it did not save the young spoon-thief and many like him from being hanged; and the crowds attending executions could be enormous. In his essay *On going to see man Hanged* the novelist William Thackeray (1811–63) wrote: '*Forty thousand persons of all marks and degrees—mechanics, gentlemen, pickpockets, members of both Houses of parliament, street walkers, newspaper writers, gather before Newgate at a very early hour*'.

As time went by, and largely thanks to the ceaseless campaigning of great reformers such as Samuel Romilly and Jeremy Bentham, the attitude of society towards the excesses of the criminal law gradually changed. The courts and the people themselves came to rebel against all the savagery. Fewer and fewer offences were punished by hanging. By 1834, the number of capital offences was reduced to 15. '*Gibbeting*'—the public display of executed corpses, was abolished in 1843.

As to the courts, in cases where the death penalty was the likely sentence juries would often acquit a defendant for whom they had sympathy, regardless of the strength of the evidence. Judges became increasingly fussy that the precise technicalities of the law should be observed. In 1840, Lord Chief Justice Denman declared that where a man had been sentenced to death, but the judge had forgotten to order that his body should be buried within the walls of the jail where he had been held, the sentence was incorrect and should be altered to imprisonment.

In 1861, the number of capital crimes was reduced to just four: murder, treason, arson in royal dockyards, and piracy with violence. The last public execution in England took place in 1868, in front of Newgate prison. The condemned man was Michael Barrett, an Irish rebel sentenced for his part in a bomb attack. The crowd sympathised with Barrett, and was so hostile towards the hangman that the execution almost caused a riot. From that time onwards, all executions were held inside prisons. As we shall see in Chapter 18, it was not until 1965 that the death penalty for murder was finally abolished; capital punishment for the remaining offences was abolished in 1998.

The history of capital punishment includes its dramatic escapes. Also, by tradition, if a hanging was unsuccessful, this was said to show a sign of divine favour, and the condemned man was reprieved.

- The greatest escapee of all time was Jack Sheppard (1702–24). A highway robber—'five times caught and four times escaped'—he became a legend in his own lifetime for his remarkable and daring escapes from the condemned cell. He was eventually hanged at Tyburn, in the presence of 20,000 spectators. Sheppard became the hero of many plays and ballads, including John Gay's *Beggar's Opera* (1728).

- In 1709, John Smith, who 'hanged for two hours', was revived by Sir William Petty, a famous surgeon. Known as 'Half-Hanged Smith', he lived for ten more years. Another extraordinary story is that of William Duell, a 16-year-old who in the eighteenth century was 'hanged' for rape and murder. As was the practice at the time, his body was bought by a local surgeon for dissection, but when he was placed on the surgeon's table Duell was found to be still breathing. He was revived, returned to prison, and later transported. Tales of horrors like this abound, and it is sometimes impossible to separate fact from fiction. In his *London—The Biography*, Peter Ackroyd writes about corpses being used to test the properties of electricity: '*One recently deceased killer was "galvanised" . . . with the result that one of his eyes opened and he raised his right hand. It is reported that the instructor . . . died that very afternoon of the shock.*'

- Another very remarkable escape, which can more easily be verified, was that of John 'Babbacombe' Lee. In November 1894, Miss Emma Keyse, a lady-in-waiting to Queen Victoria, was murdered at her home in Babbacombe, Devon. Lee had been employed by her and was charged with her murder. He denied the offence, but was nevertheless convicted at Exeter Assizes and sentenced to be hanged. Still protesting his innocence, Lee went to the gallows, but three times when the trapdoor lever was pulled it failed to open—despite working when tested before each attempt. Having survived three efforts to hang him, Lee had his sentence commuted to life imprisonment. In 1907 he was released from prison. He married in 1909 and lived the rest of his days in America, where he died in 1933, nearly 40 years after his 'execution'!

During these many centuries, in spite of appearances to the contrary, not all criminals were executed. A variety of other punishments were inflicted for less serious crimes.

IMPRISONMENT

Imprisonment has always been a favoured form of punishment. For hundreds of years the Tower of London was regarded as the premier prison in the land. Some of its more illustrious prisoners were kept in apartments, rather than cells. At the trial of (another) Bishop of Rochester in 1722, it was said to be '*generally esteemed for State prisoners, where Lords and great men are committed for their greater ease . . . else they must go into nasty country gaols, where there are no proper accommodations'*. In the nineteenth century the best-known prison was Newgate. Today the honour of being the 'flagship of the prison fleet' is claimed by Wormwood Scrubs.

In the late eighteenth century there was quite literally a prison fleet—of prison ships known as *hulks*. The old ships used to accommodate the ever-growing prison population were no longer seaworthy. Some of them were moored on the Thames off Woolwich and Deptford. There, prisoners were kept in such appalling conditions that the hulks became sickly tourist attractions. Newgate prison was particularly notorious for its insanitary conditions. In 1750 the 'unwashed prisoners of Newgate' who were brought to court for trial carried 'gaol fever' (typhus) with them. Many court users, judges and officials included, died as a result. It was thought that the way to ward off disease was to fight the foul smells with sweet-smelling flowers—the origin of the nursery rhyme, '*A ring, a ring o' roses . . .*'. To this day, by tradition, on certain days in the legal calendar judges sitting at the Old Bailey will carry small posies of flowers into court.

In fact there were relatively few prisons, and they were often grossly overcrowded. Some were little better than dungeons. Those sentenced to *hard labour* cleaned the prisons, made uniforms, and cut stone. In the nineteenth century many prisoners were made to work the tread wheel. These differed in shape and design, but the principle was similar to that of a 'hamster wheel', with the prisoners walking endlessly, turning the huge wheel to work the prison factory machinery.

Oscar Wilde

In 1895 the famous dramatist Oscar Wilde was sentenced to two years' hard labour for homosexual practices. His first months were served in Wandsworth prison. He was then transferred to Reading prison where the humane Governor, fearing for Wilde's sanity, answered his pleas and those of his friends (who included the playwright George Bernard Shaw) that he should be given special permission to write. His poem *The Ballad of Reading Gaol* has become a classic work of prison literature. One of its most quoted verses evokes the full impact of a sentence of imprisonment:

> *I know not whether Laws be right,*
> *Or whether Laws be wrong;*
> *All we know who lie in gaol*
> *Is that the wall is strong;*
> *And that each day is like a year,*
> *A year whose days are long.*

Long before his trial, Wilde had, in conversation with a friend, taken a rather different line: '*There is only one thing wore than injustice, and that is justice without a sword in her hand. When right is not might it is evil.*'

PRISON REFORM

In the eighteenth and nineteenth centuries some men and women, horrified by prison conditions, dedicated their lives to achieving reform. In fact, for all their labours, such reforms as took place came very slowly.

- *John Howard* was one of the greatest reformers. The *Howard League for Penal Reform*, which operates today, is named after him. In 1773, as High Sheriff of Bedfordshire, he was appalled by the conditions in Bedford prison. He toured prisons throughout the land, and discovered that many prisoners were actually being kept in custody longer than was necessary by jailers who would not release them until they had been paid money. As a result of his campaigning, in 1774 two Acts of Parliament were passed, one enforcing standards of cleanliness, the other providing payment for jailers, and making it an offence for them to receive money from prisoners. Even so, the improvements were far from satisfactory.

- *Elizabeth Fry* was another noted reformer. In 1813 she visited Newgate prison, and there found 300 women, with their children, who either had been tried or were waiting to be tried. They were living in terrible conditions. The filth and neglect she witnessed changed her life. From this time onwards Fry worked tirelessly in the cause of prison reform, and for the destitute.

- *Charles Dickens* was a great force for prison reform, but of a different kind. He did not actively campaign, but stirred the public conscience with his writings about the cruelties of the day. As a child of 10 living in London he had seen his father go to the Marshalsea prison for debt, and had been sent to work in a blacking factory in Hungerford Market. There he labelled bottles of blacking used for cleaning boots and shoes. At the end of each day he had to walk four miles to his lodgings in Camden Town. The experiences of the Dickens family provided the inspiration for many of his writings, and are surely the reason why he wrote so vividly about the suffering of poor children in his books. The Marshalsea prison features in his novel *Little Dorrit*. The moving and chilling account in *Great Expectations* of the death in prison of the convict Magwitch is another fine illustration of this. The two great debtors prisons in London—the King's Bench Prison and the Marshalsea, were in Southwark, south of the Thames. Imprisonment for debt was finally abolished in 1869.

We may have advanced a great deal since the days of Charles Dickens, but we shall see in Chapter 18 that to this day prison reform still remains an important issue.

TRANSPORTATION

Transportation abroad became a common form of punishment. This was particularly so in the seventeenth and eighteenth centuries, when the domestic prison service was unable to cope with all the prisoners. Large numbers were deported to America and Australia.

First they were sent to the American colonies, and by the 1760s about 1,000 'criminals' were being sent to America each year. Many of these prisoners were hardly criminals at all. In those days, you could be deported for the most trivial offences, and the movement of prisoners out of the country was exploited for commercial gain. Before the American Declaration of Independence (4 July 1776) over 30,000 men and women had been deported to Maryland and Virginia, where they were often treated like slaves. Indeed, transportation became the basis of a form of slave trade with convicts being 'purchased' in the West Indies for onward sale. The Americans, however, became increasingly hostile to this trade. Benjamin Franklin, the American statesman, was hardly sympathetic to these new immigrants. He protested: *'The instances of transported thieves advancing their fortunes is extremely rare, but of their being advanced to the gallows, the instances are plenty. Might they not well have been hanged at home?'*

The reluctance of America to accept more transported convicts led to the introduction in 1779 of the Hard Labour Bill. Convicts who would previously have been transported to America were now kept in prison, working at such useless tasks as carrying heavy stones backwards and forwards across the prison yard. One advantage of this punishment was said to be that pickpockets would lose the delicacy of touch needed to carry out their trade. The great jurist William Blackstone, who was now a judge, played a part in devising this sentence, which he described as *'a species of punishment in which Terror, Benevolence and Reformation are . . . happily blended together'*.

Transportation to the most distant colony, Australia, commenced partly in an effort to ease the crisis of prison overpopulation. In 1787, a convoy of ships left for Australia carrying over 700 convicts, including 200 women. This form of punishment continued, with the transportation of ever-increasing numbers, for many years. The main port of destination was Botany Bay. Each voyage took its terrible toll of deaths on board ship; many more met their end in the appalling conditions that awaited their arrival.

In 1853, transportation was replaced by **penal servitude**. This was a sentence of three years' imprisonment or more. Convicts were sent to prisons at Dartmoor, Parkhurst, and Peterhead, or Aylesbury for women. Broadmoor was reserved for 'criminal lunatics'. Penal servitude consisted of three stages: separate confinement, associated labour (this took place in gradual stages, with prisoners eventually being taught trades), and release on licence. This system ended in 1949.

CORPORAL PUNISHMENT

The corporal punishments which courts imposed included flogging, whipping, branding, and public humiliation in the stocks. In Tudor times the terror of robbers was so great that vagrants and beggars could be arrested by the local constable and sentenced by a Justice of the Peace to be tied to a cart and whipped *'till his or her body shall be bloody'*. An Act of 1572 provided for the punishment of 'vagabonds' with whipping and branding.

From the earliest times offenders might be placed in the *stocks*—sometimes in pairs—and have rotten food and other even less savoury things thrown at them. The *pillory* was a form of stocks into which the head or head and arms of a culprit were thrust, and in this state he was exposed to public ridicule or violence. This form of punishment could include mutilation, with the convict's ears being nailed to the pillory; it could even be murderous, with an uncontrollable crowd pelting unpopular offenders with stones. Some held in the pillory were literally stoned to death.

- In 1541 William Poyner, a Northampton man, was found guilty of perjury and was sentenced to be 'set upon the pillory at Northampton, Stamford, Oxford and Aylesbury at four several market days, with a paper [around his neck] in great letters declaring the cause of his punishment'.

- In 1597 two goldsmiths of London, Johnes and Thomas, who had 'alloyed' (mixed) silver plate with copper, were sentenced *'to wear papers here upon the pillory and to lose either [each] of them an ear on the pillory at Cheapside, and to pay either £100, and imprisonment'*.

These men, and many like them, will have been fortunate to survive their ordeals. You may be wondering if there ever was a limit to the atrocities inflicted in the name of the law (and remember the quotation from Oscar Wilde in the Preface to the first edition of this book: *'As one reads history, one is absolutely sickened, not by the crimes that the wicked have committed, but by the punishments that the good have inflicted'*). If he were alive today Mr Titus Oates would no doubt be pleased to enlighten you, if only he could bring himself to tell the truth:

- Titus Oates was a notorious rumour-monger and perjurer, described as *'the biggest liar in England'*. In 1678 he gave evidence against a number of Catholics that they were plotting to massacre Protestants, burn down London, and assassinate King Charles II. His evidence of this 'Popish Plot' led to over 30 people being executed, and Oates became a popular hero. It was later revealed to have been a pack of lies. Those executed on his word had been innocent. In 1685 Oates was sentenced to be pilloried, flogged, and imprisoned for life. His flogging—'*all around London*'—was a prolonged and merciless punishment from which he barely escaped alive. One of those implicated in the Popish Plot was Samuel Pepys, the great naval administrator and famous diarist. Pepys was imprisoned in the Tower of London, but released after six weeks, with all charges against him dropped.

- In 1732 John Waller was sentenced for perjury—he had given false evidence against several innocent people that they had robbed him. They had been convicted on his evidence, and had been in great danger of being executed before the truth was discovered. Waller was taken to the parish of St Giles's in the Fields to stand in the pillory. There the relatives of his victims were waiting for him. A contemporary report records that after no more than a few minutes '*he was most furiously pelted with large stones, pieces of bottles and cauliflower stalks, by which he was very much cut in his face and head; then a Chimney Sweeper jumped up to him and pulled him down from the Pillory and tore all his clothes off leaving only his stockings and shoes on. After that they beat him and kicked him and jumped on him as he lay on the ground till they killed him*'. Soon afterwards the Coroner's inquest sat '*on the body*' (considered the cause of death) and brought in the verdict: '*Wilful murder, with unlawful weapons*'.

The punishment of standing in the pillory was abolished in 1837. For women the law devised special delights. The *ducking stool* was in use between the early 1600s and the early 1800s as a punishment for 'scolds, witches, and prostitutes'—a *scold* being a nagging woman. It was a strong wooden armchair, into which a woman was strapped with an iron band. The chair was fastened to a long wooden beam. This was used like a seesaw on the edge of a river or pond. The woman would be ducked into the water, once or a number of times, depending on the order of the magistrates. The only redeeming feature of this punishment was that it was less severe than its predecessor, the *scold's bridle*—an iron contraption that was placed over a woman's face. It had a bar across the front that fitted into her mouth, like the *bit* on a horse's bridle, and prevented her from talking. The last recorded case of a ducking stool being used was that of Sarah Leake of Leominster, in 1817. In her case, however, the punishment lacked a certain depth, for when the stool was lowered, the pool was empty.

*

Punishments for the civilian population may have been harsh, but discipline in the army and navy was even more ferocious. For centuries there was a scale of severe penalties in the navy, designed to ensure order on board ship. The most serious penalties were available to the Admiral or Commander of the Fleet, most of which he would delegate to his Captains, and which crews were sworn to obey. They included: for murder—the culprit to be tied to the corpse of his victim and thrown into the sea, or if on land, buried alive; for stabbing another, or drawing a knife to do so—to lose a hand; for robbery and theft—to have hot pitch poured over his head and a shower of feathers shaken over him and to be cast ashore at the first point of land; for striking another with his hand—to be ducked three times; for defiance of authority, or vilifying or swearing at his fellows—to pay one ounce of silver. Captains also had authority to keep seamen in chains, deprive them of food, have them whipped, and (for blasphemy) gag them and scrape their tongues.

*

This account of punishments through the ages is by no means complete. Many books have been devoted to the subject, and the Public Record Office holds lists, which seem to be never ending, of men and women sentenced to terrible punishments. Neither is this account as bloodthirsty as it might be. Some of the eye-witness accounts of early punishments are so horrific they hardly bear repeating. You might think that the punishments described in this chapter alone were so terrible that no one would have dared to commit any crimes at all; but they did. It is interesting to wonder why, just as it is still interesting and important to ask the same question when we look at the system of punishments we have today.

17

Criminal Trials Today

'*Throughout the web of the English criminal law one golden thread is to be seen, that it is the duty of the prosecution to prove the prisoner's guilt . . .*'

Viscount Sankey, Lord Chancellor, in the House of Lords appeal in the case of *Woolmington* v *Director of Public Prosecutions*, 1935.

*

These days all **criminal** cases are heard either in the magistrates' courts or in the Crown Courts. In these courts the method of conducting a trial is basically the same, the main difference being that in the magistrates' court, magistrates try cases on their own; whereas in the Crown Court they are tried by a judge and jury. In this chapter, we shall be looking more closely at a jury trial in the **Crown Court.**

Many cities and large towns have their own Crown Court. In London there are no fewer than 12 Crown Courts. Many Crown Courts are now housed in modern buildings, but a few beautifully preserved old courts are still in use today. A visit to the remarkable Crown Court in York, with its fine carved furniture and exquisite domed ceiling, will step you back to the fabled days of the highwayman Dick Turpin.

The most famous Crown Court in the country, and possibly one of the best known in the world, is the Central Criminal Court in London. It is commonly known as the Old Bailey, being built in what used to be 'the bailey'—the name for a courtyard immediately inside a City Wall. Its dome is topped with the renowned 12-foot-high statue by Frederick Pomeroy of the *Lady of Justice*, holding her sword and scales of justice. Contrary to popular belief, she is *not* blindfolded!

The foremost court at the 'Bailey' is Court 1. It has been the scene of many of the most important criminal trials over the last century. Its interior has been re-created in countless films. Some Circuit Judges sit permanently at the Old Bailey. The most senior of these are the Recorder of London and the Common Serjeant. They wear special robes unique to their office.

All criminal trials follow the same pattern. Each trial usually takes place in 11 stages, which are quite easy to follow:

THE STAGES OF A CRIMINAL TRIAL

1 Arraignment (accusation)

2 Jury sworn in

3 Prosecution opening speech

4 Prosecution evidence

5 Defence opening speech

6 Defence evidence

7 Prosecution closing speech

8 Defence closing speech

9 Judge's summing-up

10 Jury's verdict, and if that verdict is guilty

11 Sentence

We will take a brief look at each of these stages, but first we must bear in mind that there are five vitally important principles of justice which govern every criminal trial:

- *Every person who is accused of crime must know what the accusation is.* This must be set out in writing in the form of a charge and it must state clearly what the person is alleged to have done.

- *A person can be convicted of crime only on evidence given in open court.*

  — **Evidence** means the account of events given by witnesses (from their own knowledge of the events), who must swear on oath (or solemnly affirm) that they are telling the truth.

  — **Open court** means in a court which is open to the public, that is, anyone who wishes to hear the case, including, for example, the family and friends of the defendant and the Press. Members of the public have to be over 14 years old in order to attend. They may sit in the public gallery and (it is hoped) will see for themselves that justice is being done.

- *In a criminal trial the burden of proving the defendant's guilt is always on the prosecution.* This means that it is for the prosecution to prove a defendant's guilt, not for the defendant to prove his innocence; and the prosecution must make those who have to decide what the facts of the case are (whether they be magistrates or a jury) *sure of guilt*. If they fail, the defendant must be acquitted.

- *'No man shall be condemned unheard.'* This means that whatever the case for the prosecution may be, the defendant has an equal right to have his or her case presented to the court, and to call evidence in support of that case. This was not always so. Until 1898, a defendant was not allowed to give evidence on his own behalf.

- *Trial by jury is actually a trial by judge and jury.* It is a partnership in which the two have separate parts to play—with the judge presiding over the trial and deciding all matters of law, and the jury deciding all questions of fact.

The duties of the judge and jury are therefore quite different. The judge is there to preside over the trial and to ensure that it is conducted fairly, as a referee will be in charge of a football match. He is, however, much more than a referee. He also has the very important job of deciding all matters of law and admissibility of evidence (deciding whether either side can call certain evidence). This he must do in the *absence* of the jury, because if the evidence is ruled inadmissible, the jury ought not to hear it at all.

The judge must be careful to enforce the rules relating to confessions to the police. If he believes that the confession was obtained by oppression he must 'exclude it' (make the legal ruling that it should not go before the jury). Section 78 of the Police and Criminal Evidence Act 1984 (PACE) sets out one of the most important rules of the criminal law. This is that a judge may always refuse to allow evidence to be given in court if he or she believes that *'the admission of the evidence would have such an adverse effect on the fairness of the proceedings that the court ought not to admit it'*. This means that if, for whatever reason, a judge agrees that it would *make the trial unfair* to allow any part of the evidence to count against a defendant, then the jury will not hear that evidence.

INQUISITORIAL AND ADVERSARIAL SYSTEMS

In many countries one or more judges try criminal cases alone, without juries. They have an **inquisitorial system**. In this system the judges themselves try to get at the truth by *inquiring* into the case, directing investigations, and questioning witnesses.

Our system is quite different. We have an **adversarial system**. This involves two sides, the prosecution and defence, as opponents or *adversaries*, fighting the case out before a jury—each side producing the best evidence it can in support of its case, and doing the best it can to destroy the case for the other side. The one very important qualification to this general approach is that if in a criminal case the prosecution knows of any information or evidence which might assist the defendant to present his case, they are duty bound to disclose it to the defence, and make it available to them.

The judge's responsibilities in a criminal trial are great, but the jury's role is even more important. It is the jury who must weigh up the evidence given by the witnesses and decide who to believe or disbelieve. In this way the jury actually decide all the facts of the case. As it is their duty to decide these facts 'according to the evidence', they (not the judge) must therefore say whether the defendant is guilty or not guilty.

Let us now follow the stages of a criminal trial:

1 ARRAIGNMENT (accusation)

The trial begins with the **arraignment** of the defendant. This means that the defendant is now accused in court of the offence or offences which are to be tried. This is done by the clerk of the court reading out the **indictment**, the document which contains the charge or list of the charges.

After each charge is read the defendant is asked: *'Do you plead guilty or not guilty?'* If a defendant **pleads guilty** to the charges against him, this means that he admits that he committed the offences. Then there is no need for a trial, and the judge will sentence him to the appropriate punishment (see later). If he **pleads not guilty**, he of course denies committing the offence, and we move on to the next stage.

2 SWEARING IN THE JURY

Twelve jurors are now sworn to try the case. The jury is made up of members of the public who are asked to come to court to serve on juries, usually for a period of two or three weeks.

Jurors will come from different backgrounds and different walks of life. They must be between the ages of 18 and 70, and not have any convictions themselves for any serious offence. Certain people in special categories are disqualified from sitting on juries, for example: people concerned in the administration of justice (such as judges, barristers, solicitors, police and prison officers), clergymen, and servicemen. This rule may soon be changed. People suffering from mental illness, and criminals who have been sentenced to imprisonment or to perform community service, are also disqualified. Jurors are selected at random and, provided they are not disqualified from serving, anyone can be asked.

Jurors who are chosen to serve on a jury will then be **sworn** on the holy book of their religion to try the case and give *'a true verdict according to the evidence'*. Christians will take the oath on the Bible (New Testament), Jews on the Old Testament, Muslims on the Koran, Hindus on the Gita, Sikhs on the Adi Granth. If the jurors are Quakers or Moravians, or have no religious beliefs, they will be asked to **affirm**, and permitted to make a *solemn promise* to give a true verdict according to the evidence.

A defendant has the right to **challenge** (object to) any of the jurors who are chosen to try his case, but only if he can give a good reason for the objection. For example, if a juror knows a defendant, or knows any of the witnesses in the case, that would be a good reason for objecting to him. If the judge agrees with the objection, the juror or jurors are replaced by others to make up 12.

3 PROSECUTION OPENING SPEECH

The barrister appearing for the prosecution now stands and makes a short opening statement, telling the jury what the case is all about. The purpose of this statement is to help the jury to understand what the charge is and to follow the evidence when it is given. It may be interesting to make up a simple case of our own, and see how the trial might go. In this case the barrister 'opens' his case to the jury as follows:

> Members of the jury, this defendant is charged with three offences: theft, assault, and possessing an offensive weapon, that is a large lock-knife. The prosecution say that on Wednesday 31 December 2003 he entered a pet shop where he appeared to be acting suspiciously.
>
> Eventually he was seen to withdraw a white plastic carrier bag from his pocket and place three bags of bird food into it. He started to walk out of the shop with these bags. He made no attempt to pay for them. That is why he is charged with theft.
>
> The shopkeeper shouted at him, asking what he was doing, and when she lifted up the telephone to ring for the police, the defendant jumped over the counter, pulled the telephone from her hand, and hit her. The shopkeeper was later taken to hospital, where she was treated for minor injuries to her face. That is why the defendant is charged with assault.
>
> The defendant then ran out of the shop, taking the carrier bag with him. Two customers who were inside the shop also ran out and stopped a police car which was passing by. The police found that he was in possession of a lock-knife. The prosecution say that he had it with him to cause injury. That is why he is charged with possessing an offensive weapon.
>
> The defendant has pleaded not guilty. When he was arrested by the police he said that he had not stolen anything at all. He said that he had been in the shop, and was in the process of choosing some bird-seed, because he is very fond of his 'feathered friends'. The shopkeeper had wrongly accused him of stealing, and the customers in the shop

had attacked him. As he was trying to get free, he may have hit her, but that was an accident. He could not remember taking the bags of bird-seed out of the shop. He may have, as he was in a panic and frightened of being injured, but he never intended to steal them. As for the knife, he denied that it was his, and claimed that the police must have 'planted' it on him.

It will be for you to decide what actually happened in this case. You must consider each of these charges separately. In each case before you can convict, the prosecution must make you sure that the defendant is guilty. If you are not sure you must find him not guilty. I will now call the evidence before you.

Pausing here, everyone reading this will now have a mental picture of the prosecution's case. Every mental picture will be different, and it is interesting to consider that if the jury have not been provided with photographs and plans of the scene, they will now have 12 quite different ideas of the events in question. In addition, the judge and lawyers will all have their own imagined pictures of what happened—unless the lawyers have been sensible enough to visit the scene. Still, despite this handicap, it is surprising how easy it is for everyone in court to come together in their assessment of a case. In rare cases, the jury will be taken for a 'view' of the scene.

- In 1999, legal history was made at the Old Bailey when 77-year-old Anthony Sawoniuk went on trial for war crimes. It was alleged that during the Second World War he had shot a number of innocent civilians. The judge granted a defence application to visit the scene of these events in the Republic of Belarus (part of the old Soviet Union); and so — another 'first' — for the first time in legal history a jury (together with judge, lawyers, and court officials) was flown out of the country for a 'a view' of the scene of an alleged crime.

- In 2001, during the trial of the novelist Jeffrey Archer for perjury, an Old Bailey jury was taken to view another alleged 'crime scene'; but this time it was a court—the court at the Royal Courts of Justice where the original libel action between Jeffrey Archer and the *Star* newspaper had been tried, and where it was said that he had given false evidence.

4 PROSECUTION EVIDENCE

The barrister for the prosecution now calls each of the prosecution witnesses. They give evidence from the witness box. This is almost always directly opposite the jury, so that they are facing one another, and the jury can observe the witnesses as they are giving evidence.

The victim of the offence usually goes first. In our case, this is likely to be the shopkeeper. Then the prosecution will call the other witnesses who saw what happened—the customers who were in the shop at the time. After that they will call the police officers who arrested the defendant in the street.

Finally, they will call the doctor who examined the shopkeeper at the hospital and who saw the bruises on her face, and the forensic scientist who examined the knife and found the defendant's fingerprints on the blade.

(The prosecution are not bound to call everyone who can give some evidence about the incident, but if they choose not to call a witness they must provide his or her name and address to the defence, so that the defence can call that witness if they wish to.)

When any witness is called (by either side), the same course is followed: The witness must first **swear an oath** on the holy book of his religion to tell the truth or **affirm** that he will do so. Then he gives his evidence, according to certain rules. There are always two or three stages to giving evidence:

(a) Examination in Chief

The side calling the witness (in this example the prosecution) asks questions first, in order to bring out what the witness has to say. This is the **examination in chief**. The party calling the witness is not allowed to ask questions that are designed to lead the witness into giving a particular answer. These are called **leading questions**. Therefore, in our example it would be all right to ask the shopkeeper: 'What happened on Wednesday, 31 December 2003?' It would not be proper to ask: 'On Wednesday, 31 December 2003 did the defendant enter your shop, and steal some birdseed from you?'

Another important principle relating to the type of evidence which may be given is the rule against allowing **hearsay** evidence. Witnesses may talk about what they saw and heard, but not about what other people may have told them (this is called *hearsay*). In our example, the shopkeeper who was present can of course give evidence about what happened, but the prosecution could not call her daughter as a witness to say that she was at school at the time but that her mother had told her all about it. What she said to her daughter would be *hearsay* and neither of them could tell the court about that.

In Chapter 16 we looked at the trial of the 'Suffolk witches'. The aunt who gave evidence in that case gave hearsay evidence, telling the court about all sorts of things which she claimed the children had said to her. This was obviously very unfair, because the defendants could not challenge the evidence properly, by asking questions which might demonstrate that this account was unreliable. This evidence would not be allowed in court today. The Criminal Justice Act 2003, however, makes an important alteration to this rule of evidence, for it gives a judge a discretion to allow hearsay evidence to be given in certain circumstances. He will now have the freedom to admit this type of evidence if he considers it to be 'cogent and reliable'. This still would not permit 'Suffolk-witches-type' hearsay to be given, but it will enable the court to be less rigid in its approach to hearsay evidence, where it considers there is every reason to believe that it is true.

(b) Cross-examination

The evidence of the witness may now be tested in **cross-examination** by the lawyer for the other side (in this example, the defence). The defence barrister is allowed to ask any questions provided that they are relevant to the case, including leading questions. Cross-examination is often the most interesting and exciting part of a witness's evidence, for it is the best opportunity a lawyer has to expose a witness as dishonest or unreliable.

If the defence disagrees with the witness's evidence, that should be made clear in cross-examination, and the witness should have the chance to deal with the matter. So when the shopkeeper is giving evidence, the defence lawyer would be expected to ask her about the defendant's version of events to see if she agrees with the part of it where she was involved.

(c) Re-examination

The side calling the witness now has another chance to ask the witness questions (the **re-examination**). The purpose of this is not to bring out any new evidence. It is to clear up any confusion there may have been when the witness was being cross-examined. Again, no leading questions may be asked in re-examination.

When the prosecution have called all their evidence, their case is then 'closed'. It is now possible for the defence to make a **submission** (argument) to the judge that there is no case to answer. This is called a **submission of no case** and it simply means arguing that the prosecution have failed to put reliable evidence before the court which could result in a safe verdict of guilty. If the judge agrees, he will then stop the case and direct the jury to find the defendant not guilty. If the judge disagrees, the case proceeds to its next stage.

Many 'submissions of no case' are unsuccessful, because the law is that where there is some evidence against a defendant the judge should normally leave it to the jury to decide the case. The judge is expected, however, to ensure that the jury only consider evidence which is of sufficient quality to found a safe conviction, and if the prosecution evidence is so weak that a jury could not properly convict, he should direct them to find the defendant not guilty. In Chapter 25 we will find a case where a young schoolboy was identified by a prosecution witness as being a robber. The defence did not make a 'submission of no case' at the end of the prosecution case. Nevertheless, the Court of Appeal said that the evidence was then so unsatisfactory that the judge should have stopped the case, and directed the jury to acquit.

5 DEFENCE OPENING SPEECH

After the prosecution case has finished the defence lawyer may make an opening speech, but does not have to do so. In practice defence opening speeches are rarely made. Part of the reason for this is the rather strange rule that the defence can make an opening speech only if the defendant is to be called as a witness *and* at least one other defence witness will give evidence as to what happened. So in our example, if the defendant is to be the only witness for the defence, there can be no defence opening speech.

6 THE DEFENCE EVIDENCE

The defendant may now give evidence, and his lawyer can call any witnesses to support his case. The rules for the prosecution regarding the procedure for giving evidence—Examination in chief, Cross-examination, and Re-examination—apply equally to the defence.

A defendant does not have to give evidence, but the law now is that if he does not, the jury may 'draw inferences' from his failure to do so. In other words, they may hold it against him when deciding whether he is guilty. Normally, when a defendant gives evidence he must be called as the first defence witness. This is because he is entitled to sit in court throughout the trial, and it would not be right to allow him to call witnesses, and then tailor his evidence to the evidence they have given.

The cross-examination of a defendant can be the highlight of a criminal trial. Juries will naturally be interested to see him and hear what he has to say. This is the prosecution's chance to demonstrate the case against him very directly and personally. It is often the time when the jury find that they are able to get to the truth of a case, whether it helps the prosecution or the defendant. A good cross-examination of a clever but guilty defendant can be a revealing and thrilling exercise in the art of advocacy. Unfortunately, excitement in bird-seed cases cannot be guaranteed.

What happens if a witness (whether for the prosecution or the defence) breaks his oath and tells lies? Any person who gives false evidence in court about a 'material' (important) matter may in theory be charged with the criminal offence of **perjury**, but a prosecution for perjury is rare. People are usually charged with perjury only when they have conspired together in a carefully prepared plan to give false evidence.

7 PROSECUTION CLOSING SPEECH

The prosecuting barrister will usually make a final speech to the jury explaining how, in the light of all the evidence which has been called, the prosecution say that their case is proved. He does not have to make a closing speech, and in cases where a defendant chooses to represent himself, he will rarely do so.

8 DEFENCE CLOSING SPEECH

The defence barrister always makes a closing speech, and experience shows that a good defence speech may well have a real effect on the jury's verdict. In their closing speeches barristers are allowed to comment on the evidence. Some defence closing speeches have gone down in legal history as examples of great advocacy; some even as landmark statements of our liberties.

9 JUDGE'S SUMMING-UP

There are two main parts to every summing-up:

- *The judge must first tell the jury what the law is.* This includes giving them 'legal directions' that the prosecution must prove the case so that they are sure that the defendant is guilty. He must also give directions as to what the prosecution must prove in order to make them sure. If there are several defendants charged with a number of different offences, the judge must ensure that the jury understand what the law is in each case.

  For example, in our case, dealing with the charge of *theft*, the judge must tell the jury what the prosecution must prove. He will tell them that the prosecution must make them sure of three things:

  1 The defendant took property (in our example, the bags of seed) from the shelf in the shop; and

  2 He then intended to deprive the shopkeeper of them permanently (and not return them); and

  3 When he took them he was acting dishonestly.

  If there are two or more charges the judge must tell the jury to consider them separately, each on its own merits, and make a separate decision in each case. It would therefore be possible, for example, for the jury to find our defendant guilty or not guilty of all charges, or say, guilty of theft, not guilty of assault, and guilty of possessing an offensive weapon.

- *The judge must remind the jury of the important parts of the evidence, including, of course, the evidence called by the defence.* He must do his best to give a fair and balanced summary of the facts. This does not mean that he should try to make the prosecution and the defence cases sound equally strong. Where it is clear that the evidence for one side is much stronger than the evidence for the other, a fair summing-up will reflect that.

10 VERDICT

It is the jury who must decide whether the defendant is guilty or not guilty. This decision is called their **verdict**. When the judge has finished his summing-up, the jury will go to their room, and consider their verdict in private. One of the jury is elected by them to be their foreman or forewoman. He or she will act as their unofficial chairman and spokesman, and will announce the jury's verdict to the court.

Jurors who are considering their verdict are always guarded by the court ushers, who must ensure that no one interrupts or interferes with them while they are 'deliberating'. They may not discuss the case with anyone—even family or friends—for they must not allow their decision to be influenced by people who have not heard all the evidence as jurors. These days jurors are told that they must not have mobile phones with them in the jury room.

If the jury need a long time to reach their verdict, they may be allowed to 'separate' and go home, and come back the next day to continue their discussions. In some particularly serious or sensitive cases, which have attracted much publicity, they may have to spend the night in a hotel under the supervision of the ushers. In Chapter 25 we will encounter a rare case where this system went badly wrong.

Normally a jury will have to reach a **unanimous verdict**, that is a decision upon which all 12 agree. If they have been considering their verdict for a long time and are unable to agree, the judge may permit them to return a **majority verdict**; but when it comes to jury verdicts the word *majority* has a special meaning—the verdict must be one on which at least 10 of the jurors are agreed. So a jury's verdict may be either unanimous (all 12) or 11–1 or 10–2. If the jury find a defendant not guilty of all the charges against him, then he has been acquitted, and is immediately allowed to leave the dock, and walk out of court a free man.

Double jeopardy

Until recent times, if a defendant was acquitted, he could not be placed in 'double jeopardy' and tried again on the same charge, even if after his trial further and better evidence of his guilt was found—even if he later admitted the offence! There is now an exception to this rule, for if the prosecution can satisfy the Court of Appeal that the acquittal was 'tainted' because a juror or witness has been intimidated, the court may order that the defendant should be re-tried. Following the *Stephen Lawrence Inquiry* (Chapter 20), the Law Commission proposed that where, after an acquittal, entirely 'new' evidence comes to light (such as DNA, or fingerprint testing) which is 'compelling evidence' of a defendant's guilt, the Court of Appeal should be able to order his re-trial. The Criminal Justice Act 2003 has now made this law: in the case of certain very serious offences (such as murder, manslaughter, rape, and robbery involving firearms). When this law comes into force, the Director of Public Prosecutions must first give his consent to a second prosecution. The Court of Appeal will be able to quash an acquittal and order a re-trial if it is satisfied that there is new and compelling evidence of guilt and that it is in the interests of justice to do so.

If a jury cannot even reach a majority verdict, and its members therefore *disagree*, there may be a re-trial. It is a custom that if after a re-trial the second jury also disagree, the prosecution will then drop the case and *offer no further evidence*. When this happens the judge will order that a verdict of *not guilty* be recorded, and the defendant will go free.

In England, there are only two possible verdicts: 'guilty' or 'not guilty'. If the jury are not sure of guilt they must find the defendant not guilty. In Scotland there is a third possibility—a verdict of **not proven**, meaning that there seems to be a case against the defendant but the jury cannot be sure of guilt. As in England, if a Scottish jury return a verdict of 'not proven' the defendant cannot be tried again for the same offence.

If the jury find the defendant guilty of any charge, the judge will have to pass sentence on him in respect of it. Sometimes the jury have a choice of possible verdicts, For example, they may have to decide in a wounding case whether, when the defendant inflicted the wound, he intended to do really serious bodily harm (more serious) or not (less serious). Whatever their decision may be, the judge must faithfully follow their verdict and pass sentence for the crime or crimes which the jury decide the defendant has committed.

11 SENTENCE

This last phase of the trial is a quite separate one. It is very important because, except where the defendant is in need of medical treatment, the **sentence** of the court is the **punishment** which the court must decide to impose. We will be looking at punishments later; but it is necessary to understand that at this final stage of a trial there are *rules* as to how the court should approach the question of the sentence.

It is the judge who passes sentence in a case. The jury play no part in this. Deciding what the punishment should be is always one of the most difficult aspects of the judge's duties. In some cases, as we will see in the next chapter, he may have no choice but to pass a particular sentence, but in most cases he does have a discretion. If that is the case:

- The judge must first take into consideration all the circumstances of the offence itself. He will have heard about this in the course of the trial. In particular, he must consider the effect that the offence has had on the victim of the crime.

- The judge is given information about the defendant's own personal circumstances. If the defendant has not pleaded guilty and there has been a trial, the judge is already likely to know a good deal about him—his age, family, and employment situation. He will now be told in open court if the defendant has committed any crimes before; and, if he has, his list of previous convictions will be read out. The judge must take account of the defendant's character. He is naturally expected to be more lenient towards a defendant of good character who has been a law-abiding citizen than a defendant who has been in trouble many times.

- The judge will consider any reports which have been prepared on the defendant, or for which he will ask. He will usually have a **pre-sentence report** from the probation service, which deals in detail with the defendant's background, and may give advice as to how he would be likely to respond to certain types of sentence, and a medical report where this is appropriate. He may also see references from employers or others who know the defendant well. These usually take the form of letters, but witnesses may be called to speak for the defendant in court.

- The judge must give the barrister or solicitor representing the defendant the chance to plead for leniency (a light sentence). He will point out all the features of the offence which might lessen the seriousness of it, and all the features of the defendant's personal circumstances which might call for the judge to be lenient. This plea for leniency is called a **plea in mitigation**. A plea in mitigation is regarded as a particularly difficult and important part of the art of advocacy. A good 'mitigation' might mean the difference between a defendant being sent to prison, or receiving some other form of sentence in the community.

The judge will then **sentence** the defendant. This means that after he has taken into account all the matters which have been mentioned and also any guidelines for sentence in that type of case set down by the Court of Appeal, he must now make the court order which imposes punishment on him. A formal record of this order is made by the Clerk of the Court. If a sentence of imprisonment is passed, the Dock Officer, whose job it is to guard a defendant in court, makes a record of the sentence and escorts him to prison at the end of the day.

The trial is now at an end. (Our 'bird-seed thief' was found guilty of all three offences! He was aged 20, and had been convicted of shoplifting when he was 17, and possessing cannabis when he was 19. On these occasions he had been fined by the magistrates. It will be interesting to consider the different ways in which he might be sentenced, which are set out in the next chapter.)

COMPARING CRIMINAL AND CIVIL TRIALS

How does the conduct of a civil trial differ from that of a criminal trial? In fact they are very similar. A civil trial begins with the claimant's lawyer 'opening' his case to the judge (making an opening speech) and calling witnesses as in a criminal trial; and the defendant's lawyer then calls his witnesses. There are three main differences between the procedures in civil and criminal trials:

- In a civil trial the judge normally sits alone (without a jury) to try the case. Juries are not involved at all.

- In criminal trials the prosecution lawyer makes the opening speech to the jury and the defence lawyer makes the final speech, but in a civil trial the claimant has the first and the last word. Therefore, after all the evidence has been called the defendant's lawyer will make his speech first, followed by the closing speech of the claimant's lawyer.

- At the end of a civil trial the judge does not give a verdict; he gives a **judgment** in which he sets out 'findings of fact' (tells the parties what he believes actually happened) and gives reasons for his decision as to who has won the case.

TELEVISING TRIALS

There seems to be little enthusiasm amongst the judges in this country for televising trials. The experience of the courts in American cases like the trials of O. J. Simpson and Louise Woodward has been enough to teach them the lesson that televising trials is likely to lead to unfair pressure being put upon everyone connected with the case (except perhaps the flamboyant lawyers), and to prejudice and injustice. Some lawyers, however, do regard televising trials as an essential step along the path to open justice.

Open justice is very important. It is one of the cardinal principles of our legal system, but there are many good arguments against televising trials: it would intimidate witnesses and inhibit them from coming forward to give vital evidence; it would expose the defendant to unfair pressure and publicity; it would never be possible in a television programme to present a full and balanced picture of the evidence; and it would put unreasonable pressure on jurors to bow to public opinion.

In an article written for *The Times* in November 1997, following the trial of Louise Woodward in America for the murder of a child in her care, Libby Purves stated the case against televising trials in this country:

No argument for them [televised trials] carries any weight. Some say that there is more public interest if they are on television, which makes one wonder how much more interest could be borne, in, say the Rose West trial or the James Bulger case, which weren't. Some say that justice must be seen to be done and that TV is the modern equivalent of the public gallery: hooey. The experience of watching sexy little snippets of evidence and emotion on the news has absolutely nothing in common with queuing up in the rain and accepting court discipline in order to participate in a trial as a serious observer. It never will have, not unless you force networks to screen every minute without close-ups, and force viewers to stay put on their sofas without food and drink and behave with restraint while real people's lives are being disposed of.

If you take the American route, trials become entertainment, an excuse for idle, crisp munching couch potatoes to make facile judgments about whose eyes are too close together, who isn't looking quite upset enough, who has a silly voice, and so on Sometimes the couch potatoes get fired up, and you get the kind of rankly stupid partisanship we have seen in the Woodward case and the O. J. Simpson trial. Justice, I say again, is a device for using intelligence and moral sense to contain and regulate the beast in us. Why punch holes in it?

Only time will tell whether we will choose to follow the American example. Until we do, it remains the right of every citizen aged 14 or over to visit any court and watch a trial from the public gallery. Many people do this, from professionals (such as newspaper and television reporters) to parties of school children. It is the best way of understanding how our criminal justice system works

H.M. PRISON WORMWOOD SCRUBS.

18

Punishments Today

> '*The quality of mercy is not strain'd,*
> *It droppeth as the gentle rain from heaven*
> *Upon the place beneath: it is twice blessed;*
> *It blesseth him that gives and him that takes:*'
>
> William Shakespeare, *The Merchant of Venice*.

> '*Thwackum [a Magistrate] was for doing justice, and leaving mercy to heaven.*'
>
> Henry Fielding, *Tom Jones*.

✳

In the criminal justice system anyone who has pleaded guilty or been found guilty of crime is called an **offender**, and for convenience we will call them offenders too. Only the courts have the power to **sentence** (pass judgment on) offenders who have broken the law.

PURPOSES OF SENTENCING

In the Criminal Justice Act 2003, Parliament has for the first time set out in statutory form the purposes of sentencing. There are five main purposes: **punishment, public protection, crime reduction, reparation**, and **rehabilitation of offenders**. This list is in the order in which they appear in the Act, but it is not necessarily the invariable order of importance, because that will depend on the circumstances of each case. The Act also spells out exceptions where these purposes will not be applicable, for example, where an offender is under 18, or where the sentence is fixed by-law, such as the mandatory sentence of life imprisonment for murder. Ideally, in most cases, sentencing should serve at least some, hopefully all of these purposes; but when it comes to sentencing ideals can be extremely difficult to realise.

1 PUNISHMENT

Punishment was at one time known as *retribution*. It means that the punishment should in some way pay the offender back for the harm he has done. In the first place, this will give satisfaction to the victim, for most victims of crime naturally have strong feelings about the harm done to them. Some would dearly like to get their own back in an act of vengeance. They must not do this. A victim of crime must never 'take the law into his own hands'. If that were acceptable there would be even more violence and public disorder. In the second place, it is the way in which the public as a whole can show their feelings of disapproval—sometimes, even outrage and disgust— for the crime and the offender who committed it. It is this aspect of sentencing that gives the impression that the offender has been 'brought to justice'.

2 PROTECTION

Protection means protecting the public from the offender. In the case of a violent criminal it may be necessary to send him to prison for a long time simply to protect the public from further harm. In the case of a man who 'drinks and drives', it may be necessary to take away his licence to drive, and stop him from driving for a long time to protect other road users.

3 CRIME REDUCTION

The reduction of crime was at one time known as *deterrence*. It means that the sentence should also be designed to put people off committing crime—both to deter them from offending at all, and to deter them from re-offending. The theory is that imposing particular sentences for crimes, and very severe sentences for serious crimes, will deter criminals from offending for fear of the consequences.

It is impossible to say with any scientific certainty if this theory works in practice. It may well be that quite apart from the fact that the majority of the population are decent citizens, who have no intention to commit crime, the terror of the prospect of punishment is enough to put them off doing so. If this is so, deterrence does have a general effect upon the community at large—but we know that punishment alone has never been a completely successful deterrent. If it were, there would be no crime at all. Those who argue against sentencing as a deterrent point to the days of public executions, when criminals would be hanged for stealing, and yet pickpockets would be at work in the crowd—stealing from onlookers who were watching the execution. There are modern parallels: these days heavy prison sentences are imposed on drug dealers, and yet this has not stopped people from smuggling drugs into prison.

There are many who claim that the best deterrent is not the prospect of heavy punishment but the likelihood of *detection*—of the offender being caught. It is pointed out that many crimes are committed on impulse, without much more than a moment's thought, and that most people who commit crime hope and expect to get away with it. The argument is that if people thinking of committing crime always believed that there was a very strong chance that they would be caught, that would be much the best way of deterring them from doing so.

4 REPARATION

These days, more and more sentences are designed to ensure that the offender is made aware of the harm he has done, and is required in some way to 'repair' the damage by making reparation to his victim or to the community. Certain sentences—financial compensation of victims, work in the community (known as Community Punishment)—are aimed at achieving this kind of reparation. Steps are also taken in appropriate cases to ensure that the offender understands the full effect of the harm he has caused, and apologises to the victim for it.

5 REHABILITATION OF OFFENDERS

Rehabilitation of offenders means that the sentence should, wherever possible, take into account the personal circumstances of the defendant, and look to his future. If the sentence can be constructive, it may help him to avoid getting into trouble again. A large number of offenders need treatment rather than punishment. Many offenders who are mentally ill, or who are addicted to alcohol or dangerous drugs, are not sent to prison, but are ordered to receive treatment in hospitals or drug rehabilitation centres. Like reparation, rehabilitation is becoming an increasingly important part of the criminal justice system. When it is successful, it is a very satisfying part of the court's work.

TYPES OF PUNISHMENT

The courts have available to them a whole range of different sentencing 'powers' or 'disposals' (ways of disposing of criminal cases). Many of these powers, and a number of new ones, are set out in two 'consolidating' Acts of Parliament, where attempts have been made to bring the assortment of sentencing options together. These are the Powers of Criminal Courts

(Sentencing) Act 2000 and the Criminal Justice and Court Services Act 2000. This range of sentences has now been added to, and in some cases altered, by the Criminal Justice Act 2003. As we saw in Chapter 5, this Act is an example of a statute that will come into force over a period of time. It is not possible, therefore, to say with any certainty what the law will be at the time this chapter is read. It is therefore proposed to state what the law is now (at the beginning of 2004), and give a brief idea (in smaller print) of the changes that are anticipated.

Sentences may vary enormously. At one end of the scale is that of 'imprisonment for life'; at the other is an 'absolute discharge', which means that the offender leaves the court without any penalty at all. In some circumstances, sentences are **mandatory**—the court has no choice and must pass a particular sentence; but most sentences are **discretionary**—the court has a choice and may decide for itself what the just sentence will be. There follows a selection of the main types of punishment available to the courts. The death penalty is included out of interest only.

THE DEATH PENALTY

In 1965, the death penalty in Britain was abolished for murder. It has now been abolished for all crimes committed in peacetime, including treason and piracy. Section 36 of the Crime and Disorder Act 1998 lists crimes dating back to the sixteenth century for which the offender was to 'suffer pains of death' or to be 'hanged by the neck until dead' and declares that they are now to be punishable with life imprisonment.

Last executions

- The last person to be executed for High Treason was William Joyce. He was hanged in July 1946 for broadcasting propaganda from Germany during the Second World War. His voice had come to be detested, and he was nicknamed 'Lord Haw Haw' because of his 'upper-class' accent. A difficult point of law was raised in his case. At the time of his alleged offence, Joyce was not a British subject or resident within the jurisdiction, but he was in possession of a British passport. Did he owe allegiance to the Crown? If not, he could not be convicted of High Treason. Eventually Joyce's case went on final appeal to the House of Lords, who decided by a majority of 3–2 that he did owe allegiance, and his appeal should be dismissed. In order to allow time to prepare their speeches, and avoid keeping Joyce in suspense, the Law Lords announced their decision first, and postponed giving their reasons for it until after his execution.

- The last execution in England took place in 1964, when Peter Allen and John Walby were hanged for the murder of a milkman.

- The last woman to be executed was Ruth Ellis. She was hanged in 1954 for the murder of her ex-lover, David Blakely. The case of Ruth Ellis is still talked about (it was made into a film). Ruth Ellis was the mother of two children. Her crime was apparently committed 'in cold blood', for she followed Blakely to a public house in Hampstead with a gun and shot him when he came out. She had recently suffered a miscarriage, said to be the result of Blakely's violence towards her, and was almost certainly severely emotionally disturbed at the time. She did not wish to appeal. There are few people today, including those in favour of capital punishment, who believe that her execution was justified. In September 2003, the Court of Appeal was given the opportunity to put this right, for almost fifty years after her death, Ruth Ellis's family was granted leave to appeal against her conviction. The court, however, decided that judged by 'the standards of the day' the trial had been a fair one, and dismissed the appeal.

The death penalty was carried out by hanging. Until recently, there was one prison (in London) where a scaffold remained . . . just in case.

CUSTODIAL SENTENCES

Custodial sentences are those where a defendant is deprived of his freedom. This is called being taken into **custody**. People serving custodial sentences in one institution or another are normally referred to as **inmates**.

MANDATORY SENTENCES

Certain custodial sentences are *mandatory*. For example, judges must impose a sentence of life imprisonment for murder, and under a controversial Act of Parliament, the Crime Sentences Act 1997, they must now pass a sentence of life imprisonment where a defendant has been convicted of two serious offences of violence, for example manslaughter, rape, and wounding or causing grievous bodily harm with intent to cause really serious bodily injury. In these cases, a life sentence must be passed unless the judge considers there are exceptional circumstances that would justify a lesser sentence. Again, where an offender commits a second drug-trafficking offence involving Class A drugs (see Chapter 22) a sentence of at least seven years' imprisonment must normally be passed; and when an offender is convicted of his third domestic burglary (of residential premises) the sentence must be a minimum of three years.

DISCRETIONARY SENTENCES

In all other cases sentences are *discretionary*. This means that judges have the discretion, or choice, as to what the length of the sentence should be. In these cases custodial sentences may only be imposed if the judge believes that no other method of dealing with an offender can be justified. The court will choose to pass a custodial sentence if an offender has committed a serious crime, or a number of crimes, or has shown by his past record of offending that he is likely to go on committing crimes. Custodial sentences take different forms, depending on the age of the offender.

FORMS OF CUSTODIAL SENTENCE

OFFENDERS OVER 21—IMPRISONMENT

Prisons are for offenders aged 21 or over. There are many prisons throughout the United Kingdom, and as they are designed to hold all types of criminals, the security arrangements and facilities for the inmates may be quite different. Prisons vary greatly, but they must almost all provide security— high walls and video cameras are common. Each prison will have its own rules and routines, and should offer inmates facilities for recreation and rehabilitation.

The most dangerous criminals are housed in *maximum security units*, where special arrangements will be in place. The least dangerous offenders will go to *open prisons*. These are prisons without boundary walls—the inmates will be locked up at night, but during the day they can be trusted to stay on the prison premises, or return to the prison if they are allowed out. There are several women's prisons. Most of these are open prisons. In women's prisons there are limited facilities for inmates to look after their babies.

The amount of time which an offender will actually spend in prison or in a young offender institute will vary according to the type and length of the sentence. Where an offender has been convicted of murder, the court must pass a sentence of *imprisonment for life*. At present, the Home Secretary is responsible for deciding when 'lifers' can be released **on parole**. Parole means being released on licence, and under supervision. Once released, a 'lifer' can be recalled to prison at any time. In deciding how long a 'lifer' shall serve, the Home Secretary will have regard to the opinions of the judge who tried the case, the Lord Chief Justice, the prison authorities, and the Parole Board, which advises on parole in all cases where the sentence is four years or more.

A person serving a life sentence is normally released on parole after serving about 12 years; but a life sentence can mean that the offender will actually be kept in prison for life, and that has happened in some cases. These are called 'whole life' sentences. Inmates must now be informed if they are to spend the rest of their lives in prison.

The 'Moors' murders

An offender who was given a whole life sentence was Myra Hindley. In April 1966, Ian Brady and Myra Hindley were convicted of the murder of children in the Manchester area. Brady was convicted of murdering three children; Hindley was convicted of two of these murders. After the killings they had buried their victims on the moors nearby, and so they became known as the 'Moors Murderers'.

Brady, who is now detained in Broadmoor, has never sought his release, but Hindley campaigned hard for hers. In 1997 the Home Secretary imposed a 'whole life tariff' in her case (meaning that she had to spend the rest of her life in prison) 'to satisfy the requirements of retribution and deterrence'. Myra Hindley mounted a strong legal challenge to this order, but on 5 November 1998 the Court of Appeal declared that it was lawful, although the appeal court said it was right that the Home Secretary should still be prepared to keep her case under review. In 2002, while still in custody, she died.

In almost all other cases, where the sentence is discretionary, inmates will not actually serve the entire sentence that is passed. There are complicated rules which set out how long they should actually serve. This depends upon their age and the length of the sentence passed. At the present time where the sentence is *less* than four years, prisoners will normally serve one-half of their sentences, but where the sentence is four years or more, prisoners will normally serve between one-half and two-thirds of their sentence.

There are considerable penalties if the offender commits another offence when he has been released after serving only part of his sentence. At worst, before serving any new sentence which may be imposed for the further offence, he may be required to serve out the remainder of the original sentence. Therefore, if a person sentenced on 1 October 2002 to two years' imprisonment for burglary is released after the first half of his sentence on 1 October 2003, and then commits an offence of theft on 1 November 2003, he may well be ordered to serve out the second half of his original sentence— another 12 months—*before* he begins any new sentence which he may receive for the 1 November theft offence.

In certain cases the judge may pass a **suspended sentence** of imprisonment, when the offender will not have to go to prison directly, but will have the sentence suspended (hanging over him) pending his good behaviour. This will only happen where a prison sentence is called for, but there are very special circumstances which would make it unjust to send the offender to prison immediately. If an offender is sentenced to '12 months' imprisonment suspended for two years', he will not have to go to prison immediately, but if he commits any further offence during the next two years he will have to serve this sentence.

OFFENDERS UNDER 18—DETENTION

Young offender institutions are in effect special 'prisons' for offenders over 18 years of age and under 21; but this type of detention may soon be abolished, if the minimum age for imprisonment is to be reduced to 18 years. Where custodial sentences are imposed on young offenders the emphasis should always be to provide them with training and guidance—to *rehabilitate* them.

One major criticism of custodial sentences for young offenders is that once 'inside', they may learn much more about crime and how to commit it from their fellow inmates than they knew before they were sentenced. That is why these institutions are sometimes scornfully referred to as 'Universities of Crime'.

Offenders between the ages of 10 and 18 may be sentenced to various forms of detention: in the case of children aged 10–14, where they have committed serious crime; in the case of children aged 14–17, where they have committed serious crime, *or* a number of offences. In the most serious cases of crimes by children or young persons under the age of 18 (for example, if a child commits murder) they will be ordered to be 'detained during Her Majesty's pleasure'. This is a special type of sentence, which will result in the offender being kept in custody for a number of years, until it is quite safe to release him. In cases where a child or young person is ordered to be kept in custody for a long time, he may start his sentence in one form of institution and then, when he is old enough, be transferred to a prison.

The Criminal Justice Act 2003 will make considerable alterations to sentences in custody: (1) sentences of **less than 12 months** will be replaced by a new sentence—'custody plus', which following the offender's release (after serving one-half of the sentence) will always involve a period of at least 26 weeks' post-release supervision in the community; (2) sentences **over 12 months** will be served in full, but this will mean half in custody and half in the community, with supervision being extended to the end of the sentence; (3) **serious violent and sexual offenders** will be given new sentences which will ensure that they are kept in prison or under supervision for longer periods than now. There will also be two entirely new types of sentence: (4) **intermittent custody**, which will, for example, involve the offender being allowed home to work during the week, but require him to return to prison at weekends, and (5) **suspended sentences**, in which offenders will not merely have their sentences of imprisonment hanging over them, but also be ordered to co-operate with one or more of a range of 'community requirements' (see below).

MODERN PRISON REFORM

We have already seen (Chapter 16) some outstanding examples of dedicated and enlightened people who worked with passion and self-sacrifice for prison reform. A number of independent organisations still campaign for more humane prison conditions and law reform in the area of the criminal law. The most important of these are NACRO (National Association for the Care and Resettlement of Offenders), the Howard League for Penal Reform, and JUSTICE. The first two are mainly concerned with prison reform; JUSTICE is mainly concerned with law reform and helping prisoners who seem to have a justifiable complaint about their conviction or sentence.

Many individuals also do excellent work in the cause of prison reform, trying to improve the conditions in prisons, and where possible the attitudes of prisoners. Despite their achievements, serious complaints are still made by respected and influential people about the bad conditions of prisoners, many of whom are detained in prisons that were built during Dickens' lifetime. Judge Sir Stephen Tumim, a former Chief Inspector of Prisons, was a fearless advocate of prison reform. In December 1995, his successor Sir David Ramsbotham cut short his inspection of Holloway prison for women, declaring the conditions there to be so bad that he would refuse to return until something had been done to improve them. Within a matter of weeks, improvements had begun, but in July 2003 Holloway (now the largest women's prison in Europe) was identified by the Prison Service itself as being *'the worst jail in the country'*. Conditions at the large young offender institution at Feltham have been described as *'wholly unacceptable'*. In July 2001, Sir David said it was *'utterly disgraceful that there had been virtually no change'* at this institution, and there has been talk of closing it down. His main criticisms of the prison service are of a failure to put the welfare of prisoners high enough in its list of priorities and a serious lack of facilities for rehabilitation, with the result that a large proportion of offenders, young and old, re-offend. He also points to the tragic rate of suicide amongst inmates, which for a considerable time has been steadily rising. In December 2003, a report by the Commission for Racial Equality exposed 'an alarming catalogue of racist abuse and behaviour' amongst some staff and inmates.

Courts, too, are becoming involved in the process of prison reform. In 1975 the European Court of Human Rights decided that prison authorities in England should not have prevented a prisoner, Sidney Golder, from sending a letter to his solicitor seeking advice. In 1978, the Court of Appeal accepted that it had the power on *judicial review* to consider the fairness of disciplinary decisions made by boards of prison visitors following the Hull prison riot. Lord Justice Shaw accepted that *'even disgruntled prisoners may have serious grounds for complaint'*. In 1982, the House of Lords ruled that *'a convicted prisoner, in spite of his imprisonment, retains all civil rights which are not taken away expressly or by necessary implication'*. In Chapter 19 (Human Rights) we shall find that prisoners are, in increasing numbers, testing the lawfulness of the conditions of their detention before the courts.

Recently, the *Irene Taylor Trust* was set up in memory of Lady Taylor. She was the wife of Lord Taylor of Gosforth, the late Lord Chief Justice. This organisation does outstanding work in providing concerts for prisoners, and encouraging them to appreciate and even play music themselves. This may at first sight seem to be a small advance, but it is not. Many inmates benefit from this work, and some who suffer severe psychological difficulties find that music opens up for them a world of communication they had never previously experienced.

COMMUNITY SENTENCES

Community sentences are those where the offender is not kept in custody but is allowed to remain free *in the community* on certain conditions. Most community sentences are completed without the offender committing further crime during the period of the community order, but if he or she does commit a further offence, or breaks the conditions of the order, they may be brought back before the court which passed the sentence and be re-sentenced—and possibly sent to custody.

Until recently, before any community sentence was passed on an offender he had to agree to it; it was thought that there would be no point in making an order if the offender was not willing to co-operate. Now most community sentences may be imposed without the agreement of the offender, although any order to undergo treatment—for example, for a mental illness, or for alcohol or drug addiction—can only be made with his consent.

There are currently three main types of community sentence, and they are all managed and supervised by local probation services:

COMMUNITY PUNISHMENT ORDER

A **community punishment order** used to be called 'community service'. Under a community punishment order the court may order an offender over 16 years to do unpaid work on behalf of the community for between 40 and 240 hours. The type of work may involve almost anything—helping local youth groups, painting and decorating a local Community Centre, clearing the banks of a canal, or, as in the case of the football star Eric Cantona, coaching children to play football. A range of options is open for women offenders. They may do the same work as men, or they may, for example, be asked to help volunteers at an old people's home, or at a women's refuge.

The purpose of this sentence is to punish, but at the same time to benefit the community and give the offender the opportunity to *repay* society for the wrong he has done. It will also, it is hoped, give the offender some idea of his or her real worth and value in the community, and a sense of satisfaction resulting from a good job well done. Efforts are made to ensure that wherever possible no one is disadvantaged from attending. Therefore, those with jobs will complete their hours in their free time, so as not to interfere with their ordinary work; and single parents doing this work will be given help with child care. In October 2003 a new 'enhanced' community punishment scheme was introduced to give offenders doing work greater help with solving their personal problems.

COMMUNITY REHABILITATION ORDER

A **community rehabilitation order** used to be called probation. Community rehabilitation orders can be made only in the case of offenders over the age of 16 years. In the case of children under 16, **supervision orders** are made, these are usually supervised by a **young offender team**. The two orders are largely the same in their impact, although the name of the order may depend upon whether it is imposed by the magistrates' youth court or the Crown Court.

Probation Officers play an extremely important and valuable role in the criminal justice system. Theirs can be a difficult and demanding job. They prepare **pre-sentence reports** for the courts on adult offenders. In all cases involving young offenders, reports are written by the **young offender team**. These reports are confidential and will be seen only by the defendant, his lawyers, the court clerk, and magistrate or judge; but they will be sent to the prison (or place of detention) if a custodial sentence is passed. Probation officers organise and supervise the probation orders of those actually placed on rehabilitation. They also supervise the after-care of offenders released from custody. They help to arrange places in **bail hostels** for homeless people who are charged with crime, but who have not yet been tried, and they help to run **probation hostels** for offenders who have been convicted, and who need accommodation.

Rehabilitation orders last for a maximum of three years; and the court may make conditions—for example, that the offender should live at a place directed by the probation officer, or attend a course of one kind or another. The aims of these orders are to rehabilitate the offender, protect the public from harm, and prevent further offending. This is likely to be successful only if the probation officer can get the offender to face up to his or her problems, and try to solve them in a constructive way. Special programmes are designed to reduce offending. These are based on helping offenders by changing the way they think about themselves and their actions. Those who have committed offences of violence may have to attend an 'anger management course', drivers who drink and drive may have to attend a 'drink impaired drivers course'; drug addicts a 'prescribing scheme for drugs misusers', and so on.

- X was convicted of burglary of office premises. He was found to have been abusing drugs. Following a recommendation in his pre-sentence report, he was required to attend a drug day programme, and reside at a hostel.

- Y was convicted of assaulting his wife and child. It was his first offence. There was much concern about whether he could be allowed to return home. Social Services were involved in putting the name of the family on a Child Protection Register. A recommendation was accepted that the well-being of the family would be best promoted if Y remained at home; but he was required to attend an Anger Management Programme, and another course to reduce his drinking.

As time goes by the probation officer may see the offender less frequently. If he or she makes really good progress the officer can apply to the court to revoke (cancel) the order.

COMBINED COMMUNITY PUNISHMENT AND REHABILITATION ORDERS

Combined community punishment and rehabilitation orders *combine* community punishment and rehabilitation, and are therefore called 'combination orders'. The offender will have to do a certain amount of unpaid community work *and* will have to comply with the rehabilitation requirements. In these cases, the minimum period of rehabilitation is 12 months; the maximum number of work hours is 100 hours. These are very demanding orders, especially for young people.

(Most courts would say that the young offender (the bird-seed thief) who was tried in the last chapter must spend some time in detention. After all, he did assault the woman shopkeeper, and violence in these circumstances is always taken very seriously. Or might he benefit from some form of community punishment? If he had not committed this act of violence a community sentence would have been the most likely option.)

ATTENDANCE CENTRE ORDER

An **attendance centre order** may be made if the offender is under 21 years of age. This type of order is made when the court decides that the offender should lose his leisure over a certain period. The order will require him to report to a particular place at a particular time. The order is normally made for a total of 12 hours: the maximum for an offender under 16 is 24 hours; and, for an offender over 16, 36 hours. A good illustration of an attendance centre order is when magistrates order 'football hooligans' to attend an attendance centre on Saturday afternoons—at the very time football matches are being played. This keeps them out of trouble and at the same time punishes them.

PARENTING ORDER

In the case of a child or young person convicted of crime the court may make a **parenting order**. This will require the child's parent or guardian to attend for up to three months for counselling and guidance sessions.

FINES AND COMPENSATION

In the case of most offences, the court has the power to order the offender to pay a fine and a sum of money by way of compensation to his victim. Before making any order for the payment of money the court must first enquire into the offender's financial situation to make sure that its order is one which can be met. If he fails to pay within a certain time, he may have to serve a term of imprisonment 'in default of payment'. This is how the order is enforced (see Chapter 12). Where a child under the age of 16 has been found guilty of an offence, and the court decides to impose a fine, it will normally have to be paid by his parent or guardian.

CONDITIONAL DISCHARGE AND ABSOLUTE DISCHARGE

Orders of **conditional discharge** are widely used in the magistrates' courts for minor crimes and first offenders. The effect of the order is that no penalty is imposed, on condition that the offender stays out of trouble for the period of time given. This can be anything up to two years. If the offender does commit another offence within this time he or she can be brought back to court and re-sentenced for the original offence.

An **absolute discharge** is not a punishment. It amounts to the offender being released without any conditions, and no record will be kept of this order. It is sometimes made if the court believes that the offender ought not to have been prosecuted at all.

OTHER PENALTIES

The types of punishment referred to above are the main ones, but they are not the only ones. All sorts of orders are available to meet particular situations:

- *Curfew orders* may be made, as part of community sentences or as a condition for prisoners released on licence. These orders are intended to confine the offenders to certain places or areas at certain times of day, or to enable the supervising authorities to know where they are. These new orders are now largely enforced by means of electronic monitoring ('tagging').

- Dangerous drugs, firearms, ammunition, and other weapons will be *confiscated and destroyed*. People who are convicted of dealing in dangerous drugs may have their property confiscated.

- People who are dependent upon drugs or have a tendency to misuse drugs may be made the subject of a *drug treatment and testing order* (see Chapter 22). This will often form *part* of a community order such as a rehabilitation or community punishment order which requires them also to undergo a treatment programme for their problem. It includes regular testing to show whether they are still taking drugs.

- People who commit serious motoring offences will be *disqualified from driving*—some sentences of disqualification are mandatory, and the court has no option but to pass them. If someone commits a serious crime such as burglary or robbery using a car, the car may be confiscated.

- People who commit company frauds may be *disqualified from being company directors*.

- Foreigners who commit crime in this country may be recommended for *deportation* back to their own countries.

- People who commit offences of violence in pubs may be made the subject of *exclusion orders*, and prohibited from entering licensed premises for between three months and two years.

- People who commit sex offences will be required to *register* their name and address with their local police, and keep them notified of any change of address. In the case of a serious offence (where an offender has been sent to prison for 30 months or more) this condition will last for life.

REPARATION ORDERS

A **reparation order** is a new form of order, which may last up to three months, and involve a range of activities: indirect apology to the victim, by letter or other means; work for the benefit of the community or the victim personally; or 'victim offender mediation', which may in certain cases help the offender and victim to settle their differences peacefully.

An even newer aspect of this process is the introduction of a 'Restorative Justice Programme'. This is a course which certain offenders may attend, and is aimed at bringing home to them the full consequences of their behaviour. They will then have the opportunity to make sincere apology, and a commitment to future good behaviour. Offenders are informed that this will not necessarily make a difference to their sentences, but it may do so. In 2003, the Court of Appeal reduced a sentence on a robber who had successfully completed this programme from seven years' imprisonment to five years.

MENTALLY DISORDERED OFFENDERS

There are cases in which an offender can be shown by expert medical evidence to be suffering from a mental illness. When this happens it is usually possible for the court to order that he should be sent to a suitable hospital, which will provide treatment for him and protection for the public. In some less serious cases a rehabilitation order may be made with a condition that the offender receives treatment either as an in-patient, or as an out-patient.

Wherever it appears that an offender has a serious personal problem, the court will consider whether that problem can be treated or managed as part of a *community sentence*.

The Criminal Justice Act 2003 will replace the various community orders with a new single **Community Order**. This will have attached to it one or more of the following 12 **requirements**: (1) an **unpaid work requirement** (the maximum number of hours will be increased from 240 to 300 hours); (2) an **activity requirement** (this may include such tasks as receiving help with employment problems and group work on social problems; it may also include making reparation to the victim); (3) a **programme requirement** (which will involve the offender participating in an accredited programme which will address offending behaviour, such as sex offending, anger management and substance abuse); (4) a **prohibited activity requirement** (preventing the offender from participating in certain activities, or contacting persons at risk from their behaviour); (5) a **curfew requirement** (that the offender must remain at a place specified by the court for certain periods of time—for not less than two hours or more than 12 in any given day); (6) an **exclusion requirement** (prohibiting an offender from entering certain places); (7) a **residence requirement** (that the offender must reside at a certain place during a period specified in the order); (8) a **mental health treatment requirement** (directing an offender to undergo mental health treatment under a doctor or chartered psychologist, either as a resident in a hospital or as an out-patient); (9) a **drug rehabilitation requirement** (including drug testing and treatment, and possible reviews of progress by the court); (10) an **alcohol treatment requirement** (involving specialist treatment for at least six months); (11) a **supervision requirement** (the offender must meet with the officer responsible for the supervision of his order, who will monitor his progress and assist him with problems such as employment, accommodation, and finance); and (12) if an offender is under 25, an **attendance centre requirement** (where practical activities, such as sport, will be available to occupy offenders for a certain number of hours to keep them out of trouble).

✳

The punishments which the courts may impose are changing all the time. Many judges and others involved with the criminal justice system believe that they change too quickly, leaving little time for a particular regime of punishment to settle down and be properly evaluated. There has been much debate about the desirability of laws which make it mandatory for judges to pass minimum sentences upon offenders who repeatedly commit serious crimes.

Parliament decides what punishments should be available, and the courts must pass sentences within that framework. It is important that there should be some general consistency in sentencing, and that, for instance, people who live in one part of the country are not treated differently from those who live elsewhere. The Court of Appeal—usually the Lord Chief Justice, or his deputy, the Vice-President of the Court of Appeal (Criminal Division)—gives *guidance* as to what the right sentence should be in certain types of case. This is known as the 'tariff' for the offence—for example, in February 2002, the Lord Chief Justice set out a tough tariff sentence for those who rob others of mobile phones. The court is not bound to pass a 'tariff sentence', for a judge has a discretion to do what he or she thinks right in the individual case; but he must have the tariff in mind when deciding what the appropriate penalty should be.

The Criminal Justice Act 2003 establishes a new *Sentencing Guideline Council*. This will consist of seven judicial members and five non-judicial members, under the chairmanship of the Lord Chief Justice. The Council will produce a set of sentencing guidelines for all criminal courts across a wide range of issues that are relevant to sentencing. Courts will be obliged to take these guidelines into account when deciding a sentence, the idea being that this will at least result in them approaching sentencing from a common starting point.

Sentencing offenders is one of the most difficult of all the duties a judge has to perform. The laws relating to sentencing should be simple, but they are in fact very complicated. Sometimes there are vast differences of opinion about what the right sentence in a particular case should be. Very often, when these differences arise those who express them were not in court to hear what was said, and to see the offender. The Court of Appeal has the power to reduce any sentence passed by the Crown Court. It may also increase a sentence, but only if the case has been referred to it by the Attorney-General, and the court is of the opinion that the original sentence was 'unduly lenient'. It should be a comfort for judges to know that when they have to pass sentence in a difficult case, or strong views are expressed about one of their sentences, there is another court, the Court of Appeal, which can review their decision and, if necessary, correct it.

19

Human Rights

'It is because the so-called Human Rights Act involves a significant transfer of power from Parliament to the judges that it constitutes a profound weakening of our accountable democratic traditions.'

Michael Howard QC, MP, former Home Secretary, now Leader of the Opposition, in a letter to *The Times*, 5 August 2000.

'The trouble with unwritten constitutions is that they are not written down. I am therefore grateful that when my children come to learn about government and democracy they will be able to find some basic constitutional rights set out in an accessible and authoritative text.'

Peter Thornton QC, a contributing editor to *Archbold, Criminal Pleading and Practice*, in a letter to *The Times*, 2 October 2000.

*

THE HUMAN RIGHTS ACT 1998

This chapter is not about human rights generally, but about the Human Rights Act 1998, which came into force on Monday, 2 October 2000. Every Act of Parliament has a **preamble**, or introductory paragraph, which sets out its aims. The preamble to this Act says that it is *'An Act to give further effect to the rights and freedoms guaranteed under the European Convention on Human Rights'*. The Act, then, incorporates into our law the European Convention on Human Rights and Fundamental Freedoms, otherwise known as the Human Rights Convention—or simply (as we shall call it) 'the Convention'.

As can be seen from the above quotations (and many more), opinions differ greatly as to the value of the Human Rights Act, and the impact that it is likely to have on our laws. Only time will tell who is right, but the Act has been welcomed by the overwhelming majority of judges, lawyers, and commentators as heralding a new era of human rights culture. It has already had the effect of concentrating public attention upon human rights issues, and of enlarging the scope of our 'rights and freedoms'; and, as we saw in Chapter 4, it is certainly of major constitutional importance.

*

CONVENTION RIGHTS

The origins of the **Convention rights and freedoms** are to be found in the dark days of the Second World War (1939–45). Following the widespread atrocities and destruction caused by the war, the governments of Western Europe established the Council of Europe. Its first task was to draw up a set of *universal human rights*. These rights were called 'universal' because they were intended to cross national frontiers—the boundaries of nationality and State citizenship. They would establish across Europe, and for all the citizens of Europe, a minimum standard of protection in various crucially important areas of their lives.

In 1950 the Council agreed a statement of these rights, in the Convention. The United Kingdom (UK) played a major role in conceiving and drafting this Convention, and in 1951 we signified our agreement to it. It came into force in international law in 1953, but the Convention itself was not formally incorporated into English law until the Human Rights Act 1998. This was because for many years we clung to the belief that it was for our own Parliament (and courts) to protect our rights, and nothing should be done to undermine the sovereignty of Parliament.

Before the Act came into force, therefore, those who believed that a public authority had breached their Convention rights had to apply to the European Court of Human Rights ('European Court') in Strasbourg to resolve the matter. That could be extremely expensive, and take years, but now Article 13 of the Convention, which has become part of our law, provides that wherever it is claimed that rights and freedoms under the Convention have been violated, those who say they have suffered are entitled to an 'effective remedy'. This means that they must be allowed to raise the matter of their Convention rights before the UK courts. Under the Human Rights Act, these rights can be relied upon in any court or tribunal in England and Wales, and it is only if citizens can show that they have first exhausted the remedies of these 'domestic courts' that they can take their cases to Strasbourg.

The Convention was a revolutionary document, containing a number of **Articles**. These are the statements of legal rights, known as 'Convention rights'. To the Articles have been added **Protocols** (later additions or improvements to Convention rights, rather similar in nature to the Amendments to the US Constitution).

There are three fundamental characteristics of Convention rights: each right is *inherent*—it exists as a separate and essential part of what we believe it should mean to be a free human being; it is *inalienable*—it cannot be given or taken away; and it is *universal*—it is common to all. These rights are therefore thought to represent the basic freedoms and minimum standards that are to be expected for all citizens in a democratic society.

Taken as a whole, the Convention rights embrace a wide range of human and fundamental rights. They include rights protecting individual citizens from State oppression, rights concerning their standard of living and quality of life, rights of freedom from discrimination, rights to free movement throughout the European Union, and rights of equal pay for men and women.

The Human Rights Act makes it unlawful for 'public authorities' to act in a way that conflicts with Convention rights. The expression 'public authorities' covers a wide range of public bodies including the courts, the police, local councils, government departments, and other government bodies. It also includes many private bodies which also have public functions, for example private schools. Lord Irvine was the Lord Chancellor largely responsible for the introduction of this new Act, and in a speech delivered in February 2001 he explained how all this works:

> Under the Act, all public authorities are under a wholly new obligation to respect the rights enshrined in the Convention as they discharge their functions, and the courts are under a strong duty to construe legislation, wherever possible, consistently with the Convention. Crucially, however, when national [UK] legislation cannot be construed in this way . . . the judges will not have the power simply to set aside Parliamentary legislation. That would be inconsistent with our doctrine of Parliamentary Sovereignty. Instead, the higher courts will be permitted to make a 'Declaration of Incompatibility' which will trigger a fast track legislative procedure under which the Government may, with Parliamentary approval, amend the offending legislation.

In very simple terms this means that if a UK Act of Parliament is not in direct conflict with the Convention, Convention rights will be respected by the courts. Where an Act is in direct conflict with the Convention, the judges will apply the law under the UK Act. The court may, however, then make a *declaration* that the Act is not compatible with the Convention—a **Declaration of Incompatibility**—and Parliament will be then expected to consider making a change in our law to bring it into line with the Convention.

As citizens of the UK, we like to think that by comparison with those who live in some parts of the world we are indeed fortunate. After all, we do not live in daily fear of the appalling breaches of human rights that are routine in some countries; but that does not mean that the record of the UK is blameless. Over the years, many complaints of human rights violations against the UK have been taken to the European Court, and a large number of them have been upheld. Some apologists for the UK claim that the reason for this is that UK citizens are less frightened to take their country to court than citizens of certain other countries; but that cannot excuse the fact that in so many cases the European Court has decided that the UK has violated the rights of individuals.

In this chapter we will look at some of the main Articles of the Convention and the rights that they give, and which are now incorporated into our own law by the Human Rights Act. We will also see some examples of what these rights mean and the ways in which they might affect our everyday lives. The Convention rights are extremely important, for they amount to a rich seam of freedoms and protections. They do not, however, provide us with an entirely new set of rights that have never existed before. This is because the common law already protected many of the rights given by the Convention, although they may not have been set out with clarity in a single document, or interpreted as liberally by the courts of this country as they have been in Strasbourg.

The European Court in Strasbourg includes judges from all the Member States of the European Community; it therefore includes English judges too. Lord Justice John Laws sits in the Court of Appeal; he is also an 'occasional judge' at the European Court. In a lecture on 'Human Rights' he helped judges confront some of the difficulties in understanding and applying the new Act. Two simple principles he described should be of use to everyone interested in understanding how we should approach the incorporation of the Convention into our law, and how it will affect us:

- He stressed the importance of not treating the Convention merely as a foreign importation, but of seeing it in the context of the English common law, to which (as he said) many fundamental freedoms, including those of family life, speech, religion, and assembly *are not strangers*'. He said: '*By investing the new jurisprudence [under the Human Rights Act] with the framework and discipline of the common law, we shall make moderate and balanced decisions by the use of old and well tried methods. We shall not have to invent a new world or a new language. We shall make better law than otherwise.*'

- He warned that the Act must not be used to take away rights we already have:

    '*It is a cardinal rule of the British Constitution that for the individual (as opposed to any public body) everything which is not prohibited is allowed ... We should not fall into the trap of supposing that, in the English legal system, positive law is required to mark out and guarantee the right of every citizen to say and do what he chooses ... The Convention must not be allowed to displace the principle that for the Englishman everything which is not forbidden [by the law] is allowed. Nor, for that matter, must it displace the converse principle, that for government — or any public body — everything which is not allowed [by the law] is forbidden.'*

*

THE CONVENTION ARTICLES

In the paragraphs that follow, we look at some of the main rights and freedoms that, under the positive laws of the Convention, are set out in the Convention Articles, and which are now incorporated into our law. Illustrations are given of a few of these rights—what they mean, and how they have been interpreted. Human rights law may be fascinating—it is certainly important—but it is not simple. The Articles and sample cases referred to below are intended to give a flavour of the very wide range of situations with which human rights law is now concerned. They are, however, of necessity incomplete, and do not include the interesting qualifications and exceptions that any student of the subject would soon encounter.

The 1998 Act has not been in force for long, and therefore the cases that are referred to mostly concern events that happened long before October 2000; but there are some examples of recent judgments of our own courts. Those who bring cases to the European Court make *applications* to the court for findings that they have suffered a violation of their rights, and for *relief* (compensation). Therefore those who bring cases to that court are known as *applicants*. The cases are defended by the countries concerned. In all the cases quoted in this chapter the country complained about was our own. That is why, for example, the first case quoted below is entitled *Jordan v UK*.

ARTICLE 1

Article 1 of the Convention provides that Member States are required to secure to everyone in their countries the rights and freedoms given by the Convention.

ARTICLE 2

'Everyone's right to life shall be protected by-law. No one shall be deprived of his life intentionally save in the execution of a sentence of a court following a conviction of crime for which this penalty is provided by law.'

This article does not therefore outlaw capital punishment. It is intended to prevent arbitrary killing by State authorities without due process of law. It has also been interpreted as imposing on the State a duty to investigate the circumstances of violent deaths.

- *Jordan* v *UK*. In 2001 the European Court decided that where certain persons had been killed in the fight against terrorism in Northern Ireland, and the authorities had failed to conduct a proper investigation into the circumstances of their deaths, the UK had violated its duty 'to provide some form of effective investigation where individuals had been killed as a result of the use of force'. This was a violation of Article 2.

- In *R (Amin)* v *Secretary of State for the Home Department*, 2003, the House of Lords followed the decision of the European court in the case of *Jordan*. In this case, in March 2000, while in Feltham Young Offender Institution an Asian boy, Zahid Mubarek, aged 19, had been murdered in his cell by his cellmate, Robert Stewart. Stewart, who had a Klu Klux Klan sign on his cell notice board, was know to be a violent racist, who was 'very dangerous'. In ordering a public investigation into the circumstances of Zahid's death, and why he had been put into the same cell as Stewart, Lord Bingham said that '*a profound respect for the sanctity of human life underpinned the jurisprudence under Articles 1 and 2 of the Convention . . . the State owed a particular duty to those involuntarily in its custody, and such persons had to be protected against violence and abuse at the hands of State agents. Reasonable steps had to be taken to safeguard their lives and persons against the risk of violent harm.*'

- *NHS Trust A* v *M*; *NHS Trust B* v *H*. In October 2000 (after the 1998 Act had come into force) the President of the Family Division heard applications on behalf of two NHS trusts to be permitted to discontinue treatment in the cases of two patients who were in 'persistent vegetative states'. These applications were not opposed by the patients' relatives, and the court decided that it was not contrary to Article 2 to allow these patients to die. The President ruled that Article 2 did not cover 'acts of omission' (doing nothing) when it was no longer in the patient's best interests to receive treatment, and when it was shown that '*they would die swiftly and painlessly if nutrition and hydration were withdrawn*'.

- In the case above, the patients were not conscious; but in the case of *Re B*, 2002, the same judge had to decide the case of a woman who was. In this case an adult patient was paralysed from the neck down and kept alive by ventilator. She wished artificial ventilation to be removed, even though she realised this would almost certainly result in her death. Her doctors were not prepared to do this. The judge held that the right of a competent patient to request the cessation of treatment had to prevail over the natural desire of the medical and nursing professions to keep her alive. If mental capacity were not in issue (the patient was of sound mind) and the patient, having been given the relevant information and offered the viable options, chose to refuse treatment, that decision had to be respected by the doctors.

Although people have the right to life, and not to be kept alive by artificial means, they do not have the right to die.

- In 2001, Dianne Pretty was suffering from motor neurone disease, a progressive degenerative illness that was terminal. She wished to control the time and manner of her dying, but her physical disabilities were so great that they prevented her from taking her own life unaided. She wished her husband to help her; and he was willing to do this, provided he was not prosecuted for the criminal offence of aiding another person to commit suicide. The Director of Public Prosecutions (DPP) refused to give Mrs Pretty an undertaking, or assurance, that if her husband assisted her to commit suicide he would not be prosecuted.

  Gravely ill, Mrs Pretty took her case to court, seeking a judicial review of this decision, and claiming that she had a human right to commit suicide, with assistance. The House of Lords expressed much sympathy, but held that there was no human right to assisted suicide. Mrs Pretty then took her case to the European Court of Human Rights, but that court decided that Article 2 guaranteed the right to life, and could not *without a distortion of language, be interpreted as conferring the diametrically opposite right, namely a right to die'*.

ARTICLE 3

'No one shall be subjected to torture or to inhuman or degrading treatment or punishment.'

This has been described as one of the strongest rights under the Convention; and Article 3 is one of the most important and relevant of all the Articles. It is also one which is frequently violated. **Torture** means deliberate inhuman treatment causing very serious and cruel suffering; **inhuman treatment or punishment** is that which causes intense physical and mental suffering; and **degrading treatment and punishment** is conduct that arouses in the victim a feeling of fear, anguish, and inferiority, which is capable of humiliating and debasing the victim and breaking his or her physical or moral resistance.

- In *Ireland* v *UK*, heard in 1978, the European Court had to decide whether five techniques used by the authorities when interrogating suspected terrorists in Northern Ireland were unlawful. These were described as *'wall standing, hooding, subjection to noise, deprivation of sleep and deprivation of food and drink'*. The court was not prepared to say that this conduct amounted to *'suffering of the intensity and cruelty implied by the word torture'*, but held that it was *'in clear breach of the UK's obligations on inhuman and degrading treatment'*. There had been a violation of Article 3.

- In 1998, the European Court decided that a boy aged eight who had been caned by his step-father, resulting in bruising to his buttocks, thighs, and calves, had suffered 'inhuman or degrading treatment'. The step-father admitted that he had beaten the boy with a three-foot-long garden cane, but when he was prosecuted for assault at the Lincoln Crown Court he was found not guilty by the jury, who accepted his defence that the child was a 'tearaway', and that the beating was 'reasonable chastisement'. By ruling that this conduct violated Article 3 and awarding the boy £10,000 compensation, the European Court has had a real impact upon our child protection law, and the way in which we view the disciplining of children.

- In *Price* v *UK*, the European Court had to consider the case of a disabled female British national, Adele Price, who was 'four-limb deficient' as a result of a condition caused by the drug Thalidomide. She also suffered kidney trouble. In 1995 she had been sent to prison for seven days for contempt of court. She had spent one night in a cell in Lincoln police station—'*a cell which contained a wooden bed and a mattress, and which was not specially adapted for a disabled person*'. The cell was cold, and because of her severe disability the applicant could not move around to keep warm. This was one of those pre-Act cases which took a long time to come to court. In July 2001, the court unanimously decided that she had suffered degrading treatment in violation of Article 3, and she was awarded £4,500 damages.

ARTICLE 4

'No one shall be held in slavery or servitude . . . No one shall be required to perform forced or compulsory labour.'

In this Article **slavery** and **servitude** are intended to cover the status of an individual in society and his or her condition in life. People subjected to **forced or compulsory labour** are, in the main, those who are given the status of ordinary citizens, but who are made to work under threat of penalty.

ARTICLE 5

'Everyone has the right to liberty and security of person.'

This important right limits the power of the State to arrest or detain anyone except when this is justified by procedures provided by the law. For example, it imposes duties on anyone carrying out an arrest that the person detained shall be informed promptly, in language he can understand, of the reasons for his arrest and of any charge brought against him. He must also be brought promptly before a court, where he must have the right to challenge the lawfulness of his detention.

- *Hirst* v *UK* was a case where the applicant was serving a life sentence. He had not been convicted of murder, and this was therefore a 'discretionary life sentence'— imposed because the judge thought it was necessary to protect the public. The applicant was therefore entitled to have his case reviewed by the Parole Board at regular intervals. The European Court decided that as the reviews in his case had been delayed there had been a violation of Article 5. The applicant was awarded £1,000 compensation.

ARTICLE 6

'In the determination of his civil rights and obligations or of any criminal charge against him, everyone is entitled to a fair and public hearing within a reasonable time by an independent and impartial tribunal established by law.'

This right to a fair trial includes the right to cross-examine and call witnesses, the right of a defendant to participate fully in the trial, and the right (in a criminal trial) to be presumed innocent until proven guilty.

It is generally recognised that Article 6, and the way in which it has been interpreted, will have a great influence upon the conduct of proceedings in all courts of law—not least because, as the Lord Chief Justice, Lord Woolf, said in a case heard in 2001: *'if a defendant has been denied a fair trial it will be almost inevitable that the conviction will be regarded as unsafe'*. In relation to this Article, in a case where Austria was the country complained about, the European Court also developed the concept of *'equality of arms'* which provides that for a trial to be fair each party must be afforded a reasonable opportunity to present his or her case, under conditions which do not place him at a substantial disadvantage in relation to his opponent.

- In *Golder* v *UK*, heard in 1975, the European Court found that the applicant Sidney Golder had been denied a fair trial because he had when arrested been refused the right to speak with his solicitor. There had been a violation of Article 6.

- In *Sander* v *UK*, an Asian defendant had been tried in the Birmingham Crown Court for conspiracy to defraud. Towards the end of the trial one juror complained that others had been making racist remarks. The judge was asked by the defence to dismiss the whole jury on the ground that there was a real danger of racial bias, but he dealt with the matter by making enquiries of the jury and accepting their assurance that although *'some unfortunate jokes'* had been made, there was no question of bias. He directed the jury that they must *'remember to bring in true verdicts according to the evidence'*.

  The Court of Appeal decided that the action taken by the judge had been appropriate, but the European Court held (by a majority of four to three) that the judge had not been robust enough. The comments that had been made *'were capable of causing the applicant and any independent observer to have legitimate doubts as to the impartiality of the court'*. There had therefore been a violation of the defendant's right to a fair trial. The Court, however, unanimously rejected the applicant's claim for compensation.

ARTICLE 7

'No one shall be held guilty of any criminal offence on account of any act or omission which did not constitute a criminal offence . . . at the time when it was committed. Nor shall a heavier penalty be imposed than the one that was applicable at the time the criminal offence was committed.'

The object of this Article is to provide a safeguard against arbitrary prosecution, conviction, and punishment. For example, no one should be held guilty of a criminal offence if his action was not a criminal offence at the time when he did it.

ARTICLE 8.1 AND 8.2

1. 'Everyone has the right to respect for his private and family life, his home and his correspondence.'
2. 'There shall be no interference by a public authority with the exercise of this [Article 8.1] right except such as is in accordance with the law and is necessary in a democratic society in the interests of national security, public safety or the economic well-being of the country, for the prevention of disorder or crime, for the protection of health or morals, or for the protection of the rights and freedoms of others.'

This is another right of immense importance, designed to protect the individual against arbitrary action by public authorities. It includes the idea of an *inner circle* of our personal lives in which we may be allowed to live without interference from the State.

- In 1999, the cases of *Lustig-Prean* v *UK* and *John Beckett* v *UK* were decided by the European Court. These two applicants (and others) had been members of the UK armed forces, but had then been excluded because they were homosexuals. They complained that their Article 8 rights to respect for their private lives had been violated. They also complained of violations of other Articles. The court decided unanimously that this right had been violated (and that there had also been a violation of Article 13, for despite the sympathy which had been expressed for their situation by the UK domestic courts, they had been denied the right to an effective remedy by our courts).

ARTICLE 9

'Everyone has the right to freedom of thought, conscience and religion.'

This Article is designed to protect freedom of thought, conscience, and religion, and the right of the individual to *'manifest one's religious belief'*. This means that people must be entitled to observe their religion openly.

This cannot mean, however, that in doing so they are allowed to break the law.

- In 2001, the Court of Appeal decided that a Rastafarian who used and distributed cannabis as part of his religion was still guilty of an offence under the Misuse of Drugs Act 1971.

ARTICLE 10

'Everyone has the right to freedom of expression.'

This right includes the freedom to *'hold opinions and to receive and impart information and ideas without interference from any public authority and regardless of frontiers'*. This freedom has been interpreted liberally, and in 2002 the High Court decided that where Lindis Percy had protested against the USA by defacing its flag at a US air force base in England, her conviction for using threatening and insulting words and behaviour was incompatible with Article 10. There are, however, some obvious restrictions. For example, this Article does not give anyone the right to incite crime or encourage racial hatred or disorder, or publish the most serious kinds of pornographic material.

ARTICLE 12

'Men and women of marriageable age have the right to marry and to found a family.'

This right has been interpreted as *'a right to form a legally binding association between a man and a woman'*. It does not imply the right to marry at any age— it is for the State to set the marriageable age—neither does it imply the right to divorce. The European Court has also ruled that the Article does not give the right to a married couple to be allowed to visit or live together if one of them is sent to prison.

ARTICLES 11 AND 13

These Articles give rights of *'freedom of assembly and association'* with others, and (as we have seen) the right to an *'effective remedy'* (the right to bring a complaint before the court and have the court take some action to deal with it).

ARTICLE 14

'The enjoyment of the rights and freedoms ... shall be secured without discrimination on any ground such as sex, race, colour, language, religion, political or other opinion, national or social origin, association with a national minority, property, birth or other status.'

The struggle against discrimination has been central to the whole human rights movement. We will be looking more closely at this subject in the next chapter, but it is predicted that this Article will add considerably to our domestic law, which in general has been limited to laws against discrimination on the grounds of sex, marital status, race, and disability.

*

In the two-year period before the Human Rights Act 1998 came into force, all judges and most practising lawyers received training in the purpose and provisions of the Act, and the ways in which it is likely to affect us all. When the Act first came into force it was said that there would be a torrent of human rights claims, such as to overwhelm the entire legal system. Lord Chancellor Irvine later said that the early indications were that the Act was working well: *'The picture so far emerging is good. As I predicted the prophets of doom are being proved wrong: the heavens have not fallen in, and there is no chaos in the courts.'*

During its first years in force the Act gave rise to a number of applications in English courts in which our laws, and procedures in our legal system, have been challenged. Claims of violations under the Act have often been unsuccessful, but not always so. The very fact that judges are constantly having to test the way in which our lives are affected by human rights, by *upholding them*—not merely against our own standards of fairness, but also against those expounded by foreign (and UK) judges in the European Court—is a form of guarantee that human rights will always remain high on the agenda of all our courts.

20

Discrimination and the Law

In 1920, a man named Scranton was tried for fraud. Scranton was cross-examined by Sir Ernest Wild KC for the prosecution about his dealings with a man named Tarsh. When Scranton said Tarsh was a moneylender, Sir Ernest remarked, 'A Jew, I suppose?' The case later came on appeal before Lord Reading the Lord Chief Justice, who referred to that remark and asked Sir Ernest what he meant by it. A well-known barrister named Roberts described what happened:

'Imagine the scene! The Lord Chief Justice of England, a Jew by race, of which he was intensely proud ... was asking counsel to explain an observation apparently which could have had no purpose other than to appeal to racial prejudice. The court was packed. Every eye was on Sir Ernest ... Every ear was strained to hear his answer, of which there was none. He grew red. He went white. His mouth opened and closed without the production of any sound. His eyes went up in mute appeal to the roof of the court, as though imploring providence to open up the floor so that he might sink from the scene.'

Oxford Book of Legal Anecdotes, edited by Michael Gilbert.

*

DISCRIMINATION

Discriminating against people means being prejudiced against them *and* treating them differently on account of their race, religion, or sex. Most people accept that it is morally wrong to do this, but in this country it is also recognised to be a social evil. Discrimination at its worst can lead to hatred, harassment, and violence. Victims of discrimination suffer insecurity, unhappiness, fear, and injustice. It is, in fact, one of the most obvious examples of injustice, and is *unlawful*.

The early history of our country is a story of invasion by other nations and tribes. This is something that many fail to appreciate, and so in 1996 the *Commission for Racial Equality* published *Roots of the future, Ethnic Diversity in the Making of Britain*, a book which sets out to describe the extent of migration to and from Great Britain over the past 40,000 years. From Bronze Age 'immigrants', who arrived from north-west Europe, to Celts, descendants of inhabitants of the Russian steppes; from the Romans to the Angles, Saxons, and Jutes—invaders from what is now northern Germany, southern Denmark, and the Netherlands; from the Norse Vikings to the Normans, who invaded under William the Conqueror in 1066—all are ancient ingredients of the modern 'Briton'. Since then, over a period of nearly 1,000 years, either because they were welcomed for who they were or because they were exploited for what they were, men and women from many other parts of the world have settled in this island. We should therefore understand that is wrong to imagine that our 'island race' is anything other than a mixture of peoples.

It has been the claim of some historians that Britain has, by comparison with many other countries, been a haven from oppression for ethnic and religious minorities; and there are some outstanding examples of tolerance. William the Conqueror encouraged the first Jewish settlers, and provided them with royal protection; in 1337 Edward III promised protection to '*all cloth workers of strange lands and whatsoever county they may be*'. Between 1550 and 1660 Protestant refugees, fleeing persecution in countries in Western Europe, found safety in Britain. Whatever may have motivated the tolerance, this assertion is therefore to an extent true; but even then we hardly have a record of which we can be proud.

Domesday Book records that at the time of William the Conqueror nine per cent of the population were counted as slaves. We should remember (Chapter 3) that it was not until *Somerset's Case* in 1772 that the common law of England outlawed slavery; and it was not until the Emancipation Act 1834 that all slaves in the British colonies were freed. It is well to recall that at one time great cities, such as Liverpool and Bristol, owed their prosperity to slavery—as John Mortimer reminds us, '*an easily forgotten item on our national criminal record*'.

There has always been discrimination for discrimination's sake. The reigns of several Sovereigns were deeply scarred by religious intolerance, not least that of Queen 'Bloody' Mary (1553–8) who within her short reign, and to the growing disgust of her subjects, burnt in the fires of Smithfield, and elsewhere, over 300 Protestant 'heretics'. In 1596, Mary's half-sister, Queen Elizabeth I, more tolerant in many ways, decided there were too many black people in the capital. She wrote personally to the Lord Mayor of London: '*There are of late divers blackamoors brought into this realme, of which kinde of people there are already here too many ... Her Majesty's pleasure therefore ys that those kinde of people should be sent forth of the lande.*' Until the early years of the twentieth century, serious sexual discrimination was still part of the law, women being treated as property belonging to their fathers or husbands, and denied the basic civil rights of being allowed to vote and stand for Parliament, or even to serve on juries.

The past half-century, since the Second World War, has seen a large influx of immigrants: in particular, of South Asians from India, Pakistan, Bangladesh, and East Africa; West Africans from Nigeria and Ghana; and Afro-Caribbeans from the West Indies. After the war, it became the policy of the Government to encourage these people to come to Britain, to provide a work force that could help rebuild the economy. Many of these immigrants were skilled men and women, including doctors and nurses, who made an enormous contribution to our national well-being.

One of the earliest discrimination cases to come before the courts was brought by the great black cricketer, Leary Constantine, against a hotel that refused him admission, but in the 1940s the result hardly amounted to more than a mild slap on the wrist for equal treatment:

- Leary Constantine was one of the great sportsmen of the twentieth-century—an outstanding cricketer, he was a member of the West Indies cricket team, and later knighted for his services to cricket. On 30 July 1943, he visited the Imperial Hotel in London. Although it had room for him, he was refused admittance to stay there. The Judge found that the management had no 'just cause or excuse' for doing so, and that he was entitled to damages. However, despite the fact that this had caused Constantine 'much humiliation and distress' the judge decided that he could only award him 5 guineas (£5.5s.) damages. (Even a case involving very little money could attract great lawyers. The barrister representing Constantine was Sir Patrick Hastings KC; the defendants were represented by G. O. Slade KC, later a High Court judge. The judge was Sir Norman Birkett, who had been one of the great advocates of the age.)

Some immigrants have now lived and worked in this country for many years. New generations of men and women, boys and girls, may have a foreign ancestry, but were born and educated here, and have always been British subjects. The law is that they are entitled to be treated in the same way as any other citizen. This has not always been so. In the 1950s and 1960s it was not uncommon to see advertisements for rooms to let bearing the offensive words 'no coloureds'. This was not then against the law. It was in practice just as difficult for other people belonging to ethnic and religious minorities to gain acceptance. This proved to be an important period in the development of laws against discrimination.

In the USA at this time, a number of dramatic and highly publicised cases advanced the cause of racial equality. Experiences in the USA, and the rulings of its Supreme Court, influenced attitudes in this country. In 1954 the Supreme Court ruled against school segregation. Thereafter, it repeatedly extended the protection given by the 14th Amendment to the US Constitution, which decrees that *'no State shall make or enforce any law which shall abridge (restrict) the privileges or immunities of citizens'*.

- In 1956, when the black seamstress Rosa Parks defied city law in Montgomery, Alabama, and refused to surrender her bus seat to a white passenger, she can have had little idea of the social revolution she was about to ignite. Judge Frank Johnson's ruling in her favour, that the bus company's policy of segregation was unconstitutional, helped beat a path of light through much racial prejudice, and enabled many more deprived citizens to receive justice.

- In 1965, the same judge issued the court order that allowed the black leader Martin Luther King to make his historic march from Selma to Montgomery. Judge Johnson proclaimed: 'the right to march is equal to the enormity of the wrongs that are being protested'.

It was in the same year that the Race Relations Act 1965 was steered through the British Parliament by the Home Secretary, Roy Jenkins. This Act was the forerunner of a succession of statutes designed to outlaw racial discrimination—each carrying protection against racial discrimination a stage further:

- The Race Relations Act 1965 made it a criminal offence to discriminate in hotels and public places on 'national or racial grounds'. It also set up the **Race Relations Board**, whose job it was to monitor the progress of the Act, and help people bring discrimination claims before the courts.

- In 1968, these laws against discrimination were extended to housing, employment, and insurance.

- The Race Relations Act 1976 made it unlawful to discriminate on racial grounds in relation to employment, training, and education; and the provision of goods and services. It also established the *Commission for Racial Equality*.

- The Race Relations (Amendment) Act 2000, which came into force on 1 April 2001, was influenced by the provisions of the Human Rights Act 1998, and the need to bring race relations legislation into line with the European Convention (see Chapter 19). In particular, it extends the protections given by the 1976 Act to all 'public authorities', and contains long lists of the many authorities and bodies that deal with the public.

To this day it is not possible for everyone who wishes to come to live and work in this country to do so. There are complex immigration laws that deal with these matters. Nevertheless, millions of people who belong to ethnic and religious minorities do live here, either as citizens with British nationality or as legal immigrants. Their rights against discrimination must be protected by the law, but that can be easier said than done. It would be foolish to imagine that problems of discrimination no longer exist. Prejudice still exists in the hearts and minds of many people; and it can be extremely difficult to show that prejudice has been transferred into acts of unlawful discrimination. A realisation of just how much harm can be done by prejudice to the causes of race relations and justice, and how much needs to be done to remove that harm, emerged in the course of the Stephen Lawrence Inquiry.

The Stephen Lawrence Inquiry

In April 1993 a black teenager, Stephen Lawrence, was stabbed to death as he was waiting for a bus in Eltham, London. The attack upon him has always been seen as racially motivated, and his killers have never been 'brought to justice'. Serious doubts were expressed as to the conduct of the police investigations into Stephen's murder. The Public Inquiry, held in 1998 into the crime and the investigation that followed, is a monument to the burning sense of injustice which results from acts of racial hatred and discrimination.

On 17 June 1998, in the course of the Inquiry, Assistant Commissioner Johnston on behalf of the Metropolitan Police apologised to the Lawrence family for failing to bring Stephen's killers to justice. He said that the case 'has been a tragedy for the Metropolitan Police who have lost the confidence of a significant section of the community [meaning the black community] for the way we have handled the case'. On 1 October 1998, Sir Paul Condon, the Metropolitan Police Commissioner, expressed the 'sense of shame in the Met. about many aspects of this tragic case'. The Metropolitan Police was not the only force to examine its attitudes and practices. On 14 October David Wilmot, the Chief Constable of Greater Manchester, said, 'We live in a society that has institutionalised racism, and Greater Manchester Police is no exception'.

The Lawrence Inquiry published its Report on 24 February 1999. It was highly critical of the original police investigation into the murder. It accused the police force which investigated the crime of itself being riven with 'institutionalised racism', which it defined as 'The collective failure of an organisation to provide an appropriate and professional service to people because of their colour, culture or ethnic origin'.

The Report made over 70 recommendations, which the Home Secretary has accepted. These are intended to lead to a radical improvement in the approach of the police and other sections of the community to problems of racial discrimination, and to the solutions which may eventually be found for them. Some of these recommendations, such as the suggestion that people might be tried twice for the same offence if new evidence comes to light after they have been acquitted in their first trial, have been strongly criticised, but many of them have been put into action.

In a powerful address on the *Administration of Justice in a Multi-Cultural Society, 2000*. Lord Justice Henry Brooke made the point that however careful we may think we are being, the (1997–8) statistics appear to show that there is still discrimination in the justice system itself. For example, black people are on average five times more likely to be stopped and searched by the police than white people, and the police give a formal caution more frequently to a white offender (who is not prosecuted) than to a black offender (who is). As regards sentencing by the courts, fewer people from ethnic minorities are made the subject of community orders by the courts, with a greater proportion being sent to prison. He said:

> *Nearly all the sentencing studies I have read . . . suggest that once you have peeled off the obvious reasons for differential treatment between black and white offenders—the seriousness of the offence, the past record of the offender, any obvious aggravating factors, and any obvious mitigating factors—there remains an unexplained residuum of differential treatment which cannot be so easily explained.*

In 2003, the Lord Chancellor added his voice to the call for racial equality in the justice system:

> *The justice system must convince all of society that it serves their needs irrespective of gender, race, religion, or sexual orientation. Of all the areas where constant vigilance is required, it is in attitudes to black and minority communities shown by the criminal justice system . . . They more than any other groups are the victims of crime. They are more dependent for protection on the law working effectively. All too often they have seen the system work in a way which has been unfair to their communities, often at a time when they needed the system to provide them with protection and justice.*

The strong message that discrimination is still with us, even in the justice system itself, is hitting home. Parliament is constantly passing new and tougher laws to protect people against discrimination. These laws are aimed at protecting women (and men) against sexual discrimination, and ethnic or religious minorities against racial discrimination; and while they cannot as yet claim great success, they can claim to be getting better at it all the time. There are three important areas in which *the courts* become involved in this work:

1. UPHOLDING THE LAW

It is the aim of the courts always to uphold the laws passed by Parliament against sexual or racial discrimination.

SEXUAL DISCRIMINATION

It is unlawful to discriminate against anyone because of his or her *sex* (Sex Discrimination Act 1975). In a number of cases, courts and employment tribunals have decided that sex discrimination has taken place, and have taken action to prevent it.

- El Vino's wine bar in Fleet Street London is just outside the Temple (where the barristers have their chambers) and a favourite haunt of lawyers. There it was a tradition, which became a rule, that although women could sit at the tables and drink, they could not go to the bar and order drinks, and they could not stand drinking in the bar area.

  On 2 February 1981, Mrs Gill, a solicitor, and Miss Coote, a journalist, went to the bar and asked to be served with two glasses of white wine. The barman 'politely refused to serve them', offering to serve them at their table instead. They took the matter to court, claiming unlawful discrimination.

  The Court of Appeal declared that these women had been discriminated against. They were entitled to the same treatment as male customers; and the court ordered that in future they should receive the same treatment.

- In 1989, the House of Lords heard an appeal in a case brought by the Equal Opportunities Commission against the Birmingham City Council. The Council had provided far fewer grammar school places for girls than boys, with the result that girls had to attain higher standards than boys to qualify. The Law Lords decided that this was unlawful. At the end of his speech (judgment) Lord Goff stated that discrimination would not be tolerated. He said: *'The time has come for the Birmingham City Council to accept that it is in breach of the law, and that something has got to be done about it.'*

- In 1999, Rachel Anderson was awarded £7,500 damages against the Professional Football Association. She is a FIFA-approved football agent, but had been excluded from the Association's annual awards dinner because she is a woman. The dinner was attended by 1,000 members, guests, and others, and some of the invitations had been on sale. The judge said that because places at the dinner had been on sale, this was 'not a private affair'. It was a public function, and she had been unlawfully discriminated against on the grounds of her sex.

- In the same year, an employment tribunal in Reading heard a complaint by Annette Crowley that she had been discriminated against by her employers, South African Airways. When she had returned to work eight weeks after the birth of her child, she had been required to increase the hours of her shifts at work to as many as 16 hours. Her work sometimes included driving across runways. She complained that the long hours prevented her from caring for her child, and were a safety risk. She was dismissed. The employment tribunal decided that her employers had made 'wholly unreasonable demands' upon her, and that she had been unfairly discriminated against on the ground of her sex. She was awarded three years' salary by way of compensation—a sum of approximately £50,000.

- In 2000, Deborah Stubbs, a detective in the Lincolnshire Police Force was awarded a large sum against the force having suffered a long period of serious sexual harassment by one of her superior officers.

- In March 2003, however, an employer's order to a *male* employee to wear a tie gave him the opportunity to take a sex discrimination case to court on behalf of men. Matthew Thompson, a job-centre employee, complained to the Manchester Employment Tribunal that he was the victim of sexual discrimination—his employers demanded that he wear a tie at all times, but they allowed women employees to wear T-shirts. The tribunal decided in his favour: '*The requirement to wear a collar and tie at work was gender-based, and therefore unlawful*'.

RACIAL DISCRIMINATION

A succession of Race Relations Acts have outlawed racial discrimination in a number of fields. Many cases of racial discrimination have come before the courts.

- In 1971, the licensee of the Painters Arms public house in Luton and his wife refused to serve five West Indians, saying that they had previously had trouble with West Indians at other public houses. A judge sitting at the Westminster County Court ruled that their conduct was unlawful, and awarded each of the five compensation for 'loss of opportunity' to be served there.

- In 1988, a transport authority employed Jaquant Singh as a bus inspector. He applied for the position of Senior Inspector, but the authority employed a system of 'ethnic monitoring' and he failed to get the job. He wished to prove that this was because he was being unlawfully discriminated against, but he needed evidence to do so. He applied to the court for an order that his employers should disclose all its statistical information, in order to see whether the authority had adopted a policy of racial discrimination. The Court of Appeal agreed to make the order, saying that if the statistics '*show racial or ethnic imbalance or disparities, then they may indicate areas of racial discrimination*'.

No one is free from proper complaint. Law and order agencies, and the legal profession itself, have been taken to court for discrimination:

- In 1999, a black Police Constable, Leslie Bowie, was awarded £7,000 compensation against the Metropolitan Police Force after suffering 'extreme and excessive discrimination' at the hands of a senior officer at Heathrow police station.

- In the same year, the South London Employment Tribunal decided that Maria Bameh, an employee of the Crown Prosecution Service, had been discriminated against by the Service. Her unfavourable treatment '*could only have been influenced by her ethnicity and gender*'.

- In 2001, the former vice-president of the Law Society, Kamlesh Bahl CBE, won a ruling in the employment tribunal that she had been a victim of racial and sexual discrimination by the Law Society itself.

There have been a number of cases in which black police officers have claimed that they have been discriminated against in their forces. In 2003, however, there came the kind of breakthrough in race relations which makes a difference. Mike Fuller, a Deputy Commissioner in the Metropolitan Police Force, became the first black chief constable when he was appointed Chief Constable of Kent.

Employers and others will also be responsible for unlawful discrimination if they impose conditions upon those in their charge which would have the effect of discriminating against them.

- In 1983, the Court of Appeal decided that a school requirement that pupils should all wear caps was discriminatory against Sikhs, and unlawful.

- Normally it would be unlawful to refuse to allow Sikhs to wear beards or turbans, but in two cases brought against the sweet manufacturers Rowntree Mackintosh and Nestlé, the companies were able to show that all people working in the factories had to cover up their hair. The court decided that a condition that employees must not wear beards in a sweet factory was justifiable on hygienic grounds.

OTHER DISCRIMINATION

There are other important laws which relate to discrimination:

- It is now a criminal offence to do anything to stir up racial hatred (Public Order Act 1986).

- The law has been changed to bring greater equality to homosexuals in their sexual relations with one another. The Sexual Offences (Amendment) Act 2000 finally equalised the age of consent (16) for homosexuals and heterosexuals. We learned in Chapter 5 that the Bill proposing this law was strongly resisted by the House of Lords, and only became an Act after the Parliament Act 1911 was invoked.

- In relation to a quite different minority, one of the latest in the line of statutes aimed at ending discrimination is the Disability Discrimination Act 1995 which, as its name suggests, sets out to provide equality of treatment and adequate facilities for the disabled. This Act applies in the fields of employment, transport, and services; and, as we will see below, includes the courts.

- In August 2003, a blind cricket team—the Eastern Vipers Cricket Club, from March in Cambridgeshire, won a £7,000 settlement for disability discrimination after the owners of a guesthouse had cancelled a booking they had made, when they realised that some of the team members would need to bring guide dogs on to the premises. (For the curious, 'blind cricket' is played on a normal outdoor pitch, with a large ball containing ball bearings, so the players can hear it.)

2. RACIALLY MOTIVATED CRIME

We have seen that it is a criminal offence in itself to do anything to stir up racial hatred; but the Crime and Disorder Act 1998 takes the criminal law much further than that. It provides that racial motivation for a crime shall be regarded as an **aggravating factor**, which will attract a more severe sentence. The Act introduced four main offences to deal with the problem of racially aggravated violence and harassment. These offences concern 'racially aggravated assaults', 'racially aggravated criminal damage', 'racially aggravated public order offences', and 'racially aggravated harassment'.

An offence is *racially aggravated* if the prosecution can show either the existence of 'racial hostility at the time of the offence' (for example, the use by the offender of racially hostile language) or 'that the offence was motivated wholly or partly by racial hostility' (for example, a group of white youths for no reason seek out and attack a group of black youths). If any of these offences is committed the maximum penalty which the court can pass is considerably higher than that for a similar crime which is not racially aggravated. The Criminal Justice Act 2003 takes all this one stage further. Now, in relation to most offences, the court must treat the fact that they were 'religiously or racially aggravated' as increasing their seriousness, and if it comes to this conclusion it must say so in open court. Both the Association of Chief Police Officers and the Crown Prosecution Service have indicated that provided the evidence available gives 'a realistic prospect of conviction', cases of this kind will be prosecuted.

3. CONDUCT OF CASE IN COURT

The judges themselves must do their best to ensure that their own courts are free from any prejudice and discrimination, whether intentional or not. In 1995, Lord Taylor, the Lord Chief Justice, said:

> Race issues go to the heart of our system of justice, which demands that all are treated as equal before the law. This is recognised not only in the standard embodiment of

justice as a figure blindfolded but also in terms of the judicial oath. It is therefore a matter of the gravest concern if members of the ethnic minorities feel they are discriminated against by the criminal justice system; more so if their fears were to be borne out in reality.

(Lord Taylor rightly refers to *Justice* traditionally being a figure blindfolded, but we may recall that the most famous emblem of justice—the *Lady of Justice* on top of the Old Bailey—is not. As it happens, some judges are blind. In 1998, the Lord Chancellor appointed four visually impaired magistrates, and by 2001 eight blind or visually impaired magistrates were in post. In 2000, John Lafferty, a solicitor, became the first blind recorder to preside over criminal cases in the Crown Court. In addition, in the Crown Court, on a number of occasions blind jurors have been permitted to try cases, bringing their guide dogs into court with them.)

The clear message of Lord Taylor's remarks, and those of many other senior judges, is that any person from an ethnic or religious minority who comes into court must be treated properly and with consideration, and in the same way as anybody else. The Criminal Justice Act 2003 adds to this, requiring the court to try to avoid, as far as practicable, making any order which clashes with an offender's religious beliefs. The courts' duty to avoid discrimination applies equally to the disabled:

DISABILITY

Courts now have a duty to comply with the Disability Discrimination Act 1995. Other Acts of Parliament, including the Human Rights Act, also require the courts to take account of disability. It is well known that a person's mental and physical health and abilities may influence their experience as a defendant or party to a case, or as a witness. Courts must be aware of this, and are required to have regard to their problems. They may need more time than others who are not disabled. Questions may have to be repeated or rephrased. The stress of coming to court may make their symptoms worse.

Special arrangements may have to be made in advance of the trial for the convenience and comfort of the disabled. The person with a disability may not be able to hear, read, or be understood, or fully understand what is happening. Some disabilities are so serious that they may make it impossible for the disabled person to attend court at all. Disabilities come in many forms, and whatever the disability may be—inability to walk, defective vision or hearing, or impairment of speech—all disabled people must have an equal access to justice, and their problems must be accommodated sympathetically. Therefore, if a litigant is so severely disabled that he or she cannot come to court at all, the court should be prepared to move and, if necessary, hear the case (or at least part of it) in the litigant's home or in a hospital, to ensure a fair trial. All this requires conscious thought, training, and, above all, understanding. Here are just four ways in which the judges try to make sure that they deal with everyone who comes into their courts equally, 'without fear or favour, affection or ill will'.

• Judges must ensure that everyone can understand what is being said, and can be understood. This frequently means using interpreters to translate for anyone who normally speaks a foreign language, or for any disabled person who cannot hear or speak.

• Judges must ensure that the religious beliefs of all jurors and witnesses are respected, and that when they have to swear an oath they are allowed to do so on the Holy Book of their choice, in the manner which is right for their beliefs.

• Judges must never allow any witness, whether a witness for the prosecution or the defence, to be bullied or intimidated. Judges these days receive training to make them aware of racial and cultural differences, and the need to make allowances for them.

• Judges must ensure that all those who come into their courts are treated in the same way, and are judged by the same standards. No defendant in a criminal case who appears to belong to an ethnic minority should be treated differently from any other defendant.

The Criminal Justice Act 1991 contains a provision (section 95), which is considered to be a breakthrough in the field of race relations in criminal cases. It instructs the Home Secretary to publish information each year to enable everyone involved in the administration of justice to '*avoid discriminating against any person on the ground of race or sex or any other improper ground*'. This research means that the *courts*—quite apart from anyone else involved in the criminal justice system—must keep a close check on the way in which people are sentenced, and consciously guard against discrimination.

It is interesting to note that those who are sentenced by the courts to community orders (Rehabilitation or Community Punishment) are given these very specific instructions in relation to discrimination by their supervising probation officers: '*We have a commitment to providing equal services and opportunities for all. We expect you to behave with respect towards people of different race, age, sex, disability, sexual orientation or religion. We will not tolerate any discrimination, either by you, or towards you.*'

*

The problems of prejudice and discrimination remain some of the most difficult, sensitive, and important facing society today. No one, except the most saintly, is free from all forms of prejudice; but that can never be an excuse for discrimination. It may well be that these problems will never be completely solved, but the work that is being done can make a real difference.

The force of new legislation, which is based upon the value of respecting others of a different sex or sexual orientation, and of different racial or ethic origins, is seeping slowly into the national consciousness. There is now a move in Parliament to make religious discrimination a criminal offence, although in December 2001, in the face of strong opposition from the House of Lords, the Government abandoned its attempt to make a new criminal offence of inciting religious hatred. Credit for the steady improvement goes to many people: enlightened parents, teachers, and workers in the community; role models from 'ethnic minorities'—community leaders, those in the public eye such as sportsmen and women and entertainers, who attract admiration and respect from a wide cross-section of the community, and in doing so gain acceptance for others; and not least, those of a new generation who refuse to share the prejudices of some of their elders.

Changing attitudes and prejudices is always very difficult, and can take a long time. Education and example by people of good sense and good will, and the promotion of women, disabled people, and people of merit from so-called ethnic minority groups to positions of authority, are a crucial part of this process. The courts cannot, by themselves, be expected to achieve these goals, but the law accepts that in many areas of life waiting for fair treatment is not good enough, and that all citizens are entitled to expect equal and fair treatment now. The belief that an equal justice is, so far as is humanly possible, available to all is one of the most important aspects of this work; and giving the whole community confidence that the justice system is dedicated to achieving this ideal is the special responsibility of the judges.

21

Young Persons

'When a court determines any question with respect to the upbringing of a child, the child's welfare shall be the court's paramount consideration.'
Section 1(1)(a) of the Children Act 1989.

*

This chapter is about young people up to the age of 18. It is called **young persons** because that is one term officially used for them in the *criminal courts*. The chapter could easily be headed differently, for by a Practice Direction dated February 2000, young persons when tried in the Crown Court are to be called **young defendants**; and in the *family courts* they are generally referred to as **children**. These are not the only names used for under-18s. In civil cases they are still sometimes referred to as 'infants' or 'minors', and in the criminal courts as 'juveniles'!

We all know that the law provides that there are certain things that children cannot lawfully do. That is because in this country the **age of majority**, that is, the age at which children become adults in the eyes of the law, is 18. Under that age, children cannot acquire full legal status, which means that they do not have all the rights and responsibilities of adults. There are many laws in existence which relate to this. These are just a few examples:

Under 18, a child cannot:

- Vote.

- Serve on a jury.

- Make binding contracts upon which he or she can be sued, except for *necessaries*, such as food and clothing.

- Make a will.

- Be served or drink alcohol in a pub or bar.

- Gamble in betting shops, clubs, and casinos.

- Be tattooed.

- See films certified as '18'.

Under 17, a child cannot:

- Drive.

Under 16, a child cannot:

- Marry. Children aged 16 or 17 may only marry with the written consent of their parents or a magistrate.

- Obtain a passport.

- Obtain a licence to drive a moped.

- Buy cigarettes or tobacco.

- Buy fireworks.

- Buy a lottery ticket.

Under 15, a child cannot:

- See films certified as '15'.

*

Young people may get involved with the courts in a number of ways, and much is done to ensure that when this happens, the courts, if possible, act in their best interests. It may be helpful to look at each of the main ways in which the courts may have to deal with young people.

YOUNG PERSONS ACCUSED OF CRIME

In Chapter 18, we looked at the main punishments that are available to the courts when dealing with young offenders; but how do they come to be prosecuted at all?

In this country a child under the age of ten years is *presumed* to be too young to commit a crime. Until 1998, as we have seen, children between the ages of ten and 14 were presumed not to understand the full consequences of their actions. They could not therefore be convicted of crime unless it could be shown that they knew that what they were doing was seriously wrong. The Crime and Disorder Act 1998 abolished this rule. Children in this age bracket are now presumed to understand the consequences of their actions, and are legally responsible for them.

When dealing with young persons who are suspected of committing crime, the police are not the only people involved. Their parent(s) or another adult concerned with their welfare (called 'the appropriate adult') and social services are also involved.

CAUTIONING

When police officers believe that young persons have committed offences they may, after discussing the case with a small group known as the 'cautioning panel', give them an **informal warning**. This amounts to little more than telling them in stern language not to misbehave again, although a record is kept that a warning has been given.

Sometimes the police may give a **formal caution**. If this happens the young person is not charged and taken to court, but has to attend a police station with his or her parent(s) or appropriate adult. A senior police officer will formally warn the young person of the seriousness of their behaviour, and the risk of prosecution if they offend again.

Formal cautions are only given where the offence is admitted, and adults responsible for the child agree. If not, serious consideration will then be given to prosecuting the young person in court. If a caution is administered, a record is made of it; and if the young person gets into trouble again, the court may be told about it. (This system of cautioning is also available in cases of adult crime, although the way of dealing with it is slightly different.) Sometimes when accepting a caution the young person may have to agree to behave in a particular way in future—for example, not to truant from school. Cautioning with a condition attached to it is called **cautioning plus**.

When police who are investigating a crime have reason to believe that a young person under the age of 17 has been involved, there are special rules relating to the interviewing of suspects. These are designed to ensure that they have a parent or appropriate adult present at the interview, that a lawyer can be there to protect their legal interests, and that the police questioning is entirely fair.

PROSECUTION

If the prosecuting authority (the Crown Prosecution Service—CPS) believes a young person has committed a crime and that it is necessary to bring him or her before a court, they will then be charged with the offence, and will have to appear before a **youth court**. Youth courts used to be known as 'juvenile courts'. The youth court is a branch of the magistrates' court, and justices who sit in this court are specially trained to deal with young persons.

If the young person denies the offence, the justices will hold a trial. This will take place along the lines set out in Chapter 17. If he or she pleads guilty or is found guilty, the justices will have to decide what action to take. The options open to the court are set out in Chapter 18. Youth courts do their utmost to avoid sending young offenders away from home into custody; and they will never do so without first obtaining the report of a probation officer or other social worker. They will always try to impose a constructive **community sentence** if possible, but they must also have in mind the interests of the public, and the need for innocent citizens to be protected from serious crime or repeated offending.

The justices have power to insist that the young person's parents should attend court. If the young person does not have a lawyer, the parents may be allowed to represent their child. Youth courts do not sit in public. This means that members of the general public are not allowed to sit in court, and there will be no press or media reporting of these cases. This is to protect young people from having their future lives blighted because they have been in trouble at an early age.

If a young person is charged with a very serious crime, such as murder or manslaughter, he or she will be tried in the Crown Court by a judge and jury. When that happens the public and the press are allowed into court, although the judge may make an order that the names of those on trial should not be published. In any other type of case, however serious, if a young person is sent to the Crown Court for trial, the Crown Court has the power to decide that it would be better in that particular case if he or she was tried by a youth court. If that happens, the case goes back to the youth court for trial.

The Bulger case (1)

In November 1993, two ten-year-old boys, Robert Thompson and Jon Venables, were tried in the Preston Crown Court for the horrific murder of a much younger child, James Bulger. They had taken James from a shopping centre and had battered him to death. Their trial took place in an ordinary adult court. They were convicted and sentenced to be 'detained during Her Majesty's pleasure'. The Lord Chief Justice, Lord Taylor, then said that this would mean a sentence of not less than ten years' detention.

Lawyers for the two young murderers did not appeal against their conviction in England, but in March 1998 they took their case to the European Commission of Human Rights in Strasbourg. They claimed that it was wrong for children of this age to be tried in an adult court in the full glare of publicity, and that their trial had been unfair because it had been 'frightening, humiliating and intimidating'. They said their trial had amounted to 'inhuman and degrading treatment' and was therefore unlawful.

In March 1999 the Commission decided that the two boys had been denied a fair trial because, as they had been tried in an adult criminal court, they had been 'prevented from effectively participating in their trial'. The Commission decided, though, that the trial had not amounted to inhuman or degrading treatment contrary to the European Convention on Human Rights. The case was then referred to the European Court of Human Rights to decide if our system of trying young children was flawed. The European Court decided that it was. In deciding this the Court had in mind that in many European countries children under 14 years of age are not tried in adult courts but in family courts. Also, the age of criminal responsibility in other European countries is different. In England it is ten, but in France it is 13; in Germany, Austria, and Italy it is 14; in the Scandinavian countries it is 15; and in Spain and Portugal it is 16.

Many people believe that we should not allow an outside body such as the European Court to interfere with our system of justice, but in the UK we do not hesitate to criticise the criminal justice systems of other countries, and so perhaps we should not resent it when our procedures are reflected through the eyes of others and tested in this way. It may well be that we have much to learn from the way in which the Commission and the European Court of Human Rights consider children should be tried. In February 2000, the Lord Chief Justice decided that we have. In that month, Lord Chief Justice Bingham set out in a *Practice Direction* new arrangements for the trial of young defendants in the Crown Court. Lord Bingham stated the *overriding principle* governing these trials:

> *Some young defendants accused of committing serious crimes might be very young and very immature when standing trial in the Crown Court. The purpose of such trial was to determine guilt (if that was in issue) and decide the appropriate sentence if the young defendant pleaded guilty or was convicted. The trial process should not itself expose the young defendant to avoidable intimidation, humiliation or distress. All possible steps should be taken to assist the young defendant to understand and participate in the proceedings.*

The Lord Chief Justice then went on to spell out what was expected in trials of young defendants, for example, that all involved in the trial should be on the same physical level, that the defendants should be permitted to sit with their parents and that there should be regular breaks. He went on to say, *'Robes and wigs should not be worn unless the young defendant asked that they should or the court for good reason ordered that they should.'*

The Bulger case (2)

This case has an interesting and important sequel. In 2001, after a number of years in custody, the two defendants were approaching their majorities. They would soon be adults, and no longer protected by an order of the court shielding their identities from disclosure. They therefore went to court to request permanent injunctions to restrain publication of confidential information relating to their identities, whereabouts, and appearance, especially after their release from detention.

Dame Butler-Sloss, President of the Family Division, granted these injunctions on the grounds that the disclosure of their identities on their release would have disastrous consequences for them, including 'the real and strong possibility of serious harm and death'.

YOUNG PERSONS AS VICTIMS OF CRIME

No young person should ever be sexually or physically abused. No young person should ever be treated cruelly or be neglected (in law, this means being deprived of adequate food, clothing, medical aid, or lodging). No young person should ever be harmed by an adult, and any kind of harmful conduct counts as 'child abuse'. When this happens, the child concerned should be protected by the law. As these cases are commonly known as cases of 'child abuse' we will for convenience refer to young victims as children.

There has been much debate about whether children may be punished by being smacked, or beaten in some other way. In Chapter 19 we saw a case decided by the European Court of Human Rights, when the Court said that the caning of an eight-year-old boy by his step-father amounted to 'inhuman or degrading treatment' contrary to Article 3 of the European Convention. The child was awarded damages of £10,000. This decision was hailed by some as a landmark judgment—the most important development in child protection law for over a hundred years; but although corporal punishment has now been outlawed in schools, and there are moves to prohibit the striking of any small child, it is still legal for a child to be physically chastised.

Sadly, not all cases of serious child abuse are reported to the police, and where there is no report there is little the law can do. When a report is received, the law in most cases moves swiftly to protect children by separating them from anyone who presents as a danger, punishing anyone who abuses or behaves cruelly towards them, and providing the children with a safe and healthy environment in which to live. It is a major national scandal, exposed by recent public inquiries, that children have actually been abused in some of the homes to which they have been sent for their protection.

- In 1999, Victoria Climbié was sent by her parents in the Ivory Coast to live in London with her great-aunt. They felt that her opportunities to succeed in life would be better in Europe. In February 2000, aged eight, she died having been tortured and starved to death. The great-aunt and her boyfriend were convicted of murder, and following this trial, Lord William Laming, a former Chief Inspector in the Department of Health, conducted a 15-month inquiry into the circumstances of her death. The inquiry found that on a number of occasions Victoria might have been saved by social workers, National Health Service staff, and the police if they had been aware of each other's suspicions. Following the inquiry, in September 2003 the Government announced a range of proposals to try to ensure that this could not happen again.

These were introduced by the Prime Minister, Tony Blair, who said the names of abused children had triggered previous inquiries 'echoing down the years', and which were 'a standing shame to us all'. The proposals included the appointment of an independent commissioner to protect the rights and well-being of children, and that every child in the country should be given a unique identification number, so as to ensure efficient liaison between the protection agencies for any child at risk.

When it comes to proceedings in court, much has been learned in past years about the ill-treatment of children. Judges who deal with these cases have specialist training and now have much more knowledge and understanding than before. They appreciate that it is very common for children who have been abused to feel in some way guilty or responsible for what has happened, especially if the abuse has gone on for a long time. Judges know how painful and confusing these feelings can be, and that assists them to deal with these cases sensitively in court.

Let us take the case of a child who has been the victim of crime. How does the law protect him or her, and deal with the person responsible? What happens if the person accused of abuse or ill-treatment denies the allegation?

If a young person has been the victim of crime, he or she will first be seen by a police officer who is specially trained to deal with this type of case. Police forces and all social service departments have **child protection teams**. The police officers and social workers in these teams have great experience in dealing with problems of this type. If the person accused of an offence is arrested and charged, the police and the courts will ensure that, when it is necessary, there is no contact between that person and the child they are accused of harming.

The child will first be interviewed by the police about what happened. This interview takes place in a special room. It is made as informal and comfortable as possible. Small children will find it is well stocked with toys. It will be fitted with a **video camera** to record what the child has to say. Usually a police woman and social worker will conduct the interview; but a parent or an adult friend of the child may also be present.

The interviewing of young children in these circumstances calls for considerable skill. If the child is very young, he or she will first be put at ease. It is essential that the interviewer should gain the child's confidence. Those watching the video recording of the interview (which is always made) will often find that for some time the child is playing with toys and just chatting with the interviewer. Gradually, sometimes almost imperceptibly, the child will be brought round to the subject of the case. The child will be asked questions about the case, but this will be done in an informal way. The interviewer will be careful not to tell the witness what to say.

Are you worried?

Here is a list of things that have worried some children about going to court. We would like to know if any of them worry you. Tick the box that describes your feelings best. There are no 'right' or 'wrong' answers. If you have worries that are not listed here, you can add them at the end. You can also write down your questions.

Does it worry you . . .?	Not worried	A little worried	Very worried
Seeing the defendant			
Being 'got at' by the defendant or his supporters			
Mother/father/brother/sister/grandparents being angry			
Being sent away			
Being sent to prison myself			
People shouting at me in court			
Not understanding the questions			
Not being believed			
Speaking in front of strangers			
Not understanding what I am supposed to do at court			
Crying while giving evidence			
Needing to go to the toilet			
Having my name in the newspaper			
The defendant being sent to prison			
What will happen when he gets out			
The defendant being found not guilty			

Other fears and worries that I have	Questions I would like to ask

Figure 21.1 Questionnaire for child witnesses
Source: NSPCC/Childline, *Preparing Young Witnesses for Court* (1998). Reproduced with permission.

Often the child will be expected to go over the events more than once in order to test the consistency of his or her account. Sometimes the doll the child has been playing with will be used to help the child explain and demonstrate what has happened. The advantage of this system is that there is a permanent record for all to see of what took place during the interview. This will help everyone to assess the evidence.

If children have to go to court to give evidence, they will be given a great deal of support. This will include a 'young witness pack', which has been specially devised by the National Society for the Prevention of Cruelty to Children (NSPCC) for '5–17-year-old child witnesses'. The younger witness will have a model of a courtroom with slot-in characters, and other material, which will help him or her to understand what happens at court. The pack includes a useful checklist of things that have been known to worry children about going to court, and child is able to tick the box which describes his or her feelings best. Then they can be reassured. In July 2000, the NSPCC produced a video for children entitled *Giving evidence, what is it really like?* This is intended to help children understand their role as witnesses, and cope with the experience in court. The NSPCC checklist is reproduced as Figure 21.1.

Going to court will not be a pleasant experience but much is done to try to make sure it is not traumatic—in the hope that children will understand that it is very much better to complain about their treatment than continue to be abused. There will be no publicity of the child's name. The court will order that **special measures** be taken to protect the child as far as possible. He or she will never have to be in the same room as the person who is accused of abusing or ill-treating them. They do not go into court at all, but give evidence to everyone who is in court (including the defendant) by means of a **video-link** between their room and the court. Let us picture what happens in a typical 'video-link trial':

A video-link trial

A young child aged nine says that she was assaulted by a man in a park. She has told her mother, and the police have been called. They will then go to a police station and in a specially equipped room the girl will tell a female police officer all about it. Her 'complaint', as it is called, has been videoed.

If the man is arrested and prosecuted the child will be taken to court by her parent(s), or (if she has no parent), by a close relative or adult friend. There she will meet a social worker or some other independent person who is used to dealing with these cases. After they have got to know one another, they will go into a room with a television and video recorder. The social worker will stay with her while she is in this room, and will look after her until it is time for her to go back to her parents.

Once in the room, the child will sit down facing the screen. She will first see the judge on the screen. He will tell her that it is very important to tell the truth, and will then introduce her to the lawyers (for the prosecution and defence) who will also appear on the screen. The judge and lawyers will all treat her with consideration.

Then the child will watch the video recording of her complaint to the police. At the same time, this will be seen by the people in court. She will be asked if what she said was true, and if she would like to change or add anything. Then she will be asked questions about what she has said by the lawyers.

The judge and lawyers and everyone else involved in the case will remain in court. The child will only be able to see the judge or the lawyer who is asking the questions on the television screen in her room. The people in court will be able to see her on television screens in the court. If she gets tired or upset, there will be a break. When the child has finished her evidence, the rest of the evidence in the case will be heard in open court as usual.

Normally, in these cases too, lawyers are not 'robed' — they do not wear their wigs and gowns. Even the judge will take off his or her wig and gown — to make the experience less daunting for the child. Judges always try to make sure that children are treated properly. They are never bullied by the lawyers. Children as young as five or six have given evidence in this way, although some have been disappointed that the judges and barristers were *not* wearing their wigs and gowns!

The police, social services, and the courts always try hard to ensure that in cases where children have to give evidence, they come to no harm.

CHILDREN AND THE FAMILY

However young or old we may be, we are all the children of our parents, and when it comes to the welfare of young persons in a *family situation*, they are always referred to as **children**. That is why we are doing so here.

There are many unhappy cases where parents separate, or divorce, or where for some other reason the courts have to concern themselves with 'child welfare'. It is not necessary to go into all the possibilities in this book, but it is important to point out that wherever there is a serious family problem, or there is reason to believe that a child is not being properly cared for, the courts have the power to make **orders** (give instructions) concerning the child. Whatever order is requested or being considered, the court must always be guided by what is in the *best interests of the child*.

In this connection, the most important Act of Parliament providing for the welfare of children is the Children Act 1989. At the beginning of the Act, three general principles are set out for the guidance of the courts. These are:

- *That the child's welfare shall be the paramount consideration.* (The child's best interests always come first.)

- *That any delay in dealing with a case concerning a child is likely to prejudice the child's welfare.* (Any child case must be heard as quickly as possible, otherwise the child may suffer. Sometimes there may be 'planned delays' with a specific purpose, such as obtaining an assessment.)

- *The court should only make an order if it believes that doing so would be better for the child than making no order at all.* (The courts should intervene and take some action only if it is really necessary.)

When deciding what to do in any case concerning a child, the court must go through a checklist of points. These are called the **welfare checklist**. It includes taking into account:

- The wishes of the child (if the child is old enough).

- The child's physical, emotional, and educational needs.

- The likely effect on a child of any change in the child's life and circumstances.

- The child's age, sex, background, and anything else relevant to that child.

- Any harm which the child has suffered or is at risk of suffering.

- How capable the child's parents are of meeting the child's needs.

The Children Act 1989 gives the courts a very wide range of options to deal with the very wide range of cases that come before them. The most important types of orders are likely to relate to three things:

- *Who should look after the child*: this may be parents or other members of the family, or foster parents or the local authority; and

- *Who should have contact with the child*: that is, who should see the child, and when; and

- *Where the child should live.*

Very often, whatever decisions it makes, the court will also make a **supervision order**, which means that the child's progress will be carefully monitored by a trained social worker.

Decisions made by the court can be changed if it is appropriate. If the court makes any order which does not seem to be working in the best interests of the child, all those concerned with his or her welfare may ask the court to reconsider the situation, and if necessary the court will make new orders.

In every family case the court will take into account the wishes of the child and his or her family, and the views of the Child and Family Court Advisory and Support Service (CAFCASS). CAFCASS works with children and their families and then advises on what it considers to be in the children's best interests. The court may also seek the guidance of experienced social workers and, if necessary, other, independent experts, who will know all about the 'welfare checklist'. It is important to realise that although the court must know the wishes of each child, that is only part of the story. Judges sometimes say that they understand what the child wants, but the child does not know what may be in his or her best interests; and that has to be the judge's decision.

Sometimes children ask to see the judge. This wish is rarely granted. When the judge does see the child, this will be after all the other evidence has been heard; but the judge must then tell the parties in court what the child has said, for there can be no secrets between the judge and child. This is because justice must be *seen* to be done, and the parties in the case must as a matter of fairness be given the chance to consider and answer what the child has said.

*

Some countries have a Bill (or Charter) of Rights, a written statement of the rights of every citizen. In 1990, the majority of countries signed an agreement, which sets out the rights of children, and the way in which they should be treated. It is called the *United Nations Convention on the Rights of the Child*. Set out below are some of the main conditions of this Convention. Unhappily, it must be accepted that in many countries they are not honoured.

UNITED NATIONS CONVENTION ON THE RIGHTS OF THE CHILD

1 All children should be treated equally. A child's or its parent's sex, colour, language, religion or disability should not affect this in any way.

2 When dealing with children, official groups such as the police, doctors, schools and the courts should act in what they believe to be the best interests of the child.

3 Every child has the right to life, and everything possible should be done by the Government of the country concerned to ensure that a child grows up in healthy surroundings.

4 All children should have a name, a nationality and the right to know and be looked after by his or her parents.

5   *A child has the right to express an opinion freely and for that opinion to be taken into account by those dealing with the child.*

6   *Children should be free to choose their religion and friends, as long as this does not in some way damage the rights and freedom of others.*

7   *No child should be treated or punished in a cruel or inhuman way, or be deprived of liberty.*

8   *Disabled children have the right to special care to help them enjoy as full a life as possible.*

9   *All children should have a standard of living that helps them fully develop. It is the job of parents to provide this; but if this cannot be done, the State should make sure this is being done.*

10   *Children should have a free education that helps them develop to the full.*

11   *No child should carry out work that is harmful or interferes with his or her education.*

12   *No child under the age of 15 should be allowed to join the armed forces.*

22

Dangerous Drugs

'The most horrifying aspect [of class A drugs] is the degradation and suffering and not infrequently, death, which these drugs bring to the addict . . . Consequently, anything which the courts of this country can do by way of deterrent sentences on those found guilty of crimes involving these class A drugs should be done.'

Lord Lane, Lord Chief Justice, in the leading 'drugs case' of *R* v *Aramah*, 1982.

'Drugs can do untold damage. Make sure you have the low down on drugs. You don't need to try a drug to know how it will affect you. If your mates try to pressurise you into trying drugs, they're not worth having.'

Check It magazine, published on behalf of the Metropolitan Police Service.

*

This chapter deals with those drugs that have been defined by Act of Parliament as *'dangerous or otherwise harmful drugs'*. Two of the most important of these Acts are the Misuse of Drugs Act 1971 and the Drug Trafficking Act 1994. These, and other drugs laws, are not aimed at spoiling everyone's enjoyment, but at protecting people from the effects of dangerous drugs. There is much debate as to whether they are able to achieve that aim.

All drugs that are described as dangerous and harmful are listed in an Act of Parliament. They are called **controlled drugs**, because Parliament has set out to *control* their use and supply. These drugs are then **classified** into groups, which are intended to reflect the seriousness of their danger to the public. The groups are simply long lists of the drugs that have been put into a particular category. The law says that it is a criminal offence to import, to produce, to supply, or even simply to have possession of any of these *controlled* and *classified* drugs.

Supply does not simply mean 'sell'. Someone who merely hands over a dangerous drug to a friend for his or her use commits the serious criminal offence of supplying dangerous drugs.

CLASSIFICATION OF DANGEROUS DRUGS

- *Class A* drugs are regarded as the most dangerous. They include heroin, cocaine, crack, LSD, and ecstasy. The sentences for their importation, production, supply, and use can be very severe.

- *Class B* drugs are considered to be less dangerous, but they are nevertheless harmful to the people who use them. They include amphetamines.

- *Class C* drugs are the least dangerous, and therefore are lowest in the list of seriousness. The names of the drugs listed in this category are not well known, but the better-known ones include diazepam, temazepam, testosterone and cannabis (now re-classified from being a class B drug by the Criminal Justice Act 2003).

Officers of HM Customs and Excise, often with the help of their 'sniffer dogs', are largely responsible for detecting the importation of drugs into this country. Often, Customs officials receive vital information from around the world that drugs are about to arrive. Sometimes they mount surveillance operations, which may last for months before they seize some ship or container, and systematically take it apart until they have found the secret compartments that house the drugs.

A Home Office Crime Survey has found that *'drug misuse is especially prevalent among younger people (aged 16–29)'*. It is believed that in relation to the population as a whole, only a relatively small number of young people have become addicted to dangerous drugs. Nevertheless, it would be wrong to understate the huge and heartbreaking problem this causes to them and their families.

Parliament and the courts have regard to the possible serious medical effects of taking dangerous drugs. Parliament has fixed a range of penalties for drugs offences, and the courts decide what penalties to impose within that framework. The medical effects which are set out below concern the dangers of **dependency** (addiction). They also concern the possible effects of taking an overdose.

MEDICAL EFFECTS OF DANGEROUS DRUGS

The medical effects of drug taking can be catastrophic. We all know of tragic cases where people have died after taking just one 'E' (ecstasy tablet). Generally, the possible effects of overdosing on drugs will depend upon the type of drugs concerned. The dangers increase if the drugs are in any way contaminated by unclean and dangerous methods of preparation, or if they are mixed with alcohol or other drugs, or with the risk of contracting communicable diseases through sharing needles or other drugs equipment. Much of the following information about the effects of drug abuse has been compiled by the Metropolitan Police Central Drug Squad:

DEPENDENCE AND POSSIBLE EFFECTS OF OVERDOSING

- With **analgesics** such as heroin, morphine, and pethedine, it is very likely that the drugs user will quickly become dependent upon these drugs, both physically and psychologically. The effects can be convulsions, coma, and possible death.

- With **stimulants** such as cocaine and amphetamines ('speed'), it is very likely that the drugs user will quickly become dependent psychologically. The effects can include agitation, hallucinations, convulsions, and possible death.

  Ecstasy is a stimulant drug, related to speed. It also has hallucinogenic effects, which means that it can distort the perception of reality. The effect on the brain may be that the user feels elated, but everyone can react differently to dangerous drugs and ecstasy can also cause panic, depression, and even brain damage. Physical harm can include damage to the blood cells, leaving red marks on the skin, liver damage, and even kidney failure. One very serious danger is that of 'hard raving in a hot place' after taking ecstasy. This can cause heat-stroke, and has been the cause of a number of deaths.

- With **depressants** such as the sleeping tablets which contain barbiturates, it is very likely that the drugs user will quickly become dependent, both physically and psychologically. The effects can include anxiety, insomnia, tremors, convulsions, and possible death.

- With **hallucinogens** such as LSD, the dependence upon these drugs is as yet largely unknown. The effects may include nausea and vomiting. They may also involve personality change and psychosis (severe mental illness).

- With **cannabis**, whether it is in the form of herbal cannabis, resin, or oil, the effects of dependence upon these drugs is largely unknown. Cannabis is still the most commonly used drug, with more than twice as many young people saying that they have taken cannabis at some time, as have reported using any other drug. The possible harmful effects include fatigue, paranoia, and psychosis. The Criminal Justice Act 2003 reduced this drug from being a Class B drug to a Class C drug, so that its *use* became less serious; but the Act increased the maximum sentence for *supplying* all Class C drugs from five years to 14 years. The Government has for some time been investigating whether this drug, taken in tablet form, may have a beneficial effect on those who are suffering from certain serious diseases.

This list relates to some of the drugs covered by the Act. It does not cover inhaling or sniffing glue, gas, or aerosols, but these can also be highly dangerous.

LEGAL CONSEQUENCES OF INVOLVEMENT WITH DANGEROUS DRUGS

Drugs can now be readily identified by scientists working in this field. It is generally easy to identify drugs used by drug takers by analysing samples of their blood or urine. The legal consequences of involvement with dangerous drugs will largely depend upon the type of drugs concerned and what that involvement is. Parliament has ordered that:

- The maximum penalties for *supplying* controlled drugs are: in the case of Class A drugs, life imprisonment; for Class B and Class C drugs, 14 years' imprisonment.

- The maximum penalties for merely *possessing* controlled drugs (for one's own use) are: in the case of Class A drugs, seven years' imprisonment; for Class B drugs, five years' imprisonment; and for Class C drugs, two years' imprisonment.

It is regarded as an extremely serious crime to be involved in the production or importation of dangerous drugs, or their supply to others. Anyone who deals in drugs for profit, or who smuggles drugs into a prison, will normally be sentenced to a long term of imprisonment. The length of sentence will depend upon what type of drug is involved, with the most severe punishments (often in the range of between 10 and 20 years' imprisonment) reserved for those who deal in large quantities of Class A drugs. Sentences of over 20 years have been imposed in the worst cases. New laws are now in force that make it mandatory for the courts to impose heavy sentences of imprisonment if the offender has committed previous drug-dealing offences. If someone supplies dangerous drugs, but not for personal gain, there will still very likely be a prison sentence, in particular if the drugs are Class A, but this will always depend on all the circumstances of the case.

When young people are before the courts for possessing dangerous drugs for their own use they will usually be dealt with more leniently—certainly for a first offence—and efforts will be made to help them to overcome any addiction they may have. This will usually involve the court making a Rehabilitation Order, or a Drug Treatment and Testing Order (see below), with a condition that the offender will receive counselling and treatment at a residential clinic or Drug Rehabilitation Centre.

There are police community liaison officers who are specialists in the field of drugs. They are available to give advice in schools and throughout their local communities. There are also projects throughout the country which specialise in the counselling and treatment of people addicted to taking dangerous drugs. Impressive and selfless work is done by those who help at these projects. Anyone who wishes to know more about the drugs scene and the possible effects of taking drugs will find that there is now a great deal of helpful literature and advice available.

SENTENCING IN DRUGS CASES

How do *the courts* attempt to arrive at the right sentences in drugs cases? Generally, the object of sentencing in drugs cases is to *punish* and *deter* drugs dealers and to *rehabilitate drugs* users. The Court of Appeal has, in a number of 'guideline cases', given judgments for the assistance of judges on what tariff (range of sentences) they should have in mind for the importation, sale, and distribution of Class A and Class B dangerous drugs. Judges are not bound to impose sentences within the ranges suggested in these cases, but they should always be aware of the tariff.

A leaflet entitled *Drugs—Government Action*, published in 1998, records that, *'Statistics show that almost half of young people will take drugs at some time'* and estimates that *'We have between 100,000 and 200,000 seriously addicted drug misusers in this country'*. Many people, in particular teenagers and those in their twenties, who become addicted to drugs, turn to a life of crime in order to pay the large sums of money needed to buy their supplies. That is why much crime—usually burglary and robbery—is described as 'drug related'. In 2001, it was estimated that *'around 50,000–60,000 problem drug users are arrested and prosecuted every year. This group alone may each commit 150 crimes a year—roughly 7.5 million offences.'*

Many people who are otherwise decent and well-intentioned citizens find themselves forced to turn to crime to fund their addiction to drugs, but the Court of Appeal has stated that the fact that crime—such as robbery, theft, and burglary—is drug related is not a matter that judges should take into account to reduce sentences. Offenders may well have to serve sentences in young offender institutions or prisons as a result. Any judge who has to deal with criminal cases will be aware of the appalling effects that drug taking can have upon the lives of defendants, young and old—and those who are the victims of their crimes. Courts regularly encounter, at first hand, the distressing spectacle of a procession of young people whose mental and physical health has been broken through taking dangerous drugs.

Another serious legal consequence of drug offending is that anyone caught and convicted will now have a criminal record. This can spoil their chances of getting work, for anyone applying for a job will most likely be required to reveal this on his or her CV. It will also create problems for those who wish to travel, as some countries have very strict rules prohibiting entry to foreigners who have even minor convictions for drugs offences.

DRUG TREATMENT AND TESTING ORDERS

Special Drug Treatment and Testing Orders, which require close supervision of the offender by the court itself were introduced on an experimental basis in 1998, and are becoming more widely available. These orders can be made on offenders aged 16 and over, for periods of between six months and three years. They are targeted at serious drug misusers, with a view to reducing the amount of crime they commit to fund their drugs habit. The offender will be considered suitable for an order only after careful assessment, and if he or she has a real motivation to accept treatment, and consents to an order being made. The order will provide for three things: *treatment* (this will be as part of a community sentence, such as a community rehabilitation or punishment order), *regular drug testing*, and *regular reviews by the court* of the offender's progress.

*

In October 1997, the first 'UK Anti-Drugs Co-ordinator' (known as the 'Drug Czar') was appointed to make an overall appraisal of the drugs problem in Britain, and to recommend ways of tackling it in the future. (This work has now been taken over by the Home Office.) A ten-year strategy, *Tackling Drugs To Build a Better Britain*, was developed. It had four key aims:

- *Young people*—to help young people resist drug misuse in order to achieve their full potential in society.

- *Communities*—to protect communities from drug-related anti-social and criminal behaviour.

- *Treatment*—to enable people with drug problems to overcome them and live healthy and crime-free lives.

- *Availability*—to stifle the availability of illegal drugs on our streets.

There is a move to legalise or 'de-criminalise' drug taking, but few involved with the drugs laws—either as law makers, law enforcers, law upholders, or those involved with the care of drugs users—have supported this. The Home Office, however, regularly takes advice from medical experts, and considers representations from interested bodies and members of the public, in relation to possible changes in the law.

Those who say that drugs should be available to anyone argue for personal freedom. They say that cigarettes contain an addictive and dangerous drug (nicotine), and alcohol is also a drug. They are both freely on sale to adults, yet they are potentially dangerous, and have caused much misery in the lives of many people. If these drugs are legal, why not all the others; and in particular, why not cannabis, about which there has been much controversy? This is a powerful point, and a difficult one to answer, as are so many ethical problems of this kind. One answer is that, whichever way one looks at it, two wrongs cannot make a right, and some drugs are known to take a very quick and deadly hold on those who use them. These arguments have had some effect, because they have persuaded Parliament to re-classify cannabis as a Class C drug (although those who supply it will face even harsher sentences than before). Another answer is that Parliament tries to achieve a balance between allowing people the freedom to enjoy themselves as they please, and protecting them and others from serious harm.

Many of the problems that we have in society involve trying to strike a reasonable balance between rights and duties—even rights and duties in relation to our own bodies. As with all controversial matters, the courts will uphold the laws passed by Parliament. Whether Parliament succeeds in striking a fair and reasonable balance, and whether the courts are able to give expression to this successfully, are questions that each individual is entitled to consider.

23

Animals

'We can judge the heart of a man by his treatment of animals.'
Immanuel Kant, German philosopher (1724–1804).

'A gift for the benefit and protection of animals tends to promote and encourage kindness towards them, to discourage cruelty, and to ameliorate the condition of the brute creation, and thus stimulate humane and generous sentiments in man towards the lower animals, and by these means promote feelings of humanity and morality generally, repress brutality, and thus elevate the human race.'
Lord Justice Swinfen Eady, in a case concerning a gift in a will for animal welfare, 1915.

＊

Animals are entitled to be protected against cruel treatment; and we are entitled to be protected from dangerous animals. In this chapter we will examine how the law tries to achieve both of these aims.

PROTECTION OF ANIMALS

The proper treatment of animals is governed by several Acts of Parliament. There has been much controversy about the law. Many people believe that it does not give sufficient protection for creatures which, after all, have no way of speaking up for themselves. Nearly two hundred years ago, a philosopher and great writer on law reform, Jeremy Bentham, put the case for animal welfare in this simple way: *'The question is not can they reason? Nor can they talk? But can they suffer?'* He stated the principle that *'The legislator should forbid everything which may serve to lead to cruelty'*.

Bentham's writings were so influential that in 1822 Parliament made it an offence to 'beat abuse or ill-treat any horse, mare, gelding, mule, ass, ox, cow, heifer, steer, sheep or other cattle'. Other animals that were baited and ill-treated were not so fortunate. Bull-baiting and cockfighting were still accepted 'sports', and the treatment of animals in slaughterhouses was truly appalling.

The law now is that no one may treat an animal cruelly. It is unlawful to inflict pain and suffering on an animal, or to abandon an animal in circumstances that would be likely to cause suffering.

- In November 1998 two police dogs Instructors in the Essex Police Force were sentenced (one of them to imprisonment) for cruelty to dogs at their training centre at Sandon, near Chelmsford. They had used cruel methods to train police dogs. This had included kicking and punching disobedient dogs. One dog had died.

Certain people keep and look after animals as part of their business—pet shops, kennels, riding stables, zoos. They must have a licence to keep animals, and if they treat them cruelly, they may be punished, have their licences cancelled, and be banned from keeping them in the future. Circus owners must be registered to exhibit and train performing animals. They too must allow them to be inspected regularly, to ensure they are being treated properly.

- In January 1999 Mary Chipperfield, a member of the famous Chipperfield's Circus family, was convicted of ill-treating a baby chimpanzee by hitting and kicking it. Her husband was found guilty of cruelty to a sick elephant.

The law also protects animals that live in the wild. The Wildlife and Countryside Act 1981 provides laws for the protection of wild birds, their nests, and eggs. Certain wild animals may not be taken at all.

This Act contains a very long list of these fortunate creatures. It is extremely detailed, and includes a whole range of animals as diverse as bats (all kinds), the swallowtail butterfly, the bottle-nosed and common dolphins, and the Carthusian snail! The list is updated by the Department for Environment, Food and Rural Affairs, whenever an animal (or plant) is under threat. More recent additions include the basking shark, the water vole, the giant goby fish, the fairy shrimp, and the marsh fritillary butterfly.

Other animals may not be killed by certain methods. The Wild Mammals (Protection) Act 1996 makes it an offence to inflict unnecessary suffering on any wild animal. People hunting rabbits, hares, and other wildlife can only use traps which are approved by law, and which are not likely to cause suffering. Nevertheless, some 'blood sports', such as fox hunting, are still lawful. Parliament is presently considering whether there should be a change in the law, which would ban hunting with dogs. The House of Commons has voted for abolition; the House of Lords has voted for retention.

The need to protect animals raises another important question of ethics, concerning vivisection and experimentation. Animals have been experimented on for many years by research scientists. These days, laws are in force which regulate the treatment of animals for experimentation. This work is now subject to strict controls, although for obvious reasons the distress and suffering to animals are sometimes difficult to assess.

Most people seem to agree that some kinds of research involving animals, such as testing of cosmetics, is unacceptable, and this has recently been banned. They do, however, accept the justification for the controlled animal experimentation that has led to the saving of countless human lives, and the easing of human suffering.

PROTECTION OF PEOPLE FROM ANIMALS

There are many health regulations designed to protect us from animals that might carry disease. One of the most serious of these diseases is rabies, and although the quarantine laws have now been revised, there are very strict rules requiring animals brought into this country to be examined to make sure that they are free of disease before they are allowed to mix with the general population.

What about animals that actually cause harm or injury when they get out of control, or attack people? Here the law divides animals into two categories: animals that belong to a 'naturally dangerous' species, and animals that are normally regarded as harmless. Different rules apply to each group.

NATURALLY DANGEROUS ANIMALS

The law is that any animals in this category have to be kept in conditions of strict security; and if they do any harm, their owners or keepers are responsible for it, even if they were not personally to blame. This concept of responsibility without blame is called **strict liability**; for the keeper of the animal is strictly liable for any harm it may do, regardless of fault on his part.

Animals that belong to the dangerous category naturally include wild animals such as lions and tigers. Elephants are also included. In some parts of the world, elephants may be domesticated, and are not normally thought of as naturally vicious. Nevertheless, a court has decided that because of their sheer size and unpredictable behaviour—they may become frightened and stampede—they must be regarded as dangerous.

- In 1954 Mr and Mrs Behrens worked together at a fun fair, which travelled around the country with Bertram Mills Circus. They were midgets, and were exhibited in a small booth near to the main circus tent.

  Bertram Mills had six Burmese elephants that performed in the circus. In order to reach the circus from the menagerie where they were kept, they had to pass the booth where the Behrens worked. One day, as the animals were being led past the booth, a small dog ran out, barking. This frightened one of the elephants and caused a stampede; and in a flash two of them had trampled down the booth, and injured Mrs Behrens. Her husband suffered shock. They both had to be off work, and lost earnings as a result.

The court decided that the Circus was liable for the accident, because as elephants are a naturally dangerous species of animal their owners were responsible for keeping them under control at all times. It did not matter that the damage resulted from circumstances beyond their control. Mrs Behrens was awarded almost £3,000 damages, and her husband £480.

On the other hand, bees and (as we shall see) camels have been included in the category of animals that are naturally harmless.

NATURALLY HARMLESS ANIMALS

The law is that animals that are naturally harmless do not have to be kept in conditions of strict security. All domestic animals come into this category, and Parliament has even defined what they include. A domestic animal *'means any horse, ass, mule, bull, sheep, pig, goat, dog, cat, or fowl, or any other animal of whatsoever kind of species, and whether a quadruped or not which is tame or which has been or is being sufficiently tamed to serve some purpose for the use of man'*.

If the owners or keepers of 'naturally harmless animals' allow them to escape and do harm, they will be normally be held responsible only if they can be shown to have been negligent in their handling. There are, however, two important exceptions to the general law relating to naturally harmless animals:

(a) Vicious animals

If the owner of an animal (normally harmless) has reason to believe that this particular creature is vicious because of its past behaviour, he or she has the same responsibility for keeping it secure as if it were a naturally dangerous animal. Therefore, if the owner of a horse knows that it has a habit of biting or kicking people he must keep it as secure as if it were a wild animal.

- In 1938 Mr McQuaker visited Chessington Zoo. While he was feeding a camel through a fence of wire netting his hand was badly bitten. He claimed damages against the Zoo for failing to ensure his safety, but he lost his case. He took it to the Court of Appeal.

  First the court decided that as *'nowhere in the world is the camel found in a wild state'*, it was a domestic animal. The Zoo could therefore be held responsible for the biting only if it could be shown that it was negligent because the animal was not properly fenced, or if the camel was known to have a tendency to bite people. As it was fenced, and it was not known to bite people, the Zoo was not responsible. The Court of Appeal expressed sympathy for the claimant, but said he was not entitled to damages.

(b) Dogs

Although dogs are normally regarded as naturally harmless animals, some dogs are known to be dangerous, and Parliament has passed strict laws in relation to their safe keeping. For example, the Guard Dogs Act 1975 provides that no guard dog shall be used on any premises unless its handler keeps it under control, or it is securely tethered.

The most controversial laws in relation to dogs are set out in the Dangerous Dogs Act 1991. This Act was passed in response to public outrage at savage attacks by uncontrolled dogs on members of the public, in particular, children. It contains specially harsh rules for guard dogs and certain other types of dog:

- If the owner of any dog allows it to get dangerously out of control in a public place, and it attacks someone, he or she may be punished and the court must order that the dog shall be destroyed. Any place such as a road or park is a public place, as is a building (a cinema or football ground) or form of transport used by members of the public (bus or train).

- In addition, the Dangerous Dogs Acts 1989 and 1991 list certain special types of dog that have the characteristics of 'dogs bred for fighting'. These include the Pit Bull Terrier and the Japanese Tosa. They must be kept under control at all times, and if they are taken into any public place they must kept on a leash and muzzled. If this strict law is broken—even if the dog does no harm—the owner can be severely punished and the court *must* order that the dog shall be destroyed.

This law was severely criticised, for it gave the court no choice what to do, even if it believed that the dog could do no harm. In response to this criticism, Parliament has amended the law, and a court no longer has to make a destruction order if it believes that 'the dog would not constitute a danger to public safety'.

- In November 2002 Princess Anne, the Princess Royal, pleaded guilty at the East Berkshire magistrates' court to being in charge of a dog that was dangerously out of control in a public place. This was a very rare occasion when a member of the Royal Family was a defendant in court. Her English bull terrier, Dotty, had attacked two young boys in Windsor Great Park. The court, having heard the evidence of a 'dog behaviourist', was persuaded not to order its destruction. The Princess was fined £500, and warned that the dog should be kept under strict control, and would have to be put down if a further offence was committed.

The Animals Act 1971 also protects other *animals* from dogs. This Act says that in any civil proceedings for killing or causing injury to a dog *'it shall be a defence to prove that the defendant acted for the protection of any livestock'*. This means that a farmer would be entitled to kill a dog that was attacking his sheep.

24

Laws Around the World

'But equally it [an international organization] is not a United Kingdom juri-dical person. Nor is it a foreign juridical person. It is a person "sui generis", which has all the capacities of a United Kingdom juridical person, but is not subject to the controls to which such a person is subject under United Kingdom law. It is not a native, but nor is it a visitor from abroad. It comes from the invisible depths of outer space.'

Lord Donaldson of Lymington, Master of the Rolls, giving judgment in 1990 about the status of an international banking organisation.

*

We have been concentrating in this book on the laws of England and Wales, but these nations are also part of the European Union, and as such are members of the European Community. They are also part of the greater international community of nations. We should therefore be prepared to see our laws in three quite different contexts:

- The European Community (EC) has its own constitution, its own courts and its own laws. These laws are now part of our own laws and are known as **Community law or EC law**.

- Together with almost every other nation throughout the world, we live under the rule of **International law**. International laws are those which apply between States—laws which countries agree to obey by being members of a great international organisation such as the United Nations, or by entering into agreements with one another. Formal agreements between States are called **treaties**. States will usually agree to be bound by these laws for the same reasons that they have laws in their own countries—to ensure peaceful and harmonious relations between one another. International laws are designed to promote trade between nations, avoid wars, and ensure world-wide protection for citizens.

- Every country in the world—every *Nation State*—has its own set of laws and its own legal system. These laws are called the **Laws of Nations**, and we will take a brief look at some of them later on. They may differ greatly from our own laws. For example, we no longer have the death penalty in the UK, but in America, China, Malawi, Russia, and Singapore it continues to exist.

COMMUNITY LAW

The first stage of the European Community was formed by the Treaty of Paris in 1951; the second stage by the Treaty of Rome in 1957. This second treaty is normally referred to as the 'EC Treaty'. At present the EC has 15 **Member States**: Austria, Belgium, Denmark, Finland, France, Germany, Greece, Italy, Ireland, Luxembourg, the Netherlands, Portugal, Spain, Sweden, and the United Kingdom (England, Scotland, Wales, and Northern Ireland). Yet more States are seeking to join. Included in the *First Wave* of nations which hope to join by June 2004 are Cyprus, the Czech Republic, Estonia, Hungary, and Slovenia. Following that, Bulgaria, Latvia, Lithuania, Malta, Romania, Slovakia, and Turkey hope to join.

Each of the Member States has agreed that Community laws shall become part of their own national laws. Where a particular Community law differs from a national law, Community law will be supreme. At a conference held in December 2003, the *First Wave* of nations failed to agree upon a new Constitution for the European Community.

There is now a great body of law which has come from the EC, and which we in this country must obey. The main areas of our law that are affected by Community law relate to the movement of persons and employment in EC countries, to the movement of goods, and to competition law. EC law is also concerned with issues of sex discrimination. In this book it is possible to give only a bare outline of the objectives of EC law in these four areas:

- *Movement of persons.* The free movement of persons among Member States is an important principle of the EC law. This can create major problems. For example, it is not easy for a country with a relatively high rate of unemployment to assimilate large numbers of unemployed workers and their families from other countries. Now, much EC law is designed to cope with this type of problem.

- *Movement of goods.* The free movement of goods between Member States is an equally vital principle of Community law. This affects a variety of aspects of national law, including the charging of customs duties and protecting Member States from each other's taxation systems, which may discriminate against goods being imported in order to protect the manufacturing industries of the individual States.

- *Competition law.* It is the policy of the EC to maintain and encourage competition for the benefit of the Community. The idea is for the Community to achieve a **single market**, which can compete with the great trading blocs of the world (for example, the USA, the Far East, China). Article 2 of the EC Treaty states that this is to be achieved *'by establishing a common market and an economic and monetary union'*. Already a common currency, the ECU, now known as the Euro, has come into being; and there is much debate as to whether the United Kingdom should adopt the Euro as its own standard form of currency, instead of the pound Sterling.

- *Sex discrimination.* The EC has developed laws that provide for sex equality rights, and it encourages the role of its own institutions and Member States in promoting sex equality. The EC is able to issue Directives to the Member States. These set out certain aims which the Member States must achieve, but leave the way in which they do this to the Member States themselves. One important practical step along the road towards removing sex discrimination was taken in 1975, with the issue of the Equal Pay Directive, which extends to men and women alike the principle of equal pay for *'work to which equal value is attributed'*.

The court which must decide if EC laws have been broken is the European Court of Justice (ECJ). Its decisions are binding upon each Member State. The ECJ currently consists of 15 judges and eight Advocates-general. These are nominated and appointed by unanimous agreement by the governments of the Member States.

The *judges* of this court are chosen with care for their qualities of independence and high judicial skills. The rulings of the ECJ are delivered in a single judgment, and before taking office each judge must take an oath to preserve the secrecy of the Court's deliberations.

The *Advocates-general* are not always lawyers who represent one side or the other. The parties in the case are allowed to have their own legal representatives to argue their cases. Advocates-general are there to assist the court by giving *independent* advice on the issues that have been raised in each case. In doing this they are entitled to take into account the overall effects for the EC of the Court's ruling. The Court is not bound to follow their advice, but Advocates-general tend to be highly distinguished lawyers in their own right, and their opinions are treated with great respect.

INTERNATIONAL LAW

International law is the law between States. Just like our own laws, it has grown up out of *customs*, which have developed over the centuries, and, more recently, *case law* (decisions handed down by international courts); but it has also been influenced by *treaties*. The renowned international lawyer, Professor Lassa Oppenheim, described an international custom as '*a clear and continuous habit which has grown up under the conviction that it is obligatory and right*'.

From early times States came to recognise the importance of international rules. Examples of essential international customs are maritime rules, which regulated the 'traffic' of the seas; and rules of international trade. Medieval trading cities needed to be confident that their trade with one another could be conducted honourably and fairly by rules which were agreeable to all. Cities that accepted these rules also accepted a system of arbitration which provided for special courts to decide trading disputes.

States also set up **embassies** in each other's territories. Their Ambassadors would be skilled diplomats, whose job it was to represent the interests of their own countries, and to report back on the activities and policies of the country to which they were sent. Sometimes, these embassies were—and still are—little more than bases for spying. Today, we have embassies in countries around the world, and those countries have embassies in London.

Rules of **diplomatic immunity** protect citizens of any country who work in its embassy abroad. These rules grant special privileges to ambassadors and their staff to escape detention and prosecution in the countries in which their embassies are situated; but they have often been abused, and are much criticised. They even allow senior diplomats to claim immunity from prosecution for quite serious crimes. When this happens here, we may ask the country concerned to 'waive' (give up the right to) diplomatic immunity; but they will rarely do so. Then, all we can do is to ask the diplomat to leave the country. At the lowest level of crime, it is not unknown for embassy employees to build up literally hundreds of unpaid parking fines.

One remarkable example of the protection given to diplomats is the *diplomatic bag*. This is the right of senior embassy officials to carry luggage—'bags'—through customs without being searched. Normally the diplomatic bag receives complete immunity, but customary international law does make an exception where it is necessary to search luggage 'to save life and limb.' Therefore, customs officials could, for example, seize diplomatic bags which contain guns and dangerous drugs.

The Dikko case

In 1985, Dikko, a former Government Minister in Nigeria, fled to England. The Government in Nigeria wanted his return there to face charges of theft, but were not confident that they could persuade an English court to make an order for his extradition. The Nigerian authorities therefore arranged for him to be kidnapped, drugged, and 'posted' back to Nigeria in a wooden crate—an unusual diplomatic 'bag'—bound for Lagos. The crate was seized at the airport. The Foreign Secretary ruled that the duty to 'protect life and limb' was more important than the diplomatic protection given to cargo, and Dikko was released.

THE UNITED NATIONS

The most important international body in the world today is the **United Nations** (UN). Its headquarters is in New York, and most of the independent nations in the world are members. The UN has its own **Charter**, which sets out the principles by which it acts. It has many functions, but the most important of these is set out in Article 1 of the Charter:

> To maintain international peace and security . . . and take effective . . . measures for the prevention and removal of threats to peace, and . . . the suppression of acts of aggression or other breaches of the peace.

This would not perhaps have been of any importance in the days of bows and arrows or cannon guns, but the first half of the twentieth century witnessed two World Wars and the use of nuclear weapons. The world discovered how wars between nations, which might well have treaties with other nations promising to defend them in case of attack, can quickly spread to cover entire continents, and threaten the whole planet. Some countries now have weapons of mass destruction that can be launched by rocket or plane, striking targets thousands of miles away. The peacekeeping work of the UN and its international peacekeeping force are therefore of critical importance to the future of mankind.

All member nations are required to contribute to this work. They are all part of the *General Assembly* of the UN, which acts like its parliament, but the most vital responsibility for world peace rests with the *Security Council*. The Security Council has 15 members. Only five of these are permanent members (China, France, Russia, Britain, and the USA); the rest are elected by the General Assembly every two years. The Security Council has immense influence over the course of international events. In 2003, one of the greatest criticisms of leaders of the USA and the UK was that they took their countries into war with Iraq without first obtaining the approval of the Security Council.

Many specialised agencies work under the overall control of the United Nations. These help to foster international co-operation, for example in the fight against dangerous drugs, and give relief to the poor and needy throughout the world. Their names usually explain the spheres of their work. They include: the *World Health Organisation*, the *International Labour Organisation*, the *Food and Agriculture Organisation*, and *UNICEF* (originally called the United Nations International Children's Emergency Fund). Over the years UNICEF has provided many millions of destitute children throughout the world with food, clothing, and basic medical supplies. Nevertheless, widespread famine and appalling poverty still exist.

INTERNATIONAL COURT OF JUSTICE

What happens if there is a dispute between nations? They should no longer need to go to war to settle it, for the UN has its own International Court of Justice, which is based in The Hague. This court consists of 15 judges (no more than two may come from the same State). They may decide cases by reaching majority decisions. Although the court cannot force States to obey its decisions, they are usually respected and obeyed.

If a State refuses to abide by the Court's judgment, the matter will be reported to the Security Council, which will decide what action to take. The actions that may be taken against a nation in default of its international or human rights obligations are known as **sanctions**. It will be appreciated that sanctions may be very difficult to mount against a foreign country. They may range from political isolation (such as suspending a country's membership of the UN) to economic sanctions (such as a trade blockade), to the use of military force, as in the operation against Iraq to liberate Kuwait.

INTERNATIONAL HUMAN RIGHTS

In Chapter 19 we saw that the Council of Europe has its own Convention on Human Rights which, following the Human Rights Act 1998, is now part of our law. The Convention rights are upheld by the European Court of Human Rights in Strasbourg. Beyond that, a vitally important part of the work of the UN is to pronounce upon and protect human rights *worldwide*. The UN General Assembly frequently debates human rights issues and has passed many Resolutions and Declarations on human rights. The UN also has a *Human Rights Commission*, which has drafted important treaties on human rights, and hears complaints from individuals who claim to have been denied basic human rights in their own counties.

The UN Human Rights Commission employs many people to investigate cases where individuals 'arrested' by State authorities have simply 'disappeared', or been imprisoned or executed without trial. The Commission also investigates cases of torture and religious intolerance. These cases are heard by an International Criminal Tribunal, sitting in The Hague. This Tribunal was established within the framework of the UN. It has been described as an 'ad hoc' Tribunal, meaning that it is set up to hear particular cases as and when they arise. It has already tried several Bosnian war crimes suspects, and is still doing so. As we will see, this Tribunal has now been superseded by a new permanent International Criminal Court. These are examples of cases that have been before the Tribunal:

- In August 2001 one of these war crimes suspects, General Radislac Krstic, was convicted of genocide, having being concerned in the massacre of at least 7,500 Muslim men and boys at Srebrenica in July 1995. He was sentenced to 46 years' imprisonment.

- On 3 July 2001, the Serbian leader, Slobodan Milosevic, appeared before The Hague Tribunal. He had been indicted as a war criminal charged with crimes against humanity, including the mass murder, persecution, and deportation of over 700,000 ethnic Albanians. After he lost power, he was arrested by the authorities in his own country and extradited to The Hague. There, he refused to be represented by lawyers or to recognise the jurisdiction of the Tribunal, declaring it to have no authority to try him. The Tribunal thereupon ordered that pleas of not guilty should be entered on his behalf, and for many months he has been on trial for these crimes, and for the crime of genocide.

THE NEW INTERNATIONAL CRIMINAL COURT

In 2002, a new International Criminal Court came into being as a result of 120 nations signing a treaty—'The Rome Statute of the International Criminal Court'. This treaty came into force on 1 July 2002, and was largely the work of the UN; but it established a *permanent* court which will, itself, be an *independent* international organisation. The Court will comprise three divisions: a Pretrial Division, a Trial Division, and an Appeals Division. Its 18 judges have been specially chosen for their competence in criminal law and procedure, and as representing the world's principal legal systems. The first UK judge on the court is Sir Adrian Fulford, who is also a judge of the High Court. This court is expected to take over the work of the Tribunals.

Not every case with international implications has, however, been dealt with by an international tribunal. In some cases it has been necessary for domestic courts to make important decisions. In November 1998, a case came before the House of Lords which has been recognised as a watershed in attempts to bring to justice those accused of human rights violations. Until their Lordships' ruling in this case, it had been thought to be a rule of international law that all Heads of State were immune from prosecution for offences committed by them during the time they were in office. This immunity is called *State Immunity*; it was formerly called *Sovereign Immunity*.

The case of General Pinochet—Part 2

We first met this case in Chapter 7. General Augusto Pinochet was the Head of State in Chile between the years 1973 and 1990. In September 1998, while he was in hospital in England, the Spanish authorities applied for a warrant for his arrest and extradition to Spain. The grounds of this application were that during his time as Head of State, he had been responsible for 'genocide, torture and terrorism', and implicated in 3,178 murders or 'disappearances' including the torture and disappearance of a number of Spanish citizens in Chile. General Pinochet was detained on this warrant, but applied for his release on the grounds that as Head of State at the time of these alleged events, he was immune from prosecution for crimes said to have been committed in that capacity.

In November 1998, in a landmark ruling, the House of Lords decided by a majority of 3–2 that General Pinochet could have no immunity in respect of acts of torture and hostage taking carried out on his instructions during his time in office. In his leading speech Lord Nicholls said, '*That applied as much to Heads of State, or even more so, as it did to anyone else; the contrary conclusion would make a mockery of international law.*' As we have seen in Chapter 7, this ruling had to be set aside, and a new hearing was held.

The new hearing took place before seven Law Lords. Four Law Lords (making the majority) ruled that as General Pinochet was Head of State of a country that had ratified (signed up to) the International Convention against Torture and other Cruel, Inhuman or Degrading Treatment or Punishment 1984 (which in 1988 came into effect in Chile, Spain, and the UK) he had no sovereign immunity in relation to acts of murder or torture committed after that date. The remaining three judges reached decisions at either extreme end: one decided that General Pinochet had not lost his sovereign immunity at all, and could not be extradited; but two decided that he had no immunity from extradition at all, and could be extradited even for offences committed before 1988.

The result of this decision was that the court decided that General Pinochet had no immunity from extradition in respect of only three of the many offences which were the subject of the proceedings—three offences of torture and conspiracy to commit torture said to have been committed after 1988. In fact, the Home Secretary later decided—on the basis of medical evidence—that General Pinochet was in such a poor state of health that he could no longer face proceedings. Pinochet returned to Chile, where authorities there have been attempting to bring proceedings against him.

Another extraordinary criminal case that had strong international connections was the Lockerbie trial. This was a unique case because it became necessary to fashion out of nothing a new kind of court to try what was really a 'domestic' crime, of murder by blowing up an aircraft over Lockerbie in

Scotland. The case was heard by Scottish judges applying Scottish law, but by international agreement it was transferred out of the country.

The Lockerbie trial

On 21 December 1988, an American passenger jet was blown up over Lockerbie in Scotland, with the loss of all 259 passengers and crew, and 11 Lockerbie residents. It was soon established that this was an act of terrorism, and suspicion fell upon two Libyans — Abdul Ali Al-Magrahi and Lamin Fhimah.

After many years of diplomatic pressure and the imposition of stringent economic sanctions against Libya, the Libyan Government finally agreed to their extradition to stand trial. This was to be by a Scottish court using Scots law and procedure, but at a neutral venue — Camp Zeist in the Netherlands. The US Department of Justice paid for the families of the victims to attend the trial, or to watch it by CCTV. After a trial lasting nearly 12 months the three judges convicted Al-Magrahi, but acquitted Fhimah. Al-Magrahi appealed against his conviction, but his appeal was dismissed, and the Libyan Government has now paid very substantial sums by way of compensation to the families of the victims. Legal commentators have applauded the fact that international negotiations eventually produced a unique compromise solution which made the trial possible.

THE ENVIRONMENT

There is now a vast body of environmental and conservation laws aimed at protecting the environment and endangered species. These laws deal with everything from atmospheric pollution to trading in wild birds.

International conferences are held to discuss these problems, and attempt to solve them by agreement. One of the earliest of these environmental agreements was the International Convention on the Regulation of Whaling 1948, aimed at ensuring the preservation of whales. Other Conventions have, for example, made regulations to preserve elephants from slaughter by poachers engaged in the ivory trade, and other animals from the trade in fur.

THE LAWS OF NATIONS

There are many differences between the internal laws of our own country and those of other nations. In this chapter, it is only possible to give a few of the many thousands of examples of how laws vary in different parts of the world:

- Judges in France, Germany, and Italy are 'career judges.' They do not become judges having first practised as lawyers for a number of years (as in the UK). They are trained for a judicial career early in life, and after leaving University must go on to take examinations which are specially designed for the education of judges.

- In many countries, both in Europe and throughout the world, judges sit alone to try cases without juries. For example, in France, although trivial cases will be dealt with by one judge sitting alone (called a *Magistrat*) more serious cases are usually tried by a panel of three trained judges. In some countries juries are only used in the most serious cases, such as homicide (where death has been caused) or rape.

- Punishments vary greatly from country to country. Many countries still have capital punishment.

Capital punishment

In the USA, different states have in recent years used at least five different methods of execution: hanging, shooting, death in the gas chamber, electrocution, and lethal injection. Twelve states actually offer the condemned man a choice between the last two. In some states, a condemned man or woman may wait as long as 14 years on 'death row' before being executed (in the next chapter we will see a case in which the Privy Council decided that it was inhuman to keep a defendant waiting five years for his execution). On the other hand, in China executions by shooting may take place within a few hours of sentence of death being pronounced.

Other countries such as Singapore and a number of Middle Eastern countries have also retained corporal punishment (flogging). In some Middle Eastern countries mutilation by amputation is still a form of punishment.

- Each of a number of important European countries including France, Germany, Switzerland, and Austria, has its own **code of civil laws**. A code of laws is a set of written laws which are carefully worked out to provide a statement of the leading rules of law on any given subject. The French Code is known as the *Code Napoleon*, and was one of Napoleon's proudest achievements. Other countries which also have codes of laws include Egypt and Japan. The Republic of China has a Criminal Code of laws, which came into force in January 1980, and work is in hand to provide the Chinese people with a Civil Code.

RELIGION

Throughout the world vast numbers of people are ruled by the laws of their religion. Two of the most important of these are Islamic law and Hindu law. A huge part of the world's population is affected by these laws. They may be very different from ours in many ways, but they should be respected as representing the deeply held beliefs and values of countless people.

- *Islamic law* consists of a great number of divinely revealed rules which every faithful Muslim must observe. Unlike Western legal systems, where laws may easily be changed, these laws, decreed by Allah and revealed to mankind through his prophet Mohammed, were given to man for all time. In Islamic countries society must adapt itself to these laws; the laws are not to be altered to adapt to society.

  The highest source of Islamic law is the Koran. Islamic law is followed by approximately five hundred million people—about one-sixth of the world's population. It provides a code of behaviour and also important social rules. These include the right of a man to have four wives. In England if a man (or woman) has more than one spouse, he or she commits the criminal offence of bigamy.

- *Hindu law* applies to over four hundred million Hindus. The great majority of Hindus live in India, although many also live in Pakistan, Singapore, Malaysia, and countries on the east coast of Africa (for instance, Uganda and Kenya). Although the Hindu legal system is one of the oldest in the world, many Hindu laws have been adapted to meet the changes in society. For example, within the ten years after India achieved independence from the UK, its Parliament had passed the Hindu Marriage Act of 1955, which reformed and unified the Hindu marriage laws.

*

The *laws between nations* and the *laws of nations* are fascinating subjects that provoke interesting and revealing comparisons of how people across the world think and behave. Over the years very many distinguished books have been written about them, and these have had a profound influence in forming and shaping the State of world order. One of the earliest and most famous works on international law was published in 1625. Written by the great Dutch jurist Hugo De Groot who, in the academic fashion of the day, 'latinised' his name to 'Grotius', *On the Laws of War and Peace* was a dissertation both on the laws which should bind nations when dealing with each other, and on the way in which nations should treat each other's citizens in times of peace and war. These laws have been greatly developed over the years. For example, the humane treatment of prisoners of war is now governed by the Geneva Conventions, which rule that they should not be intimidated, humiliated, or mistreated.

There seems to be no limit to man's greed. Whether it be the Arctic (just ice and water) the Antarctic, the sea, air space, or even the depths of outer space, man is happy to lay claim to the lot, and there must be international laws to deal with these claims. There seems to be no limit to man's thirst for violence. It is, of course, a terrible reflection on the narrow thinking and selfishness of mankind that even to this day, wars are in progress throughout the world, and there are fears of yet more to come. The UN and other international agencies have done remarkable work in both these areas—solving national boundary and territorial disputes, and preventing wars; but the UN, despite all its efforts, could do nothing to prevent the Middle East Wars of 1968 and 1973, the Falklands War, the war in the Congo, the Kuwait War, and the Bosnian War. In March 1999 the forces of NATO (North Atlantic Treaty Organisation) were mobilised against the Serbs to prevent further violations of human rights but without the final approval of the UN. The war against Saddam Hussein's Iraq, in 2003, was another war declared without the approval of this organisation.

Acts of international terrorism are now being countered by international action. In September 2001, following the attack on the New York World Trade Center and the Pentagon in Washington, the nations of NATO immediately joined in declaring the attack to be an 'act of war'. They pledged military support to their partner, the USA, in fighting the terrorists, whoever they may be, and bringing them to justice. In January 2002, during the war in Afghanistan, which followed this act of terrorism, there was much international concern about the conditions in which the USA was detaining and questioning al-Quaeda and the Taleban prisoners at its Camp X-Ray base in Cuba, and its plans to try them and punish them. These prisoners have now been kept in strict conditions of custody for many months, raising serious issues about breaches of their human rights.

It is a fact that, for all the great human rights activities of the UN and other organizations, whole peoples are still being terrorised and massacred in the name of religious, tribal, or national rivalry. The work of the Nuremberg War Crimes Tribunal, set up by the Allies at the end of the Second World War, has been carried on by other international criminal tribunals, and will soon be taken over by the new International Criminal Court. The international community of nations is awakening to its own powers to take action against the criminals, whoever they may be, who are persistently breaching human rights. Joint international efforts and co-operation are on the increase. These, and the rule of international law, are seen as possibly the only hope—certainly the best hope—for peace and respect for human rights in the years to come.

25

Some Interesting Cases

'Not everyone, however, loves McDonalds.'
Mr Justice Bell, giving judgment in the 'Mc.Libel' case, June 1997.

✳

There are so many interesting cases that it is difficult to choose just a few for this book. In addition to those we have already come across, these are a varied selection, to give the reader an idea of how the courts have to deal with different aspects of our lives.

'*R v [versus]*' *means* and is pronounced 'The Queen (or King) *against*'— indicating a criminal trial. If there are two or more *names*, as in *Tolley* v *J. S. Fry and Sons Ltd* (the first case below) this means Tolley *against* J. S. Fry and Sons Ltd, for they are the names of the parties the claimant and the defendant in a *civil* trial. Lawyers referring to a civil case do not actually use the word '*against*'; they use the word '*and*'. If this case were being discussed either in or out of court it would be talked of as 'Tolley and J. S. Fry and Sons Ltd'. Almost all the claimants in civil cases were at the time of this case called plaintiffs. It is tempting to keep calling them that, for old times' sake, but it is better to move with the times, and they will now be referred to as claimants.

The cases we will be looking at in this chapter are a mixture of civil and criminal cases, starting off with a civil case. Some of them may be rather old, but they have been chosen because of their particular interest, or because they are still very relevant to the law as it is today. It is still quite common for nineteenth-century statutes, and cases heard within the last hundred years, to be quoted in the courts.

Some of the criminal cases are notorious. The cases of *R* v *Evans* and *R* v *Christie* are the subject of a film called *10 Rillington Place*. This address, where several murders were committed, became so notorious that its name was later changed. Some are of special interest and controversy—many people believing them to be examples of grave miscarriages of justice. We should not let this small selection of cases give us the impression that all criminal trials are controversial. The vast majority of convictions in criminal cases are accepted as being right.

TOLLEY v J. S. FRY AND SONS LTD (1931)

At the time of this case Cyril Tolley (the claimant) was a famous amateur golfing champion. Fry (the defendants) were, and still are, well-known makers of chocolate. It has always been an important principle of amateur sport that players do not play for money. Nevertheless, Fry published an advertisement in the *Daily Sketch* and the *Daily Mail* showing Tolley with a bar of their chocolate sticking out of his pocket. Even worse was the 'poem' that went with it:

> *The caddie to Tolley said, Oh, Sir*
> *Good shot, Sir. That ball, see it go, Sir!*
> *My word how it flies,*
> *Like a cartet of Frys*
> *They're handy, they're good, and priced low, Sir!*

Tolley had no idea that this advertisement was to be published. He did not even eat Fry's chocolate. When he found out about the advertisement he sued them for defamation of his character. He claimed that anyone seeing it would assume that he was being paid by Fry to advertise their products and that he had therefore breached his amateur status.

Tolley won his case, and Fry were ordered to pay him £1,000 damages. They might also have had a strong word with their resident poet, kindly described by Norman Birkett KC, the eminent lawyer who appeared on their behalf, as a 'frustrated muse'. (Birkett later became one of the judges who presided over the Nuremberg War Trials, held at the end of the Second World War.) Tolley's case was taken on appeal right up to the House of Lords, and had an important effect upon the law, for it has helped to protect everyone against commercial exploitation.

DONOGHUE v STEVENSON (1932)

This is often referred to as the case of the 'snail in the bottle'. Perhaps it might better be described as the case of the 'snail that never was', but despite being concerned with such a lowly creature it has become one of the most important cases in the civil law of negligence.

Miss May Donoghue (by the time of the trial she was Mrs McAlister), the claimant, was a shop assistant who together with her friend visited a cafe in

Paisley, Scotland. Her friend bought her a bottle of ginger beer, which had been made by Mr Stevenson, the defendant. Miss Donoghue said she opened the bottle and poured some ginger beer into a tumbler which contained some ice cream, and drank it; but when her friend started to pour out the rest of the ginger beer a decomposed snail floated out of the bottle.

Miss Donoghue brought a claim in the Scottish courts for compensation against Mr Stevenson, claiming that as a result of his negligence she had suffered shock and gastro-enteritis. She was a 'pauper', who could hardly afford to bring the case in the Scottish courts, but the point of law in the case—whether Mr Stevenson owed a duty to take care in relation to persons who bought his ginger beer—was considered so important that the case was sent to London to have it decided by the House of Lords.

The case took a long time to argue. In all, the speeches (judgments) of the Law Lords take up nearly 60 pages in the law reports. In a famous judgment Lord Atkin set out the principle of law to be applied in cases of negligence, which has been followed by the courts ever since. Simply stated it is: *People do owe a duty to take reasonable care to avoid harming anyone whom they might reasonably expect could be affected by their actions.* The court therefore decided that a manufacturer of ginger beer would owe a duty of care to the people who bought it, and if Mr Stevenson had manufactured a bottle of ginger beer that contained a snail, he would be negligent.

The case was then sent back to the court in Edinburgh for it to decide whether there had in fact been a snail in the bottle. After hearing all the evidence (one is tempted to say, after *all that*) the court decided there had not! May Donoghue may have lost her case but her name has lived on in the courts ever since.

PARIS v STEPNEY BOROUGH COUNCIL (1951)

This was another important case in the law of negligence, because it advanced the principle set out in *Donoghue* v *Stevenson*. In 1942, Mr Paris (the claimant) took up employment with Stepney Council (the defendants) as a garage mechanic. He had previously lost the sight of an eye. In 1947 he was working underneath a vehicle and using a hammer to remove a bolt, when a chip of metal flew off and entered his good eye. This caused such a severe injury that he was left totally blind.

Mr Paris claimed damages for negligence, saying that the Council had failed to ensure his safety by providing him with a protective eye visor. He won his case 'at first instance' in the High Court (judge score: Paris 1, Stepney Council 0), but this decision was overturned by the Court of Appeal, where the Lord

Chief Justice Lord Goddard gave the lead judgment (judge score: Paris 1, Stepney Council 3). The case went to the House of Lords, where the Law Lords decided by a majority of 3–2 that the Court of Appeal was wrong, and so Mr. Paris won his case (although the judge score was now: Paris 4, Stepney Council 5!).

The battleground in this case was a simple one. Mr Paris argued that as his employers knew he was blind in one eye, and as they realised that an accident of this kind might happen, they owed him a special duty of care to protect him from injury. On the other hand, the defendants said that just because Mr Paris was blind in one eye did not mean that they had to treat him differently from any other worker. In a decision said by Lord Normand to 'be of considerable importance' the House of Lords came down in favour of Mr Paris. Lord Normand said: 'The test is what precautions the ordinary, reasonable and prudent man would take for the particular individual to whom the duty of care is owed'; and so if anyone has a disability, it is a relevant matter to take into account when deciding what precautions to take for his safety.

Applying this test, the court ruled that whether or not goggles should have been supplied to a two-eyed workman was one matter; but having regard to the risks involved in this type of work they should certainly have been supplied to a one-eyed workman. This and other cases have given rise to the principle that 'you must take a claimant as you find him'. And so if, for example, in a road accident, a motorist negligently knocks down and injures a man who has an 'egg-shell' (particularly thin) skull, and he suffers a greater injury than someone with a normal skull, the motorist nevertheless has to compensate him for this greater injury.

R v EVANS (1950); R v CHRISTIE (1953)

These two murder trials are really inseparable, and are often quoted by those who argue that capital punishment should never be reintroduced.

In 1949, Timothy Evans, together with his wife and child, lived as lodgers with Reginald Christie in his small house at 10 Rillington Place, Notting Hill Gate, London. In November 1949 Evans's wife and child were strangled to death. Evans was interviewed by the police, and made a confession to their murders.

On 11 January 1950, Evans was tried for murder at the Old Bailey. He denied these crimes. He said that Christie was involved in the murders, and that he had confessed to them only because he was so 'upset'. On 13 January, at 2.10 p.m. the jury retired to consider their verdict. They returned at

2.50 p.m. They found Evans guilty, and he was sentenced to death. On 9 March, Timothy Evans was hanged at Pentonville prison.

One of the most important witnesses against Evans was his landlord, Christie. It was Evans's case that Christie must have committed the murders. Indeed, his barrister put to Christie in cross-examination: '*Well Mr Christie, I have got to suggest to you that you are responsible for the death of Mrs Evans and the little girl; or if that is not so, at least you know very much more about the deaths than you have said?*' Christie replied, '*That is a lie.*'

It was clear that everyone believed Christie. They had no reason not to. It was pointed out that Evans had admitted the murders, and Christie had for years been a Special Constable, who had assisted the work of the police.

Three years later the bodies of four more women, including Christie's own wife Ethel, were found at 10 Rillington Place, and on 22 June 1953 Christie himself stood in the same dock at the Old Bailey. He was charged with murdering his wife. She had been strangled in December 1952—long after Evans had been executed—but it was discovered that some of the bodies were of women who had been killed *before* Mrs Evans met her death. They must have been hidden away at 10 Rillington Place at the very moment when Christie was giving his deadly evidence against Evans. Christie was found guilty. He was sentenced to death, and on 15 July 1953 he too was hanged.

Naturally, this case gave rise to very great concern. After Christie's trial many highly respected people were convinced that Evans had been wrongly convicted. The author Ludovic Kennedy wrote a compelling book, *10 Rillington Place*, exposing Evans's conviction as a shocking miscarriage of justice. Kennedy had to explain away Evans's confession. He demonstrated that because Evans was of low intelligence and had a very weak personality, it was quite possible that when he learned of the deaths of his wife and child he went into a state of shock, and in this condition bowed to the strong questioning of the police and confessed to the killings. Kennedy suggests that at that time, Evans would have experienced strong feelings of guilt that he had not protected his family from Christie, and would have felt responsible for their deaths.

After this case, official inquiries were held. Many people believe that these were very unsatisfactory, and resulted in a 'whitewash', designed to give the criminal justice system the appearance of infallibility. After all, it would be very difficult to admit that the system had allowed an innocent man to be executed (and it is always easier to deny this when a defendant has been hanged, and he is no longer there to protest his innocence). The matter was debated in Parliament. The debate still continues. There are still some people who think that Evans may have been guilty, but most believe that if the Evans' jury had known the truth about Christie, Evans would never have been convicted. Indeed, knowing what we do now, he would not even have been prosecuted.

This case is often used by those who argue against the reintroduction of the death penalty. In particular, they rightly say that the experience of a number of cases has shown that 'confessions' made to the police by vulnerable people of low intelligence, who are 'suggestible' (they readily agree to suggestions put to them), have later been proved to be unreliable.

BOLTON v STONE (1951)

This is another civil case. On 9 August 1947, the claimant, Miss Bessie Stone, was standing outside her home in Beckenham Road, Manchester, when she was hit by a cricket ball. The ball had been struck a mighty 'six' by a batsman, who had hit it right out of the Cheetham Cricket Ground. The evidence was that to hit this 'six' the batsman had to hit the ball 80 yards to the boundary, over a seven-foot high boundary wall and then another 20 yards into the road! This had been done once or twice in the past; but it was very rare.

The court decided that the members of the cricket club were not responsible in law for the claimant's injuries, as the chances of anyone being injured in this way were 'so remote' that a reasonable person would not have foreseen (antici-pated) them. In the next case, though, the situation was rather different.

MILLER v JACKSON (1977)

In 1972, a housing estate was built adjoining the Lintz Club cricket ground in Burnopfield, County Durham. One of the houses was bought by Mr and Mrs Miller. Their garden was only 32 yards from the centre of the pitch. There was a six-foot high boundary wall; but time and again balls were hit out of the ground and either hit the roof of their house or landed in their garden.

The court decided that there was a real risk that one day a member of the Miller family would be injured, and it was unreasonable to *'expect the claim-ants to consent to live behind shutters and stay out of their garden on summer weekends on account of the cricket'*. Accordingly, the playing of cricket on the ground was an 'actionable nuisance'—meaning that the club was committing the *tort of nuisance*.

The court awarded the Miller family £400 damages, and said that if any harm came to them in the future the club would be responsible. Mr and Mrs Miller had, however, voluntarily chosen to live near to the cricket ground and *'since the court had to weigh the interests of the public at large against those of the individual, and it was in the interests of the inhabitants of the village that they should keep their cricket ground'*, the Court of Appeal then decided, by a majority of 2–1, that it was not right to grant an injunction against the club, preventing the playing of cricket on the ground.

R v CRAIG AND BENTLEY (1952)

On Tuesday, 9 December 1952, Christopher Craig and Derek Bentley appeared in Court 1 at the Old Bailey. They were charged with murdering a policeman, Sidney George Miles. Craig was then 16 years old and Bentley was 19. The case attracted great public interest, and was tried by the Lord Chief Justice, Lord Goddard.

At about 9.30 p.m. on the night of 2 November 1952, the two defendants were caught attempting to burgle a building in Tamworth Road, Croydon. The police were called, and Detective Sergeant Fairfax and PC McDonald found them. They were hiding behind a chimney stack on the flat roof of the warehouse.

DS Fairfax told the court that when he was about six feet away from the youths he shouted, *'I am a police officer. Come out from behind that stack.'* Craig shouted back, *'If you want us come and get us.'* Fairfax rushed up behind the stack and grabbed hold of Bentley, and then started to advance towards Craig. He said, *'As we got to the corner of the stack, Bentley broke away from me, and as he did so he shouted, "Let him have it, Chris". There was then a flash and a loud report, and I felt something strike my left shoulder which caused me to spin round and fall to the ground.'* He went on to describe how he managed to knock Bentley to the ground, and when he searched his pockets he found a knuckle-duster and a knife. This was not denied by Bentley.

DS Fairfax held Bentley and managed to move him across the roof. According to the officer, Bentley said, *'He'll shoot you'*. DS Fairfax said to PC McDonald, *'He got me on the shoulder'*, and Bentley said, *'I told the silly bugger not to use it'*. Craig continued to fire at the police, first at PC Harrison, who came up the stairs on to the roof, and then at PC Miles who followed him. Craig fired again, and PC Miles fell dead with a bullet straight between the eyes.

As PC Harrison tried to disarm Craig by throwing things at him, Craig shouted, *'I am Craig. You have just given my brother twelve years. Come on you coppers. I am only sixteen.'* (The day before the shooting his brother had been sentenced to twelve years' imprisonment for robbery.) The police started to take Bentley downstairs, and he shouted out, *'Look out Chris; they're taking me down'*. This was followed by another burst of firing from Craig. There were clicks, and then a shot. By now Craig's weapon was out of ammunition, and he dived off the roof. He was badly injured, but he survived, saying, '*I wish I was dead. I hope I've killed the lot.*'

Although Craig pleaded not guilty, there was never any chance that he would be acquitted. His defence was that although he may have been responsible for PC Miles's death, he did not intend to kill him or do him serious bodily harm; that the gun went off 'accidentally' in the struggle on the roof. Bentley was also prosecuted for murder on the basis that he incited (encouraged) Craig to begin the shooting by saying, '*Let him have it, Chris*'. The law is that if you incite another person to commit a crime you are equally guilty if he does so.

Bentley's defence was that when they went out together that night he had no idea that Craig had a gun; and he did not use these words at all. His barrister was to claim that if he had used them they meant, '*Let him have the gun*', not, '*Shoot him*'. Bentley also claimed that as he was under police arrest at the time PC Miles was killed, he could not have been involved in his murder. During the course of Bentley's evidence Lord Goddard asked him many questions which must have made it obvious to the jury that he did not believe him.

At this time capital punishment was still in force. As Craig was under 18 at the time of the killing he could not be sentenced to death. That no doubt explains why, when he was on the roof, he said, 'I am only sixteen', but Bentley was 19, and he could be hanged. The judge's summing-up was very hostile to both youths, and from Bentley's point of view, literally deadly.

On 11 November, the members of the jury retired to consider their verdict. Only a short time later they returned. They found Craig guilty of murder. When asked if they found Bentley guilty or not guilty, the foreman said '*Guilty, with a recommendation to mercy*'. This meant that the jury hoped that although Bentley would have to be sentenced to death, the sentence would later be commuted by the Home Secretary to life imprisonment.

Derek Bentley was illiterate and was of low intelligence. When Lord Goddard sentenced Craig to be detained 'during her Majesty's pleasure' (the equivalent of a life sentence for a young offender) he said, '*In my judgment and evidently in the judgment of the jury you are the more guilty of the two*'. Nevertheless, all pleas for mercy for Bentley were turned down by the Home Secretary, whose job it was to consider recommendations for leniency, and Bentley was hanged. DS Fairfax was awarded the George Cross for his bravery that night, and Police Constables Harrison and McDonald were awarded the George Medal.

It is almost certain that the reason why Bentley was executed was that the Home Secretary wished to send a strong *deterrent* warning to criminals that the police must be protected at all costs. There was great disquiet at the time, and has been ever since, that justice was not done in this case. Derek Bentley's sister, Iris, campaigned for many years for recognition of this, and achieved some success. Bentley's body was removed from prison grounds to an open cemetery, where the inscription on his headstone reads, '*A victim of British Justice*'. After Iris's death, the Bentley family fought on, arguing that Bentley's mental age was that of a child, that he was not given a fair trial, and he should never have been convicted.

In November 1997, the newly formed *Criminal Cases Review Commission*, which investigates possible miscarriages of justice, asked the Court of Appeal to reconsider this case. On 30 July 1998, nearly 46 years after he was hanged, the Court of Appeal finally quashed Bentley's conviction. In a historic judgment, Lord Bingham, Lord Chief Justice, said that in directing the jury Lord Goddard had failed to deal properly with important matters of law, and that: '*far from encouraging the jury to approach the case in a calm frame of mind, the summing-up had exactly the opposite effect*'. He then used these stirring words: '*It is with genuine diffidence that the members of this court direct criticism towards a trial judge widely recognised as one of the outstanding criminal judges of this century. But we cannot escape the duty of decision. The summing-up in this case was such as to deny the appellant that fair trial which is the birthright of every British citizen.*'

GILLICK v WEST NORFOLK AND WISBECH AREA HEALTH AUTHORITY (1985)

This case posed a fascinating legal puzzle for the Law Lords.

In this country it has for many years been a criminal offence for a man to have sexual intercourse with a girl under the age of 16 years. The law says that a girl who is under this age cannot consent to having sexual intercourse. At the time of this case the claimant, Mrs Gillick was the mother of five girls, all under the age of 16. The health authority that was responsible for medical care in her area was the West Norfolk and Wisbech Area Health Authority.

The Department of Health and Social Security had circulated a document to all the health authorities in the country, giving guidance on contraceptive advice and treatment to young people, including children under the age of 16. Mrs Gillick claimed that as girls under 16 were not allowed to have sexual intercourse, it was wrong for doctors employed by the health authority in her area to give this kind of advice without the knowledge and agreement of the girls' parents. She asked for an assurance that medical advice of this kind would not be given to her daughters without her consent. This was obviously an important **test case** (one that could have an impact far beyond the parties concerned) because if she won, all parents throughout the country would be in the same position.

When the case was first heard by a High Court judge he ruled in favour of the Health Authority and the Department, and said that doctors could give 'family planning' advice privately to girls under 16 if they believed it was in their best interests.

The case was then taken before the Court of Appeal, which ruled in favour of Mrs Gillick. This court agreed that as it was against the law for anyone to have sexual intercourse with a child under 16, parents had the *right* to be consulted in these cases. They had a right to know what advice was being given to their children, and a doctor could give this kind of advice without their knowledge only with the consent of a court.

When the case came before the Law Lords they decided (by a majority of 3–2) that if a doctor considered that it was in the best interests of an individual child to give advice of this kind, he or she should be able to give it. It would all depend on the degree of intelligence and understanding of the particular child and the doctor's judgement of what was best for her welfare. If a doctor honestly believed that it was necessary for her physical, mental, and emotional health to give this advice privately (without her parents' knowledge) then the doctor could do so.

R v SOUTHBY (1969)

The defendant was playing in an amateur football match, and deliberately struck an opponent. The blow killed him. The defendant was prosecuted for *murder*! The jury found him guilty of the less serious charge of manslaughter. This meant that they were sure that the victim had died as a result of an unlawful act, but were not sure that the defendant had intended to kill or cause grievous (really serious) bodily harm.

R v GINGELL (1980)

The defendant fouled an opponent in a rugby match, causing three fractures of his face. His sentence of six months' imprisonment was later reduced by the Appeal Court to two months.

In 1985, a similar case came before the magistrates at Clacton, Essex. This concerned a foul in a football match when an opponent's jaw was broken. The magistrates ordered the offender to pay £250 compensation to the victim. It happens that the players involved were women—the match was a 'women's friendly'!

R v X (1993)

The name of the child who was defendant in this case is not given, because that would be unfair. This case came before the Court of Appeal, and the judgment of the court, delivered by Lord Justice Steyn (now a Law Lord) makes remarkable reading. He began the story of the case with these words:

> On 28 March 1991, [X] a schoolboy aged thirteen years, was on his way to school. He was identified to police officers by [Y], who was aged seventeen, as the person who four weeks earlier had attempted to rob him. The police officers arrested [X]. He was charged. His trial took place in November 1991 . . . The trial lasted three days . . . He was convicted of assault with intent to rob . . . the judge sentenced [X] to 15 months detention . . . The truth is that [X] was wholly innocent of the offence. The conviction and sentence was an appalling disaster.

In fact, as the Lord Justice went on to explain, X's mother had been able to prove that the identification of her son was completely mistaken. The Court of Appeal was also satisfied that the judge was mistaken in allowing the case to go before the jury at all, because there were many weaknesses in the identifi cation evidence, and when they were added up it was plain that there was a very strong possibility that the schoolboy had been wrongly identified. The court said, 'In our judgment the judge ought undoubtedly to have withdrawn the case from the jury.'

What were the weaknesses in identification in this case? Here are some of them: Y had first told the police that his attacker was aged 16 to 18, but X was 13; Y had said his attacker was 5 feet 11 inches, X was 5 feet 7; Y had said his attacker had 'some stubble on his face', X had not yet started to shave; Y had said that his attacker was light skinned, X was of dark Afro-Caribbean com- plexion; Y had said that his attacker had a distinctive zig-zag pattern in his hair, so had X but he had been given this haircut *after* the attack; Y said his attacker had worn a brown jacket, but X did not have one, and when his home was searched no brown jacket was found.

After considering all the evidence carefully the Lord Justice said '*in our judgment the conviction was not only unsafe and unsatisfactory, but . . . [X] was wholly innocent*'. Nevertheless, he had served about six months of his sentence before he was released. This case is a good illustration of the care that must be taken with evidence of identification, and how it is possible for an identifica- tion case to result in a miscarriage of justice. In these cases, judges must give strong warnings to juries about the special need for care when considering identification evidence.

R v PIETERSON AND HOLLOWAY (1995)

The defendants were charged with robbing two people who worked at a club in Marston, Oxford. It was said that three men had entered the club wearing scarves or balaclavas over their heads. One of them had a gun; the others were armed with sticks. They all threatened the staff, who handed over the keys to the safe. The men then stole £5,800 and put this money into a holdall, and ran off.

The police were called to the club. They had with them a tracker dog, called Ben, and within minutes Ben led them to an alleyway nearby and to a strap from the holdall that had been used by the robbers. Later the holdall itself was found in a flat occupied by one of the defendants, where the police also found some of the stolen property. Two of the three men were arrested.

The defence argued that the actions of the dog should not be admitted in evidence—after all, a dog could not give evidence in court! The judge decided that this evidence should be put before the jury, and the defendants were convicted (the police never found the third man). When the case came before the Court of Appeal the judges decided that it would be proper to place this type of evidence before the court, but only if the jury received evidence that the dog had been properly trained to follow a scent and was reliable. In fact there had been no such evidence in this case. The evidence from Ben's police handler had simply been, *'Ben is a German shepherd and will be eight years old in December 1993. He commenced his training at one year old in the Thames Valley Police and had six years' experience of the work required of him.'* The jury had not received any detailed evidence of the dog's experience and reliability.

Nobody knows what Ben made of all of this, but he would probably have been delighted to have sniffed out an important principle of law—that the work of tracker dogs can under certain conditions be put in evidence. He might also have been interested to learn that the defendants in fact lost their appeal—there was so much other evidence connecting them with the crime, the court decided the convictions were safe. Or perhaps he would have just preferred a bone.

R v YOUNG (1995)

Normally all the discussions that take place in the jury room when the jury are considering their verdict are kept a strict secret, and if the case then goes to appeal the court will refuse to enquire into them. This case was a rare exception.

In March 1994 the defendant appeared at the Crown Court at Hove charged with two murders. The members of the jury retired at the end of the trial to consider their verdicts, and after staying in a hotel overnight they eventually found the defendant guilty of both charges. He was sentenced to life imprisonment.

It was later discovered that while in the hotel four of the jurors had met together in one of their rooms and conducted a session with a ouija board, at which they had 'contacted' one of the dead victims and had asked questions and received answers which showed that the defendant was guilty!

In the court of appeal, the Lord Chief Justice, Lord Taylor described the scene:

> The word 'ouija' is simply a combination of the French word 'oui' and the German word 'ja' and therefore means 'yes, yes'. A ouija board is used at a séance to seek messages from the spirits of absent or deceased persons. In this case there was no formal board. Letters of the alphabet were printed on scraps of paper and a glass was used as a pointer. Those present each put a finger on the glass which then moved towards a succession of letters, thereby purporting to reveal a message.

The 'messages' were harmful to the defendant's case. The court also heard that they had been discussed with other jurors at breakfast the following day. One of them became so concerned that after the trial he consulted a solicitor and provided a written statement about what had happened.

When the judges in the Court of Appeal learned of these matters they decided that they were so unusual and important that they ought to take them into account. They agreed that the behaviour of the jury had been improper and that 'what occurred during this misguided ouija board session may have influenced some jurors and may thereby have prejudiced the defendant'. The court quashed the convictions and ordered a re-trial.

BRADSHAW v ATTORNEY-GENERAL OF BARBADOS (1995)

We have already learned that our Law Lords sitting in the Privy Council are the final court of appeal from a number of other countries, including Barbados. In this case, two men who had been convicted of murder in Barbados had been sentenced to death, in 1985 and 1986 respectively. They each lost a number of appeals, and in 1993 the Court of Appeal in Barbados dismissed their final appeals. By this time they had been 'on death row' awaiting execution for over seven years.

Section 15 of the Constitution of Barbados reads, 'No person shall be subjected to torture or to inhuman or degrading punishment or other treatment'. It was argued before the Privy Council that to execute men who had been under sentence of death for so long would amount to 'inhuman or degrading punishment' in violation of this constitution.

The Privy Council agreed with this argument, and held that where it was proposed to execute a defendant five years or more after sentence the delay would be so great as to make the punishment inhuman or degrading. Accordingly, sentences of life imprisonment were substituted for the death sentences.

This judgment had a profound impact upon the fate of other prisoners in Barbados who had also been awaiting execution for many years. It has also been used to save the lives of prisoners in other Commonwealth countries. Even if we think that capital punishment can be justified, we may still feel that keeping a man or woman for five years in the 'condemned cell' is inhumane.

Condemned prisoners in the USA are regularly executed more than ten years after their sentences. On 3 February 1998 at Huntsville Prison in Texas, USA, Karla Faye Tucker was executed by lethal injection after spending 14 years on 'death row'. In January 2004, Charles Singleton, a severely mentally ill prisoner suffering schizophrenia, was executed in Varner, Arkansas. He had been on death row for many years following his conviction for a 1979 murder, and was put to death after being forcibly fed anti-psychotic drugs in order to make him lucid enough, under court guidelines, to be executed.

McDONALD'S CORPORATION v HELEN STEEL AND DAVID MORRIS (1997)

This defamation case began on 28 June 1994 and ended when the judge, Mr Justice Bell, gave his judgment on 19 June 1997. It is recorded in the *Guinness Book of Records* as the longest civil trial in British history.

The two defendants had published a fact sheet entitled, '*What's wrong with McDonald's. Everything they don't want you to know*'. The leaflet accused the food chain of being responsible for starvation in the Third World, of destroying vast areas of Central American rainforest, of serving unhealthy food with a very real risk of cancer of the breast or bowel, heart disease, and food poisoning, of lying when it claimed to use recycled paper, of exploiting children with its advertising and marketing, of cruelty to animals, and of treating its employees badly—all the while deceiving the public and hiding its true nature behind a 'clean, bright image'.

The claimants sued for defamation. Ms Steel and Mr Morris defended themselves. They fought the case every inch of the way. They cross-examined many witnesses called by the claimants (who were represented by a team of lawyers) and they called many witnesses themselves. This was in itself a great feat of endurance and commitment on their part. The trial lasted 314 days. The judge had the awesome task of assimilating all the evidence, and of making many important findings of fact.

The judge decided that most of the serious allegations made against McDonald's were untrue. He awarded the claimants a total of £60,000 damages against Mr Morris and £55,000 damages against Ms Steele; but he did find that McDonald's were responsible for exploiting children in their advertising campaigns, and that they were 'culpably responsible' for certain cruel practices used in the rearing and slaughter of some of the animals (battery and broiler hens) which were used to produce their food. After a lengthy appeal hearing, the defendants achieved even greater success, having the total award of damages reduced to £40,000.

R v MATTAN (1998)

In September 1952, a Somali, Mahmood Mattan, was executed at Cardiff Prison for the murder of Lily Volpert, a Cardiff pawnbroker. Her throat had been cut with a razor, and she had been robbed of £100. At his trial Mattan denied murder, claiming that he had been nowhere near the scene at the time. The main evidence against him was that of an eye-witness, who swore that he had seen him at the scene of the crime at the time of the murder.

For many years Mattan's family, convinced of his innocence, fought for his conviction to be reviewed and overturned. At last, in February 1998, his case came back before the Court of Appeal. It had been the first to be reviewed by the new *Criminal Cases Review Commission*, set up specially to investigate possible miscarriages of justice. The Commission discovered that the description given by the eye-witness, right down to a distinctive gold tooth, also matched that of another Somali called Tehar Gass. Gass was himself accused of a quite different murder in 1954, and it was later revealed that he had attended Lily Volpert's pawnbroker's shop on the very same day as the killing. Gass was found to be insane and was sent to Broadmoor Hospital. Upon his release from hospital he was deported back to Somalia.

In the Court of Appeal the prosecution accepted that there were many inconsistencies in the eyewitness's evidence, and that if the full story about Gass had been known at the time—some of it *was* known, but had not been disclosed to the defence at the trial—Mattan would never have been convicted. The court also heard that the eyewitness who had given such damning evidence against Mattan was himself later convicted of the attempted murder of his own daughter—with a razor—and he too had become a possible suspect in the Volpert murder!

The Court of Appeal decided that Mattan's conviction all those years ago was 'demonstrably flawed', and he should never have been convicted. The story of Mahmood Mattan is a truly tragic one. When he married there was so much local prejudice that he and his wife had to live apart. At his trial he was described by his own counsel as a *'half-child of nature, a semi-civilised savage'*. He went to his death protesting his innocence, and his wife, convinced of it, vowed that one day she would clear his name. Forty-six years later, with the help of her family and lawyers, she did so.

Lord Justice Rose gave the judgment of the court. He expressed its *'profound regret'* at what had happened, and went on to say that this case had a *'wider significance'*. The points he then made may provide a fitting epitaph for this terrible case, and for the death penalty itself:

1.   *Capital punishment was not perhaps an appropriate culmination for a criminal justice system which was human and therefore fallible.*

2.   *In important respects criminal justice law and practice had, since that trial, undergone major changes for the better.*

3.   *The new Criminal Cases Review Commission (which investigated this case) was a necessary and welcome body.*

4.   *No one associated with the criminal justice system could afford to be complacent.*

5.   *Injustice of the present kind could only be avoided if all concerned in the investigation of crime and the preparation and presentation of criminal prosecutions observed the very highest standards of integrity, conscientiousness and professional skill.*

R v DIEDRICK (1999)

This case illustrates how individual citizens can, with sufficient determination, influence the course of justice.

On the morning of Boxing Day 1994, as she was about to leave for a holiday in the United States, Joan Francisco, a gynaecologist, was murdered in her flat in Pimlico. She had been strangled. Suspicion fell upon her ex-boyfriend Anthony Diedrick. He was arrested in 1995, but was not charged because Crown Prosecution lawyers considered that there was insufficient evidence against him. Joan's mother and sisters, however, remained convinced of Diedrick's guilt, for he had already been in trouble for causing criminal damage at her flat, and had recently been stalking her.

The members of the family chose a different route to bring Diedrick to justice. They decided to pursue their case through the civil courts, and in 1998 brought civil proceedings against Diedrick for the killing. The case was heard by Mr Justice Alliot, and they succeeded in obtaining a historic civil court judgment that Diedrick was the killer.

The family now threatened to launch a private prosecution; and demanded a meeting with Sir Paul Condon, the Metropolitan Police Commissioner. He ordered the police to carry out a further investigation. This time DNA testing of three tiny bloodstains on Joan's T-shirt revealed them to bear traces of Diedrick's blood—said to have come about when Joan inflicted scratches on her killer as she tried to fight him off.

The Crown Prosecution Service now took over the case, and Diedrick was prosecuted. On 13 October 1999, nearly five years after the killing, he was convicted of murder, and sentenced to life imprisonment. After the verdict, Joan's sister Margrette said, '*I know Joan would be proud of my family's commitment to not giving up when others had. For nearly five years our family waged an arduous campaign and fought against the odds, and the legal system, to bring this case to trial.*'

R (ON THE APPLICATION OF QUINTAVALLE) v HUMAN FERTILISATION AND EMBRYOLOGY AUTHORITY (2003)

This was another case which posed important and difficult ethical problems.

Since 1990, the Human Fertilisation and Embryology Authority (HFEA) has been the official body authorised to license *in vitro* fertilisation (IVF) treatment. In this case the parents of a child called Zain, who was born with a life-threatening blood disorder, wished to undergo IVF treatment together with genetic diagnosis, with the aim of choosing an embryo that would produce a healthy child with the same tissue type as Zain. They hoped that a transplant of stem cells from the new baby's umbilical cord might cure Zain's disease.

The HFEA was prepared to grant this licence, but the claimant, who acted on behalf of a campaigning 'pro-life' group, sought judicial review of this decision. He said that the Authority had no power to grant a licence that permitted the use of tissue typing to select between healthy embryos. This would mean that the life of one healthy embryo with the wrong tissue type might be forfeited to produce another with the right one.

The Court of Appeal and the House of Lords decided that the HFEA had been right to grant the licence. The arguments before these courts were highly technical, and centred upon what activities were permitted by the Human Fertilisation and Embryology Act 1990, and by the rapid advance in science since the passing of that Act. The appeal judges concluded that Parliament had not intended to prohibit all cloning. It was right for the HFEA to approve the couple's IVF treatment so as to ensure that the embryo did not have a life-threatening genetic blood disorder (like Zain); and it was also lawful to permit the testing to determine whether the embryo had the same tissue type as Zain, so as to use cells from the newborn child to cure him.

Not everyone agrees with the judges. Later the same year, the Archbishop of Canterbury, Dr Rowan Williams, expressed a contrary opinion. He said that human embryos should never be used as 'designer babies' for the purposes of research—even if that might result in saving lives. Asserting the church's position, he said, *'That no individual is there simply for the use of another seems to me a basic ethical principle'*.

*

The cases we have looked at are just a tiny selection of the many thousands of cases which have been and are being decided by the courts. Almost all of these are interesting for one reason or another. They may involve real human concerns, a new point of law, or even obscure points of law of interest only to the lawyers who specialise in that particular field.

Many cases will be considered too 'ordinary' to be included in the law reports or the newspapers, but we may be sure that they all have this in common—that they are of the greatest interest and importance to the people who are actually involved in them. They are likely to find the experience of going to court, whether it is good or bad, a memorable one.

Most people who do go to court will appreciate that in a system operated by human beings, justice for everyone is an ideal that may always be out of reach. If they believe they have been given a fair hearing, even those who lose do not usually have feelings of resentment against the system. They understand why that has happened; some even find themselves agreeing with the court's decision! Nevertheless, the impressions of all those who go to court as to how they were treated and of the way in which the court reached its decision will probably stay with them, and affect the way in which they see our system of justice, for the rest of their lives.

Questions

CHAPTER 1 Introduction—The Royal Courts of Justice

1 What is your idea of justice?

2 Do you believe the courts are able to give people justice? What factors might prevent a court from doing justice in a particular case?

3 Research one of the cases referred to in this chapter and prepare the case for each side for presentation in court.

CHAPTER 2 The Law and its Importance

1 Imagine a day in which no one is bound by laws. Consider some of the likely consequences.

2 'Law links the past to the future. The law is a story of our moral progress as a people.' Explain what you think this means.

3 Think of any activity in which you or other people take part, and make a list of the rules and laws that might apply.

CHAPTER 3 The Invisible Palace—Part 1. Judge-Made Law — Common Law and Equity

1 What is the Common Law? Find illustrations of its importance over time.

2 What is the law of Equity, and how did it come into being?

3 What are the advantages and disadvantages of judges making law, as in the Common Law?

CHAPTER 4 The Invisible Palace—Part 2. The Constitution

1 Discuss the advantages and disadvantages of an unwritten constitution.

2 'The constitution may be an illusion, but it is an illusion which works.' Describe what this means.

3 What is meant by our legal rights and duties? Think of examples of duties owed by the citizen to the State and duties owed by the State to the citizen.

CHAPTER 5 The Palace of Westminster. Our Chief Law Makers—Parliament

1 What are the key functions of Parliament? What do you consider are the key functions of effective government?

2 What is meant by the Royal Assent to a Parliamentary Bill? What is the effect of the Queen giving her Assent to a Bill? What happens if the Queen does not wish to assent to a Bill?

3 Should the House of Lords be an 'elected' chamber or an 'appointed' chamber? What are the advantages and disadvantages of each system?

CHAPTER 6 Our Chief Law Enforcers—The Police

1 How was law and order kept before the first police forces were established in the nineteenth century?

2 *'The police perform many duties which are vital to the well-being of society.'* Discuss this in the light of your understanding of the role of the police in the twenty-first century.

3 Do you believe that the public has a 'love–hate' relationship with our police? If so, why should this be? What steps do you think could be taken to improve the relationship between the police and the public?

CHAPTER 7 Our Law Upholders—The Judiciary

1 In what ways do judges uphold the law?

2 What is meant by judicial independence? Why is this so important?

3 What qualities would you expect to see in a good judge?

CHAPTER 8 The Legal Profession

1 What are the two branches of the legal profession? What are the main differences between them?

2 Lawyers are expected to protect the interests of their clients fearlessly but what are the limits on their duties to their clients?

3 What is meant by legal professional privilege? Who enjoys this privilege — the client or the lawyer? How important is it?

CHAPTER 9 Solicitors

1 Compare the role of the 'family' solicitor with that of a specialist solicitor practitioner.

2 What opportunities do solicitors have for being courtroom advocates?

3 Who else apart from a qualified solicitor might work in a solicitor's office? How might one become a solicitor without going to university?

CHAPTER 10 Barristers

1 What is a barrister's role both in and out of court?

2 What is an Inn of Court? Why should all barristers have to be members of an Inn of Court (and eat dinners) before being permitted to practise at the Bar?

3 What are the advantages and disadvantages of a divided legal profession?

CHAPTER 11 The Work of the Courts—Part 1. The Courts

1 What are the main criminal courts and the differences in their functions?

2 What are the main civil courts and the differences in their functions? How do civil courts differ from tribunals?

3 What is the advantage of the system of binding precedent?

CHAPTER 12 The Work of the Courts—Part 2. Criminal and Civil Cases

1 What are the main differences in trials for civil and criminal cases? Thinking back to Chapter 1 and the idea of justice, do you think that the criteria for justice should be different in civil and in criminal cases?

2 What is an 'either-way' offence? Give two examples of these offences.

3 Imagine you are a solicitor. Prepare one case both for the prosecution and for a defendant in the magistrates' court, and another for a claimant and for a defendant in the county court.

CHAPTER 13 Judges

1 The American tradition of democracy has established the idea that certain judges should be directly elected by the people. Our judges are appointed until they retire. What are the advantages and disadvantages of both systems?

2 Describe the roles of the most senior judges in England and Wales.

3 How would you set about deciding facts in a case? How influenced would you be by the appearance and body language of a witness?

CHAPTER 14 Legal Robes

1 What are the advantages and disadvantages of the dress code of courtroom lawyers and judges?

2 Would you keep wigs or replace them with some other headdress? Describe the types of headdress worn in court in two other countries.

3 Assuming that the courtroom dress code of judges and advocates is reformed, what proposals would you make for that reform, and why?

CHAPTER 15 Criminal Trials through the Ages

1 What is the importance of *Bushell's Case* in the development of our criminal law?

2 What fundamental principles of English criminal law were established during the nineteenth and twentieth centuries?

3 What are the advantages and disadvantages of the jury system nowadays?

CHAPTER 16 Punishments through the Ages

1 Why do you think our history of punishments is such a cruel and savage one?

2 Discuss the extent to which you agree with Sir Winston Churchill's warning that '*the measure of a country's civilisation is the way it treats its prisoners*'.

3 Corporal and capital punishments are highly emotive issues. What is the current stance in relation to these punishments today, and what do you think it should be?

CHAPTER 17 Criminal Trials Today

1 What are the three most important principles in ensuring that a defendant in a criminal case has a fair trial?

2 What are the main differences between an adversarial system and an inquisitorial system of criminal procedure? Which system, in your opinion, has the better potential for doing justice, and why?

3 Why is it important that members of the public should be allowed to attend trials? What are the arguments for and against televising trials?

CHAPTER 18 Punishments Today

1 The Criminal Justice Act 2003 sets out five main principles of sentencing. How would you list them in order of importance? Give reasons for your prioritising.

2 In your view, what are the main purposes of custodial sentences?

3 What are the main functions of a probation officer? Why might this be satisfying work?

CHAPTER 19 Human Rights

1 What is the effect of the Human Rights Act 1998?

2 What improvements have been made to our approach to human rights since the Human Rights Act, 1998 came into force?

3 What, in your view, are the most important Human Rights Convention Articles? Justify your choices.

CHAPTER 20 Discrimination and the Law

1 Why is it important to have laws preventing discrimination? Are these laws effective?

2 Outline five kinds of discrimination that the law seeks to eliminate.

3 How might the laws against discrimination be improved?

CHAPTER 21 Young Persons

1 What special measures may be in place when a young witness gives evidence to a court of law? Can you think of ways of improving the system?

2 What special provisions may be in place when a young defendant is tried for a serious crime? Can you think of ways of improving the system?

3 Do you think that children are treated fairly by the courts dealing with the breakdown of relationships between parents? If not, why not?

CHAPTER 22 Dangerous Drugs

1 Explain the classification of dangerous drugs used in legislation making them illegal. Is it right for the law to become involved to prevent the supply and taking of all 'dangerous' drugs, or only some of them?

2 Which in your opinion is more serious — supplying small amounts of Class A drugs to friends, or supplying large amounts of Class B drugs to others for profit?

3 Are the legal consequences of drug offending a sufficient deterrent? If not, what more should be done to deter people from taking drugs?

CHAPTER 23 Animals

1 What particular ethical issues are highlighted in the law relating to the protection of animals?

2 In what circumstances should it be necessary for someone who keeps any kind of animal to have a licence? Give reasons for your opinion.

3 Explain the classification in the law relating to the protection of humans from animals. Discuss what alterations, if any, you might make.

CHAPTER 24 Laws around the World

1 In what ways does European Community law impact on how we live our lives in the UK?

2 What function does the United Nations serve? The UN has not been able to prevent wars breaking out. Why do you think that is?

3 What are the main ways in which international law (law between nations) assists in making the world a better place?

CHAPTER 25 Some interesting Cases

1 Outline four principles of law that have emerged from the cases described in this chapter.

2 In your opinion which of the following men who were executed suffered the greatest injustice and which the least injustice, and why — Timothy Evans or Derek Bentley or Mahmood Mattan?

3 Why are the cases of *R v Anthony Diedrick* and *R (On the application of Quintavalle) v Human Fertilisation and Embryology Authority* (2003) of importance?

Some Useful Reading

Berlins, M. and Dyer, C., *The Law Machine* (Penguin)
A good book for the beginner. The authors are expert in the field of communicating interesting facets of the law.

Blom-Cooper, L., *The Law as Literature* (Bodley Head)
Louis Blom-Cooper has included some wonderful legal gems in this book, which demonstrates so well how the words of lawyers and judges can reach the heights of fine language.

Lord Denning, *Landmarks in the Law* (Butterworths)
A superb and approachable collection of cases which have become landmarks in the story of our laws — told by one of the greatest judges of our age.

Devlin, P. (LORD DEVLIN), *The Judge* (Oxford University Press)
Lord Devlin's significant book may not be for beginners, but it contains many remarkable philosophical musings and insights on the law, and the way in which judges should operate to the advantage of justice.

Drinker-Bowen, C., *The Lion and the Throne* (Hamish Hamilton)
This biography of Sir Edward Coke brings to life in the most vivid way an extraordinary (feared, fearless, and hated) lawyer, judge, and jurist—who lived during one of the most colourful periods in our history—the reigns of Queen Elizabeth I and King James of England.

Gibson, B., *Human Rights and the Courts—Bringing Justice Home* (Waterside Press)
A simple, clear, and most helpful summary of a wealth of human rights information.

Goodman, A., *The Walking Guide to Lawyers' London* (Oxford University Press)
A beautifully illustrated guide to 'Legal London', which is accompanied by excellent historical and contemporary commentaries.

Grayson, E., *Sport and the Law* (Butterworths)
In this book the author, for many years the leading specialist in the field of sport and the law, covers this fascinating and wide-ranging subject with interest and humour.

Hyam, M., *Advocacy Skills* (Blackstone Press)
One of the best books on advocacy, written by a senior judge who knows as well as anyone the importance to courtroom lawyers of acquiring these skills.

Moore, L., *The Thieves' Opera* (Viking)
A captivating account of the lives and (legal) times of Jonathan Wild and Jack Sheppard, two of the most colourful and notorious criminals in eighteenth-century England.

Partington, M., *Introduction to the English Legal System* (Oxford University Press)
This is an excellent, highly informative, and comprehensive introduction to the law, written with great clarity by a distinguished Law Commissioner and Professor of Law.

Williams, G., *Learning the Law* (Sweet & Maxwell)
This book has for many years been part of the staple reading of those with a serious interest in studying to become lawyers.

Index